TIMELINE OF KINGS & QUEENS

TIMELINE OF KINGS & QUEENS

Gordon Kerr

This 2008 edition published by Barnes & Noble, Inc.,
by arrangement with Canary Press.

Barnes & Noble, Inc.
122 Fifth Avenue
New York, NY 10011

ISBN: 978-1-4351-0868-4

Printed and bound in China

10 9 8 7 6 5 4 3 2 1

COVER & INTERNAL DESIGN
Anthony Prudente on behalf of Omnipress Limited
Layout by Vivian Foster

Contents

Introduction

'The first art of a monarch is the power to endure hatred.'
Seneca, Roman Philosopher 1st century CE

Even royal families themselves agree that the concept of monarchy is a curious one. The word itself has no clear definition. It can mean different things in different countries, and a monarch's job description also changes over time, depending on the changing will of their subjects. In some places the king or queen wields unlimited political power, and in others, they do little more than appear on postage stamps.

Today 'absolute' monarchy – where a sole ruler has complete control over the populace, regardless of any written constitution or elected parliament – tends to be associated with tyrannical and less progressive societies. However, there was a time when Europeans generally believed that their rulers had been chosen by God, and nurtured a direct relationship with the divine. In the eyes of the people this gave them a right to rule their subjects with an iron fist. The appalling acts of Vlad the Impaler and Ivan the Terrible are famous examples, while Henry VIII was so convinced of his ordination by God, that he was willing to renounce the pope and reject his own children in order to reinforce his position as head of the brand new Church of England.

The French revolution, and the ideological changes of the Enlightenment, as well as the rise of secularism, helped put an end to this kind of thinking in Europe, and as a result, 'constitutional', or limited monarchy has become the most prevalent form of European monarchy. Belgium, Denmark, Netherlands, Norway, Spain, Sweden and the United Kingdom have a parliamentary system – the head of which is a prime minister, or a president. The king or queen is the 'head of state', thus echoing the ideas of Napoleon Bonaparte, the first man to proclaim himself as the embodiment of a nation rather than as its divinely appointed ruler.

The history of Europe can be characterised, and categorised, by the personalities and actions of the ruling monarchs of the time. Rich, powerful, influential, sometimes murderous, inbred or just plain insane – these eccentric individuals give European history colour, not to mention some much needed glamour and intrigue. This book explores the lives of some of the most influential men and women who have ever lived, and through the timeline, shows the fascinating connections between the royal houses of Europe.

CHARLEMAGNE TO MEDIEVAL KINGDOMS

800–1399

800 **Holy Roman Empire** Pope Leo III's coronation of Charles I the Great (Charlemagne), king of the Franks, founding father of both the French and German monarchies, as *Imperator Romanorum* (Emperor of the Romans), in St Peter's church, Rome, marks the beginning of the Holy Roman Empire.

802 **England** Egbert, driven into exile by Offa of Mercia, returns from Charlemagne's court to become king of Wessex; he maintains the independence of Wessex against Mercia. **Bulgaria** Around this time, Krum becomes khan and embarks upon expansion of his territory. **Byzantine Empire** Finance minister Nikephoros I deposes and exiles Empress Irene to become emperor; he reorganizes the empire.

804 **Denmark** Godfred becomes king. **Venice** Giovanni Galbaio, according to tradition, the eighth doge – chief magistrate and leader of the 'Most Serene Republic of Venice' – flees, with his family, to Mantua, in the face of opposition from the pro-Frankish Obelerio degli Antenori, who becomes doge; he accepts Frankish protection and war with Byzantium ensues.

810 **Denmark** King Godfred is murdered by a servant; his nephew, Hemming, becomes king. **Italy** Pepin, son of Charlemagne and king of the Frankish Kingdom of Italy (north Italy), dies; his son, Bernard, succeeds him.

811 **Venice** Obelerio degli Antenori goes into exile in Constantinople; Agnello Participazio becomes doge, and during his reign he reclaims land and refortifies the city; the Venice we know today emerges, a city of canals centred on the Rialto. **Bulgaria** Khan Krum defeats the Byzantines and kills Emperor Nikephoros I. **Byzantine Empire** On the death of Nikephoros, Staurakios I, who has been co-emperor with his father, becomes emperor, but abdicates in favour of his brother, Michael I Rangabe, another co-ruler since 803.

812 **Denmark** On the death of King Hemming, Sigfred and Anulo dispute the crown; Anulo dies in battle; the throne is fought over until the 10th century, when Denmark is unified.

813 **Holy Roman Empire** Louis the Pious is crowned co-emperor of the Franks with his father, Charlemagne. **Byzantine Empire** Michael I Rangabe is heavily defeated by the Bulgarians and abdicates in favour of the general, Leo V the Armenian; Michael II the Amorian becomes emperor.

814 **Holy Roman Empire** The death of Charlemagne; Louis the Pious succeeds him as Holy Roman Emperor and king of the Franks. **Bulgaria** On the death of Krum, Omurtag becomes ruler and concludes a 30-year peace treaty with the Byzantine Empire.

816 **Rome** Stephen IV is elected pope.

817 **Bavaria** Holy Roman Emperor Louis the German becomes king. **Rome** Paschal I is elected pope; he tries to curb the increasing power of the Roman nobility.

818 **Italy** Holy Roman Emperor Louis the Pious makes King Bernard of Italy a vassal of his cousin, Louis' son, Lothair; Bernard plots against him and is discovered and blinded, as a result of which he dies; Lothair becomes king of Italy.

820 **Byzantine Empire** Michael II the Stammerer, from a family of soldier peasants, assassinates Emperor Leo V during Christmas mass in Hagia Sophia, to become the first emperor of the Phrygian dynasty; his direct descendants will rule the Byzantine Empire for more than 200 years.

824 **Rome** Eugene II is elected pope. **Holy Roman Empire** The nine articles of the *Constitutio Romana* establish the authority of the Holy

Roman Emperors in Rome, advancing imperial pretensions there. **Pamplona** Íñigo Arista revolts against the Franks and establishes the Kingdom of Navarre.

825 **England** Egbert defeats Beornwulf of Mercia at the battle of Ellendun, and takes control of the Mercian dependencies in south-eastern England; Kent, Surrey, Sussex, East Anglia and Essex submit to Wessex.

827 **Venice** Giustiniano Participazio, son of previous doge, Agnello, exiles his younger brother, Giovanni, to become doge; during his reign, work is begun on the construction of the first Basilica di San Marco. **Rome** Valentine becomes the 100th pope, but dies after a few months; Gregory IV succeeds him.

829 **England** Egbert of Wessex conquers Mercia, and Northumberland accepts his overlordship; he is recognized as Bretwalda, the first sole ruler of Britain. **Venice** Giovanni I Participazio, brother of Giustiniano Participazio, becomes doge. **Byzantine Empire** Theophilus, becomes the sixth and last of the iconoclast emperors.

830 **England** Egbert of Wessex defeats the Welsh, but loses Mercia again.

831 **Scotland** The legendary date of the genesis of the flag of Scotland; it is said to have appeared to King Óengus II the night before a battle against the Angles. **Byzantium** Byzantine emperor, Theophilus, forbids the usage of icons. **Holy Roman Empire** Louis the Pious is reinstated as emperor of the Franks, following the end of the first civil war of his reign. **Bulgaria** Malamir, grandson of Krum, becomes ruler.

832 **Venice** The former doge, Obelerio degli Antenori, tries to reclaim the dogeship – he fails; Doge Giovanni Participazio kills him and displays his head in the marketplace.

833 **Great Moravia** The Central European Slavic Principality of Great Moravia is founded when Prince Mojmír I unifies the two neighbouring principalities of Nitra and Moravia.

836 **England** Egbert of Wessex is defeated by the Danes. **Venice** Giovanni Participazio is deposed following a revolt; Pietro Tradonico is elected doge; he is a warrior doge who is also illiterate. **Bulgaria** Presian, nephew of Malamir, becomes khan; he extends Bulgarian control over Slavic tribes in Macedonia.

THE STONE OF DESTINY
838

The Stone of Destiny – also known as the Stone of Scone – is a block of sandstone which measures 40 cm (16 in) wide, 66 cm (26 in) long and 28 cm (11 in) high. It weighs 152 kg (336 lb), and the passion this stone has inspired over the past 700 years far outweighs its rather drab appearance. It has been revered for centuries as a holy relic, it has been fought over by nations and has been used successively as an important part of enthronement ceremonies by Dalriadic, Scottish, English and British monarchs. On St Andrews Day, 30 November 1996, the Stone of Destiny returned to Scotland and can be seen here in Edward I's coronation throne.

838 **England** At Hingston Down, Egbert of Wessex beats the Danes and the west Welsh. **Scotland** The Stone of Destiny, the coronation stone of the kings of Scotland, is placed at Scone Palace, Scotland. **Ireland** Feidlimid mac Cremthanin becomes high king of Ireland.

840 **England** Egbert dies, having consolidated west Saxon domination of the south-west and south-east of England; Æthelwulf, who has been his father's sub-king, is crowned, at Kingston upon Thames, as king of Wessex, Kent, Cornwall, the west Saxons and the east Saxons. **Holy Roman Empire** Lothair I succeeds Louis the Pious as Holy Roman Emperor. **Venice** Holy Roman Emperor Lothair I recognizes the independence of Venice and its authority over its lagoon.

842 **Asturias** Alfonso the Chaste dies, after reigning for 51 years, having secured his realm against the Moors and taken Lisbon in 798; Visigoth Count Nepocian, briefly usurps the throne, but is defeated by Ramiro I at the Battle of the Bridge of Cornellana; Ramiro changes the system of succession by removing the election process, which could see his family ousted from the monarchy. **Pamplona** Basque chieftain Íñigo Arista is chosen as the first king of Pamplona, which would later become the Kingdom of Navarre. **Holy Roman Empire** Louis the German, king of East Francia and Charles the Bald, king of West Francia, swear the Oaths of Strasbourg, an alliance against Holy Roman Emperor Lothair. **Byzantine Empire** Following the death of Emperor Theophilus, his widow, Theodora, becomes empress, serving as regent for her son, Michael III the Drunkard; she reintroduces the veneration of icons.

“The Holy Roman Empire is neither Holy, nor Roman, nor an Empire.”

Voltaire

843 **Scotland** Kenneth MacAlpin is thought to have united the Kingdom of Scotia, becoming described by some as being the first king of Scotland (Alba) as well as king of the Picts. **West Francia** In keeping with the custom of partible or divisible inheritance, as opposed to inheritance by primogeniture, in the Treaty of Verdun, the three sons of Louis the Pious divide the Carolingian Empire into three kingdoms; the Kingdom of France becomes a distinct state for the first time; Charles II the Bald becomes king. **Middle Francia** Lothair is given the central portion comprising the Low Countries, Lorraine, Alsace, Burgundy, Provence and the Kingdom of Italy, which consists of the northern half of the country; he receives the title of emperor, but is only nominal overlord of his two brothers. **Eastern Francia** Louis the German becomes king of East Francia, which would eventually evolve into modern-day Germany.

844 **Wales** Rhodri Mawr becomes the first ‘Prince of all Wales’. **Italy** Louis II the Younger, son of Emperor Lothair I, is crowned king of Italy. **Rome** Sergius II is elected pope without seeking the authority of Holy Roman Emperor Lothair; Lothair invades, but is pacified when he is crowned king of Lombardy.

846 **Great Moravia** Following the death of Mojmír I, East Francia king, Louis the German confirms Rastislav as the second king of Great Moravia; King Rastislav attempts to limit the interference of Louis in his country's affairs.

847 **Rome** Leo IV is elected pope; he improves Rome's fortifications to thwart the Saracen menace.

850 **Asturias** Ordoño I, son of Ramiro I, founder of the Pérez dynasty, becomes the first king of Asturias to ascend the throne without an election; during his reign, Asturias becomes more commonly known as León.

852 **Pamplona** García Íñiguez becomes king; he has been regent since his father, Íñigo Arista, was paralysed in battle against the Vikings, in 842; he continues his father's fight against the Vikings and the Moors. **Bulgaria** Boris I becomes khan.

855 **Provence** Charles, youngest son of Holy Roman Emperor, Lothair I, becomes king when Lothair divides his realm of Lotharingia between his three sons. **Holy Roman Empire** Louis II succeeds Lothair as Holy Roman Emperor. **Rome** Benedict III is elected pope. **Byzantine Empire** Empress Theodora is displaced from her regency; her son, Michael III, rules alone.

856
England Æthelbald, second son of Æthelwulf, becomes king of Wessex after forcing his father to abdicate; he marries his widowed 16-year-old stepmother, Judith, and her father, Charles the Bald, Holy Roman Emperor, is furious; the marriage is annulled on the grounds of consanguinity.

858 **Scotland** Domnall mac Ailpín, brother of Kenneth I, becomes king of the Picts, as Donald I. **Rome** Nicholas I is elected pope; he consolidates the power of the papacy.

860 **England** Ethelbert, third son of Æthelwulf, becomes king of Wessex; unlike his predecessors, he does not appoint another member of his family as under-king of Kent; his reign is blighted by Viking raids. **Kievan Rus'** Around this time, Rurik, a Viking chieftain, comes to power in Ladoga and Novogorod, founding the Rurik dynasty that will rule Kievan Rus', the state centred on the city of Kiev, and then Russia, for the next 700 years.

862 **Scotland** Constantine I, son of Kenneth MacAlpin, becomes king of the Picts; his son, Donald II, and his descendants, will represent the main line of the kings of Scotland.

863 **Provence** When King Charles dies childless, the kingdom is split between his brother, Lothair II, and Emperor Louis II.

864 **Bavaria** Carloman, son of Louis the German, becomes king. **Venice** Pietro Tradonico is assassinated; Orso I Participazio is elected doge. **Bulgaria** Boris I converts to Christianity, following an invasion by the Byzantine Empire. **Great Moravia** King Rastislav has to acknowledge the supremacy of Louis the German, after the East Franks invade.

865 **England** Ethelred, fourth son of Æthelwulf, becomes king of Wessex.

866 **Galicia and Asturias** Alfonso III the Great becomes king; he consolidates his kingdom.

867 **Rome** Adrian II is elected pope. **Byzantine Empire** Basil I, Michael III's former courtier and chamberlain, is crowned co-emperor; Basil assassinates Michael to become sole ruler of the Byzantine Empire; he is the first ruler of the Macedonian dynasty that who transform the empire into the greatest power in Europe.

868 **Portugal** The First County of Portugal is declared by Christian warlord Vímara Peres, as a fiefdom of the Kingdom of Asturias, after the reconquest of the region north of the Douro river from the Moors; at the time, counties possess the same status as kingdoms in Iberia; Vímara, first count of Portugal of the House of Vímara Peres, rules over a city – today's Porto – known as Portucale; the County of Portugal will survive for two centuries.

869 **Holy Roman Empire** Emperor Louis II allies with eastern Emperor Basil I against the Saracens. **Byzantine Empire** Basil I begins to secure his family's tenure on the throne by crowning his son, Constantine, co-emperor.

870 **Byzantine Empire** Basil I crowns another son, Leo, co-emperor. **Great Moravia** Louis the German, king of East Francia, has King Rastislav blinded and imprisoned; Svatopluk I is chosen as king; during his reign, the country will achieve its maximum territorial expansion.

871 **England** Ethelred dies at the Battle of Merton; his brother, Alfred the Great, becomes king of Wessex, the fifth and youngest son of Æthelwulf to become king; he styles himself 'King of the Anglo-Saxons' and spends his reign defending his kingdom against the Danish Vikings.

872 **Rome** John VIII is elected pope; he reorganizes the papal Curia, the governing body of the Roman Catholic Church.

873 **Portugal** Lucídio Vimaranes takes his father's place in Portucale, but dies shortly after; Count Diogo Fernandes inherits the title through marriage to Lucídio's daughter.

875 **Provence, Holy Roman Empire and Italy** On the death of Louis II, Charles II the Bald becomes king and emperor. **Norway** Harald Fairhair, Viking king, subdues Orkney and Shetland, and adds them to his kingdom.

876 **East Francia** Louis the Younger becomes king.

877 **Scotland** Constantine I dies fighting the Vikings; Áed mac Cináeda, son of Kenneth MacAlpin, succeeds him as king of the Picts. **France** Louis the Stammerer becomes king of the West Franks and Provence. **Italy** Carloman, eldest son of Louis the German, king of East Francia, becomes king.

878 **England** Alfred defeats the Vikings under Guthrum, at Ethandune; the Treaty of Wedmore divides England between the Anglo-Saxons and the Danes. **Scotland** Giric mac Dúngail becomes king of the Picts, known simply as Giric.

879 **West Francia** On the death of Louis the Stammerer, his sons Louis III and Carloman II become joint kings of France. **Provence** Bishops and nobles elect Boso, a nobleman of Provence, king, the first non-Carolingian king in western Europe for more than a century; he strengthens his position by marrying the daughter of Emperor Louis II. **Italy** Charles III the Fat becomes king. **Byzantine Empire** Basil I begins to secure his family's tenure on the throne by crowning his son, Constantine, co-emperor, but Constantine dies soon after; Basil's youngest son, Alexander, takes his place. **Kievan Rus'** Rurik, prince of Novogorod, and founder of the Rurik dynasty, dies around this date.

880 **Bavaria** Carloman abdicates, following a stroke, and dies; his brother, Louis the Younger, already king of East Francia and Saxony, becomes king.

881 **Venice** Giovanni II Participazio, son of Orso I Participazio, is elected doge. **Holy Roman Empire** Charles III the Fat is crowned Holy Roman Emperor.

882 **France** Louis III of France dies; Carloman II rules alone. **Pamplona** Fortún Garcés becomes the last king of the Arista dynasty. **East Francia** Louis the Younger dies without an heir; his brother, Charles the Fat, Holy Roman Emperor as well as king of Italy, becomes king, reuniting the entire East Frankish kingdom. **Rome** Marinus I is elected pope. **Kievan Rus'** Oleg becomes ruler of all the Rus people and captures Kiev from Viking warlords, making it his capital and laying the foundation for the great state of Kievan Rus'.

884 **France** Holy Roman Emperor and king of East Francia, Charles the Fat, becomes king also of West Francia. **Rome** Adrian III is elected pope.

885 **Rome** Stephen V is elected pope. **Byzantine Empire** Basil I dies in a hunting accident; his belt is caught in the antlers of a deer and he is dragged 16 miles (25.75 km); Leo VI the Wise becomes emperor; the Byzantine Empire enters a golden age.

886 **England** Alfred the Great makes a treaty with the Danes formalizing the partition of England with the Danelaw – northern and eastern England – coming under Danish control.

887 **Provence** Louis the Blind becomes king. **East Francia** Charles the Fat is deposed and dies the following year; the Slovenian Arnulf of Carinthia, illegitimate son of Carloman of Bavaria, is elected king. **Venice** The elderly and much-loved Giovanni II Participazio retires, and Pietro Candiano is elected doge; he becomes the first doge to die in battle when he is killed, the same year, attacking the Narentines; his great-nephew, Pietro Tribuno, is elected doge; during his reign he has constructed a huge wall from eastern Olivolo to the Riva degli Schiavoni, turning Venice into a *civitas* or city.

888 **Western Francia** Charles the Fat dies; Odo, count of Paris and son of Robert the Strong, count of Anjou, is elected king; he is chosen for his courage and skill as a soldier. **Italy** Following the death of Charles III the Fat, Italy falls into disunity until 963, with many rulers claiming to be king.

889 **Scotland** Around this time, Donald II, son of Constantine I, becomes king of the Picts, now known as king of Alba. **Bulgaria** Boris I abdicates, in favour of his son, and becomes a monk; Vladimir becomes khan.

890 **Norway** Around this time, Harald I Fairhair becomes the country's first king.

891 **Holy Roman Empire** Guy III of Spoleto, descended from Charlemagne through marriage, becomes Holy Roman Emperor. **Rome** Formosus is elected pope.

892 **Holy Roman Empire** Lambert II of Spoleto becomes Holy Roman Emperor.

893 **Bulgaria** Former King Boris I comes out of retirement when his son tries to revert to paganism; Vladimir is defeated and blinded by his father; Boris's third son, Simeon I the Great, one of the most famous figures in Bulgarian history, becomes khan; during his reign, Bulgaria extends its empire over territory between the Aegean, the Adriatic and the Black Sea.

894 **England** Northumbrians and East Angles swear allegiance to Alfred the Great, but promptly break their truce by attacking the south-west of England. **Great Moravia** On the death of Svatopluk I, the kingdom is divided between his three sons, against his stated wishes; the country is weakened.

896 **Germany** The eastern Franks invade and conquer Italy under the leadership of Arnulf of Carinthia; he is elected Holy Roman Emperor. **Rome** Boniface VI is elected pope, following riots in Rome; Boniface dies, possibly of gout; Stephen VI is elected pope. **Bulgaria** Simeon I defeats the Byzantine Empire at the Battle of Bulgarophygon.

897 **Rome** The remains of Pope Formosus are exhumed and put on trial in the notorious ecclesiastical trial known as the Cadaver Synod; he is found to have been unworthy of the pontificate; Pope Stephen VI is imprisoned and strangled, following the Cadaver Trial; Romanus is elected pope, but is deposed three months later; Theodore II is elected pope.

898 **West Francia** Charles III the Simple, posthumous son of Louis the Stammerer, becomes king of France. **Rome** John IX is elected pope.

899 **England** The death of Alfred the Great; he is succeeded by Edward the Elder as king of Wessex; during his reign, he conquers Mercia, East Anglia and Essex. **East Francia** Louis the Child becomes the last Carolingian king of East Francia; his reign is plagued by Magyar raids from Hungary.

900 **Scotland** Constantine II, cousin of previous king, Donald II, becomes king of Alba; during his reign, he fights with the Vikings and the English. **Rome** Benedict IV is elected pope. **Serbia** Archont Petar, also known as Predimir, is prince of Duklja, on the Adriatic Coast; Hvalimir I, Sylvester, Tugemir and Hvalimir II rule in the early years of the 10th century; Duklja consists of Montenegro, north-eastern Herzegovina and Koplik, in Albania.

901 **Holy Roman Empire** Louis III the Blind, usurper king of Provence, becomes Holy Roman Emperor.

903 **Rome** Leo V becomes pope for 30 days, before being deposed and murdered by antipope Christopher.

904 **Rome** Antipope Christopher is ejected; Pope Sergius III succeeds Pope Leo V as the 119th pope, beginning the 30-year era of the Pornocracy, a time of great excess and violence; he is the only pope to have ordered the murder of another pope, and the only pope to father an illegitimate son who also became pope; he is also the first pope to be depicted wearing the triple-crowned papal tiara.

905 **Pamplona** Fortún Garcés is deposed by a coup and retires to a monastery; Sancho I Garcés, son of García Jiménez, king of another part of Navarre, becomes the first king of the Jiménez dynasty.

907 **Great Moravia** Weakened by its division among the sons of Svatopluk I, the country is finally destroyed in a Hungarian attack and vanishes as a state.

910 **Galicia, León and Asturias** On the death of Alfonso III, his kingdom is divided between his three sons; García becomes king of León; Ordoño becomes king of Galicia and Fruela becomes king of Asturias.

911 **Provence** Hugh of Arles, brother-in-law of Louis the Blind, becomes king, although he never uses the royal title. **East Francia** Louis the

Child dies aged 18; Conrad I, son of Conrad, duke of Thuringia, is elected king. **Rome** Anastasius III, possibly the illegitimate son of Sergius III, is elected pope.

912 **Venice** Orso II Participazio, unrelated to the previous Participazio incumbents, is elected doge; he establishes better relations with the Byzantine Empire. **Byzantine Empire** Leo VI's brother, Alexander, who has been co-emperor since 879, becomes co-emperor with Leo VI's son, Constantine VII Porphyrogennetos. **Kievan Rus'** Igor becomes ruler; he twice tries to conquer Constantinople.

913 **Rome** Lando is elected pope, but dies six months later; he is the last pope to use a papal name that has not been used previously, until Pope John Paul I in 1978. **Bulgaria** Simeon I decisively defeats the army of the Byzantine Empire and is recognized as tsar (emperor) by Patriarch Nicholas.

914 **León and Galicia** Ordoño, king of Galicia, also becomes king of León after the death of his brother, García. **Rome** John X is elected pope.

915 **Holy Roman Empire** Berengar of Friuli, grandson of Louis the Pious, is elected Holy Roman Emperor.

916 **England** The Mercian warrior queen Aethelflaed conquers Wales.

918 **England** By this date, all Danes south of the Humber have submitted to King Edward the Elder.

919 **East Francia** Henry I the Fowler is elected king as the only man capable of holding the kingdom together in the face of internal rivalries and raids by the Magyars; he is the first of the Ottonian dynasty and is reckoned to be the first king of the medieval state of Germany and founder of the Holy Roman Empire of the German nation; Arnulf the Bad is a rival king until 921.

OTTONIAN DYNASTY
919

The Ottonian dynasty was a succession of kings of Germany. It is also regarded as the first dynasty of the Holy Roman Empire. Although Henry I the Fowler was never emperor, he is considered to be the founder of the imperial Ottonian dynasty. Under the Ottonian rulers the kingdom of the Eastern Franks became Germany and the union of Germany with the Holy Roman Empire started with the coronation of Otto I the Great (pictured) in Rome in 962. The Ottonian dynasty became extinct after the death of Henry II in 1024.

Left is a woodcut entitled 'The Genealogy of Heinrich de Vogler' from *Liber Chronicarum* by Hartman Schedel.

920 **England** The Saxons retake East Anglia from the Danes. **Byzantine Empire** Romanos I, son of a former imperial guardsman and father-in-law of Constantine, becomes co-emperor, and then quietly usurps the throne.

922 **France** Robert I, brother of Odo, becomes king of France.

923 **France** Robert I dies in battle, possibly killed in single combat with his great rival, Charles the Simple; Rudolph, Robert's son-in-law, succeeds him.

> **“*And thus it has reached us that the English nation, by the compassion of God, eagerly desired to be converted to the Christian faith, but that the 'sacerdotes e uicino' neglect it and refrain from kindling by exhortation the desires of the English.*”**

Pope Gregory the Great

924 **England** Edward the Elder dies leading an army against a Welsh–Mercian rebellion; Ælfweard, possibly a hermit, becomes unlikely king of Wessex; he is never crowned and is killed, possibly on the orders of his older half-brother, Athelstan, who becomes king; he can claim to be the first king of England, if not *de jure*, then de facto. **Portugal** Count Mendo Gonçalves, son of Count Gonçalo of Galicia, marries Mumadona Dias, daughter of Onega Lucides and Diogo Fernandes, and becomes count of Portucale; Ramiro II, son of Ordonho II of León, was the first to bear the title 'King of Portuguese Land'. **Holy Roman Empire** Holy Roman Emperor Berengar is assassinated by one of his own men, leaving no heirs; the title remains vacant until 962.

925 **León** Fruella II's son, Alfonso Froilaz, becomes king; the sons of Ordoño II, Sancho Ordóñez, Alfonso and Ramiro, rebel against him, drive him out and divide the kingdom among themselves; Alfonso IV gets León, Froilaz is left with Galicia.

927 **Pamplona** Jimeno Garcés, brother of Sancho I, becomes king. **Bulgaria** Simeon I dies of heart failure; Peter I becomes tsar.

928 **Rome** Pope John X is imprisoned and possibly murdered by wealthy and powerful Roman noblewoman, Marozia, and her husband, Guy of Tuscany; Leo VI is elected pope; Stephen VII becomes pope for seven months.

930 **Norway** Erik Bloodaxe, oldest son of Harald Fairhair, becomes king; he quarrels with his brothers and has four of them killed.

931 **León** Alfonso IV of León abdicates, in favour of his brother Ramiro II, and enters a monastery. **Pamplona** García Sánchez I becomes king, aged 12. **Rome** John XI, son of Pope Sergius III and Marozia, is elected pope; his mother is Roman ruler and ensures his appointment, but exerts authority over him. **Norway** Eric Bloodaxe becomes second king of Norway. **Rome** John XI is elected pope.

932 **Rome** Marozia is overthrown and imprisoned; her son, Pope John XI, comes under the control of his younger brother, Alberic II, who styles himself as 'Prince and Senator of the Romans'; the pope's power is restricted to purely spiritual matters. **Venice** Orso II Participazio retires; Pietro II Candiano, son of Pietro I Candiano, doge in 887, succeeds him.

933 **Provence** ceases to be a separate kingdom when Hugh of Arles exchanges it, with Rudolph II, for the Kingdom of Italy.

934 **Burgundy** Rudolph II becomes king of a reunited Burgundy. **León and Galicia** The former king, Alfonso IV, tries to regain the throne, but is defeated and blinded by Ramiro II; he returns to his monastery. **Pamplona** García Sánchez I comes of age and begins to rule. **Denmark** Gorm the Old founds Denmark's first ruling dynasty, lasting until 1448. **Norway** Haakon, brother of Erik Bloodaxe, returns from England, where he has been fostered by King Athelstan, and with the support of Norwegian nobles, ousts Erik from the throne; Haakon takes the throne as Haakon I and reunites the country.

936 **France** Louis IV becomes king. **Germany** Henry the Fowler dies; he has united the German states into a single kingdom; Otto the Great becomes king. **Rome** Alberic II secures Leo VII's election to the papacy.

937
England Athelstan defeats a large army of Scots, Irish and Danes at the Battle of Brunanburh, northern England, securing the submission of King Constantine II of Scotland; he claims the title 'King of all Britain'.

937 **Burgundy** Conrad the Peaceful becomes king of Burgundy on the death of his father, Rudolph II.

939 **England** Edmund I becomes king; he regains control of Mercia from the Vikings and reconquers the Five Boroughs of the Danelaw. **Venice** Pietro Badoer Participazio, son of previous Doge Orso II Participazio, is elected doge. **Rome** Stephen VIII is elected pope.

942 **Venice** Pietro III Candiano is elected doge. **Rome** Marinus II is elected pope.

943 **Scotland** Constantine II abdicates and retires to a monastery, after reigning for 43 years; he will be the second-longest reigning Scottish monarch; Malcolm I, son of Donald II, becomes king.

944 **Byzantine Empire** Romanos I is deposed by his sons, and forced to become a monk; followers of Emperor Constantine VII revolt and send Stephen and Constantine into exile.

945 **England** Edmund I conquers Strathclyde, but Cumberland and Westmorland are annexed by the Scots. **Italy** Lothair II takes control of Italy, and rules until 950. **Kievan Rus'** Igor is killed while collecting tribute from the Drevlians; his wife takes terrible revenge on his killers and becomes regent for Igor's heir, his young son, Sviatoslav; she is the first ruler of Rus' to convert to Christianity.

946 **England** Edmund I is murdered by the exiled thief Leofa, at a party at Pucklechurch; his brother, Edred, becomes king; a sickly man, he can only eat the juices of already-chewed food. **Rome** Agapetus II is elected pope.

950 **Portugal** Gonçalo Mendes becomes count of Portugal.

951 **León** Ordoño III becomes king; during his reign he has to deal with rebellion and Muslim attacks. **Italy** Otto I of Germany invades and is crowned 'King of the Lombards'; the Kingdom of Italy is now ruled within the Holy Roman Empire, with the emperor as monarch.

954 **Scotland** Malcolm I is killed; his brother, Indulf, succeeds him. **France** Lothair, son of Louis IV, becomes king of France, aged 13.

955 **England** 14-year-old Edwy the Fair, King Edred's nephew, is chosen by the nobility as king; he feuds with his family and the Church. **Germany** Otto the Great, king of the Germans, defeats the Magyars at the Battle of Lechfeld, near Augsburg, and the Slavs at Reichnitz. **Rome** John XII, son of Alberic II, is elected pope; his papacy is immoral and scandalous; he loses papal territories.

956 **León** Sancho the Fat, half-brother of Ordoño III, becomes king.

957 **England** King Edwy is defeated in battle at Gloucester, but, fearing civil war, agrees to the country being divided along the Thames; Edwy rules Wessex and Kent in the south, and his brother, Edgar, rules north of the Thames.

958 **Denmark** King Harald Bluetooth becomes king, and accepts Christianity. **León** Ordoño the Wicked, son of Alfonso IV, usurps Sancho the Fat's throne, supported by disaffected nobles and the Kingdom of Castile.

959 **England** King Edwy dies, aged only 18 or 19; Edgar I the Peaceable becomes king, consolidating and uniting the kingdom. **Byzantine Empire** Constantine VII dies, possibly poisoned by his daughter-in-law, Theophano, or his son, Romanos, who becomes emperor as Romanos II.

960 **León** Sancho the Fat regains the throne with the support of Navarre.

961 **Germany** Otto II the Red becomes king. **Norway** Haakon I is mortally wounded in the Battle of Fitjar, in which he finally defeats the sons of Erik Bloodaxe; Harald II Greycloak, third son of Erik Bloodaxe, becomes king; his rule does not extend beyond the west of the country.

962 **Scotland** King Indulf is killed fighting Vikings at the Battle of the Bands, near Cullen; he is succeeded by Dub mac Maíl Coluim, son of his predecessor, Malcolm I. **Holy Roman Empire of the German Nation** Otto the Great is crowned Holy Roman Emperor; he is arguably the first true emperor, as he becomes the guarantor of the independence of the Papal States, the first emperor to do so since the Carolingian Empire; the Holy Roman Empire at its peak will encompass Germany, Italy, Burgundy, Austria, Switzerland, the Netherlands, Liechtenstein, Luxembourg, the Czech Republic, Slovenia, Belgium and parts of France, Italy and Poland.

963 **Luxembourg** is founded with the acquisition of Lucilinburhuc (modern-day Luxembourg Castle) by Siegfried, count of Ardennes. **Poland** Mieszko I, of the Piast dynasty, son of the legendary Siemomysł, founds the Kingdom of Poland. **Byzantine Empire** Romanos II dies, aged 26, possibly poisoned by his wife, Theophano; Nikephoros II Phokas, a brilliant military commander, seizes power and becomes emperor; he marries Theophano.

964 **Rome** Benedict V is voted pope by the people of Rome; Leo VIII is appointed antipope by Holy Roman Emperor Otto I and is elected pope after Benedict is deposed.

965 **Rome** Pope Leo VIII is deposed; John XIII is elected pope.

966 **León** Ramiro III becomes king, aged 5; two nuns act as regents – his aunt, Elvira Ramirez, who styled herself queen, and his mother.

967 **Scotland** King Dub is assassinated; Cuilén, son of Indulf, who was probably involved in his predecessor's murder, becomes king. **Holy Roman Empire** Otto II the Red becomes emperor.

969 **Byzantine Empire** Nikephoros II Phokas is assassinated by Theophana and others; one of the leaders of the assassination plot, John Tzimiskes, nephew of Nikephoros II, becomes Emperor John I; he successfully defends the empire from barbarian invasion. **Bulgaria** Boris II becomes tsar.

970 **Pamplona** Sancho II Garcés Abarca becomes king; he is the first to use the name 'King of Navarre'; in other places he is styled 'King of Aragón'.

971 **Scotland** King Cuilén is murdered when a hall he is in is deliberately set on fire by a Scottish noble, Amdarch, whose daughter Cuilén has been accused of raping; Kenneth II, son of Malcolm I, becomes king. **Serbia** Petrislav, son of Hvalimir II, becomes prince of Duklja and Travunia.

972
Rome Pope John XIII is possibly murdered by the jealous husband of a lover.

972 **Kievan Rus'** Sviatoslav I is killed by the Pecheneg khan, Kurya, having expanded east and south, making his kingdom the largest state in Europe.

973 **England** King Edgar I is crowned at Bath by St Dunstan, 14 years after becoming king; the coronation, described in a poem in the *Anglo-Saxon Chronicle*, forms the basis of the current British coronation ceremony; shortly after, at Chester, six British kings, including the kings of Scotland and of Strathclyde, submit to Edgar. **Rome** Benedict VI is elected pope; two months after his election, he is imprisoned and strangled on the orders of Crescentius I, son of Theodora, Roman senatrix, and mother of Marozia. **Sweden** Eric the Victorious becomes king; he reduces the power of the nobility.

974 **Rome** Benedict VII is elected pope.

975 **England** Edward the Martyr's succession to the throne, aged 13, is contested by supporters of his half-brother, Ethelred, but with Dunstan's support, Edward is acknowledged by the Witan and crowned king; factional fighting characterizes his reign.

976 **Ireland** Brian Boru becomes king of Munster. **Norway** Harald II is killed in Denmark by Haakon Sigurdsson and Harald Bluetooth, the Danish king; Haakon II Sigurdsson becomes king. **Venice** The unpopular and despotic Pietro IV Candiano is killed in a revolution against his efforts to create a monarchy; Pietro I Orseolo, one of his opponents, is elected doge; he restores the city, seriously damaged in the revolution, with his own money. **Austria** Leopold of Babenberg is appointed margrave of Austria; the Babenberg family rules Austria until 1246. **Bulgaria** Tsar Boris II and his brother, Roman, are held as 'honorary hostages' in Constantinople; to ensure the dynasty will die out, Roman is castrated (Boris only has daughters). **Byzantine Empire** Basil II the Bulgar-Slayer, nephew of John I Tzimiskes, becomes emperor; he restores Syria to the empire and wages war successfully against Bulgaria. **Kievan Rus'** Civil war breaks out between Oleg and Yaropolk, legitimate sons of the late ruler, Sviatoslav; Oleg is killed and Yarolpolk becomes prince of Kiev.

977 **Bulgaria** Boris II is accidentally killed by border guards who mistake him for a Byzantine noble; his brother, Roman, becomes tsar, ruling jointly with Samuil.

978 **England** Ethelred II the Unready becomes king of England at the age of 10, following the assassination of Edward the Martyr, his half-brother, possibly by servants of his stepmother, Ælfthryth (Elfrida); Ethelred develops the system of paying the Danes not to invade, known as *Danegeld*. **Kiev** Vladimir becomes grand prince of Kiev. **Venice** Doge Pietro I Orseolo suddenly joins a Benedictine monastery, later becoming a hermit; Vitale Candiano, possibly fourth son of the 22nd doge, Pietro IV Candiano, is elected doge.

979 **Venice** Vitale Candiano abdicates for health reasons; the wealthy but illiterate Tribuno Memmo is elected doge.

980 **Kievan Rus'** Vladimir, illegitimate son of Sviatoslav I, kills his half-brother, Yaropolk, and becomes sole ruler. **Belarus** Ragnvald Olafsson, prince of Polatsk, a Scandinavian who settled in the area, is killed by Vladimir the Great, grand prince of Kiev, after his daughter refuses to marry him; Vladimir I becomes ruler.

983 **Germany** Otto III is elected king, aged 3. **Rome** John XIV is elected pope.

984 **León** Ramiro III loses his throne to Bermudo II the Gouty, son of Ordoño III, king of Galicia, following defeats at the hands of the Moors and his unpopular attempts to establish an absolutist monarchy.

985 **Rome** John XV is elected pope.

986 **France** Louis V succeeds Lothair as king of France. **Denmark** Sweyn I Forkbeard becomes king of Denmark.

987 **France** King Louis V dies in a hunting accident; he is the last Carolingian emperor; Hugh Capet, son of Hugh the Great, duke of France and Hedwige of Saxony, daughter of Henry the Fowler, is elected king; his descendants will rule France until 1328.

988 **Kievan Rus'** Vladimir I converts to Christianity.

990 **Serbia** Jovan Vladimir becomes prince of Duklja; he allies his country with Byzantium, to avoid the expansionist aims of Bulgaria.

991 **Venice** Pietro II Orseolo is elected doge; he expands Venetian territory.

992 **Poland** Boleslaw I becomes king and greatly expands its territory; he unifies all the territories that traditionally make up Poland, and is the first ruler to be crowned king.

993 **Burgundy** Rudolph III becomes king of Burgundy.

994 **Pamplona** García Sánchez II becomes king.

995 **Scotland** Kenneth II is assassinated, possibly by Finnguala, daughter of Cuncar, Mormaer of Angus, whose only son Kenneth had been killed; Constantine III, son of King Cuilén, succeeds him. **Sweden** Olof Skötkonung, son of Danish king Sweyn Forkbeard, becomes king; he unites the Swedes with the Goths and welcomes Christianity in his kingdom. **Norway** Haakon II is killed by a servant, in his pigsty; Olaf I Tryggvason, great-grandson of Harald Fairhair, becomes king; he builds the country's first Christian church and has ambitions to rule a united Christian Scandinavia.

996 **France** Robert II the Pious becomes king; famine and revolution characterize his reign. **Holy Roman Empire** Otto III becomes emperor; he harbours ambitions to revive the power and glory of ancient Rome with himself as emperor; he revives Roman and Byzantine traditions and ceremonies. **Rome** Gregory V is elected pope, aged only 24; he is the first German pope.

997 **Scotland** Constantine II is killed in factional fighting; he is the last of the line of Áed to be king; Kenneth III, son of King Dub, succeeds him. **Bulgaria** Samuil becomes sole ruler, the first of the House of Comitopuli; his rule is characterized by war with Byzantium; he gains control of most of the Balkans and southern Greece. **Serbia** Samuil of Bulgaria conquers Duklja and takes Prince Jovan Vladimir prisoner; he marries Samuil's daughter and the Bulgarian tsar restores his lands to him.

998 **Rome** Otto III of Germany retakes the city of Rome and reinstates his cousin Pope Gregory V after mutilating and blinding his rival, the antipope, John XVI.

999 **Wales** Llewelyn ap Seisyll becomes king of Deheubarth and Gwynedd in south-west and north-west Wales. **León** Alfonso V becomes king, aged 5; his mother acts as regent. **Portugal** Mendo Gonçalves becomes 3rd count of Portugal. **Rome** Sylvester II is elected pope; he is the first French pope and introduces Arabic knowledge of arithmetic, mathematics and astronomy to Europe.

1000 **Norway** Olaf I Tryggvason dies in the Battle of Svolder, in which he is fighting an alliance of his enemies; the country is split into three areas of control divided between Olaf the Swede and Danish king Sweyn Forkbeard, with the remainder controlled by Erik Hakonarson, a vassal of Sweyn. **Hungary** The Hungarian state is founded by Stephen I; he acts against paganism and extends his territory.

1002 **Ireland** The previous king, Máel Sechnaill, surrenders the title of 'High King of all Ireland' to Brian Boru. **Germany** Otto III dies fighting the Romans; in the face of opposition, Henry II is elected king. **Bulgaria** All-out war breaks out between Byzantine Emperor Basil II and Bulgarian Tsar Samuil; Basil defeats Samuil.

1003 **Rome** John XVII is elected pope, but dies five months later; John XVIII succeeds him; he is controlled by the Roman Crescentii family.

1004 **Pamplona-Navarre** Sancho III the Great becomes king; during his reign, the kingdom becomes known as Navarre; he brings Castile, León and other territories under his control. **Italy** Henry II, king of Germany, becomes king.

1005 **Scotland** Kenneth III is killed in battle by Máel Coluim mac Cináed, son of Kenneth II, who becomes king, known as Malcolm II.

1008 **Portugal** Alvito Nunes becomes count of Portugal. **Venice** Otto Orseolo, third son of previous doge, Pietro II Orseolo, is elected doge; at 16, he is the youngest in Venetian history.

1009 **Rome** Pope John XVIII abdicates; Pietro Martino Boccapecora is elected pope as Sergius IV.

1012 **Rome** Benedict VIII is elected pope; he will promote peace in Italy by allying with the Norman settlers, defeating the Saracens and subjugating the Crescentii family.

1013 **England** The Danes invade England under Sweyn Forkbeard; Ethelred II flees to Normandy, and Sweyn takes control of England.

1014 **England** Sweyn Forkbeard dies only five weeks after his victory over Ethelred; Sweyn's son, Canute the Great, is proclaimed king by the Danish army, but is forced out of England with Ethelred being restored to the throne. **Ireland** High King Brian Boru decisively defeats the Vikings at the Battle of Clontarf, but is stabbed in the back in his tent by a Viking chief; Máel Sechnaill mac Domnaill of Meath becomes king again. **Denmark** Harald II becomes king. **Norway** On the death of Sweyn Forkbeard, Olaf II Haraldsson returns from fighting the Danes in England and declares himself king; he controls more of the country than any predecessor. **Holy Roman Empire** Henry II of Germany is crowned Holy Roman Emperor. **Byzantine Empire** In the Battle of Kleidion, Basil II defeats the Bulgarian army and massacres 15,000 prisoners. **Bulgaria** All of the Bulgarian survivors of the Battle of Kleidion are blinded, apart from 1 in every 100, so that they can be led home; Samuil is reported to die of a heart attack when he sees them; Gavril Radomir becomes tsar.

1015 **England** The Viking king, Canute the Great, invades England. **Bulgaria** On the orders of Byzantine agents, Gavril Radomir is killed while hunting by his cousin, Ivan Vladislav, who takes the throne.

CANUTE THE GREAT
REIGN: 994/995–1035

Canute (Cnut) I, or Canute the Great, was King of England, Denmark and Norway and also overlord of Schleswig and Pomerania. He was the son of the sea-king Sweyn Forkbeard, a member of the Jomsburg Vikings.

Canute was considered to be a wise and successful king, but he is perhaps best remembered for the legend of commanding the waves to go back. According to the popular story, Canute grew tired of all the flattery from his subjects, such as 'You are the greatest man that ever lived'. To try and prove a point, that he was not in fact the 'greatest man who had ever lived', he used all his powers to try and turn back the waves. Of course he was not successful, proving his point that even a king's powers have certain limits!

Canute died in 1035, at Shaftesbury in Dorset, and was buried in Winchester. He was succeeded by Harthacanute, reigning as Canute III.

1015 **Belarus** Bratislav becomes prince of Polotsk. **Kievan Rus'** Sviatopolk I becomes prince of Kiev.

1016 **England** Edmund Ironside becomes king on 23 April, but dies on 30 November 1016; his territories are ceded to Canute, who becomes king of England; he executes the most powerful English chieftains and marries Emma of Normandy, widow of Ethelred the Unready. **Serbia** Prince Jovan Vladimir is beheaded by Bulgarian ruler Ivan

Vladislav; he is canonized, the first Serbian saint; Jovan's uncle, Dragimir, succeeds, ruling both Duklja and Travunia; Duklja becomes a vassal state of the Byzantine Empire for the next 20 years.

1017 **England** Canute divides the country into the earldoms of Wessex, Mercia, East Anglia and Northumbria. **Portugal** Ilduara Mendes marries Nuno Alvites and becomes countess of Portugal.

> ***"Let all men know how empty and worthless is the power of kings. For there is none worthy of the name but God, whom heaven, earth and sea obey."***

Canute the Great

1018 **Bulgaria** Ivan Vladislav is killed by Basil II's invading Byzantine army; Presian II comes to power and leads the resistance for a brief period before submitting; the First Bulgarian Empire ends, and Bulgaria becomes part of the Byzantine Empire.

1019 **Sweden and Norway** sign a treaty at Kungälv. **Denmark** Canute I the Great becomes king. **Kievan Rus'** Iaroslav the Wise murders his three brothers and comes to power; he begins the unification of Russia when he unites the principalities of Novgorod and Kiev for the first time; during his reign, Kievan Rus' will reach the height of its power.

1020 **England** Canute the Great codifies the laws of England. **Italy** Italian towns, including Rome, Florence and Venice, become city-states. **Poland** Around this time, Boleslav I creates a powerful Polish state.

1022 **Ireland** Máel Sechnaill mac Domnaill, high king of Ireland, dies; a profusion of various contenders for the title follows, but none is successful until 1072. **Sweden** Anund Jakob becomes king.

1023 **Wales** Rhydderch ab Iestyn, ruler of Gwent and Morgannwg, seizes Deheubarth. Iago ab Idwal ap Meurig becomes king of Gwynedd. **Spain** The judge-governor of Sevilla seizes power as Abbad I, therefore founding the Abbadid dynasty.

1024 **Rome** John XIX, brother of previous Pope Benedict VIII, is elected pope. **Germany** Henry II dies childless; Conrad II, a Franconian nobleman, is elected king, the first of the Salian dynasty.

1025 **Poland** Mieszko II Lambert becomes king. **Byzantine Empire** Basil II dies childless, having greatly expanded the Empire; Constantine VIII, his co-emperor and brother, becomes sole ruler.

1026 **Venice** Tired of his appointments of members of his family to positions of power, the Venetians depose Pietro II Orseolo; Pietro Barbolano is elected doge.

1027 **Holy Roman Empire** Conrad II, king of Germany, is crowned Holy Roman Emperor.

1028 **León** Alfonso V is killed by an arrow while besieging a Muslim-held town in northern Portugal; Bermudo III, son of Alfonso V, becomes the last king of the Pérez dynasty. **Portugal** Mendes Nunes becomes count of Portugal. **Norway** Olaf II dies in the Battle of Stiklestad fighting against discontented subjects; he is canonized and becomes Norway's patron saint; Canute the Great, already king of England, Denmark and parts of Sweden, becomes king; his northern empire is one of the most powerful in Europe. **Germany** Conrad II has his son, Henry III, elected co-king. **Byzantine Empire** Zoe, daughter of Constantine VIII, becomes empress; her husband becomes Romanos III.

1029 **Spain** García Sánchez, count of Castile, is assassinated by a party of exiled Castilian noblemen as he enters the church in León where he has gone to marry the sister of Bermudo III; Sancho III of Navarre makes his son, Ferdinand, count of Castile.

1030 **France** Henry I of France revolts against his father, Robert I.

1031 **France** Henry I becomes king, having shared the throne with his father Robert I for five years. **Hungary** Emeric, only son and heir of Stephen I, is killed by a wild boar while hunting. **Poland** Bezprym, brother of Mieszko II Lambert, becomes duke of Poland.

1032 **Burgundy** The Holy Roman Emperor, Conrad II, becomes king of Burgundy; Burgundy is absorbed by the French monarchy. **Venice** Doge Pietro Barbolano is forced to abdicate in favour of his predecessor, Otto Orseolo; Orseolo is close to death, however; a relative, Domenico Orseolo, attempts to seize power, but his attempt is not welcomed by the Venetians, who are against the establishment of a hereditary monarchy; wealthy merchant Domenico Flabanico, who has no noble ties, is elected doge. **Rome** Benedict IX is elected pope; aged only 20, he is one of the youngest popes. **Poland** Bezprym is murdered; Mieszko II Lambert returns to the throne.

1034 **Scotland** Duncan I, son of Crínán, lay abbot of Dunkeld, and Bethóc, daughter of Malcolm II, become king and queen. **Poland** Mieszko II Lambert dies, probably murdered by members of the Polish aristocracy; peasants revolt in favour of paganism; priests, monks and knights are killed and cities, churches and monasteries are burned; the Czechs invade from the south and Poland is divided among local rulers until 1039. **Byzantine Empire** Empress Zoe of Byzantium murders her husband, Romanos III, and marries her chamberlain, elevating him to the throne of the eastern Roman Empire as Michael IV the Paphlagonian.

1035 **England** Canute's younger son, Harold I Harefoot, becomes regent in England, while his half-brother, Harthacanute, king of Denmark, fights against Magnus I of Norway. **France** Normandy, in the north of France, grows powerful. **Navarre-Aragón** On his death, Sancho III of Navarre, having done his utmost to unite the kingdoms of Spain, divides his kingdom between his sons; Ramiro I becomes count, and later the first king of Aragón; he turns it into an autonomous state; García Sánchez III becomes king of Navarre; Ferdinand receives Castile. **Norway** Magnus I the Good, illegitimate son of Olaf II, becomes king. **Serbia** Around this time, Stefan Dobroslav I Vojislav, cousin of Jovan Vladimir, declares independence for Duklja.

1036 **England** Edward the Confessor attempts to seize the throne from Harold I.

1037 **England** In the absence of his brother, Harthacanute, Harold I assumes the crown of England. **León** King Bermudo III is killed fighting his brother-in-law, Ferdinand, count of Castile, in the Battle of Tamarón; the Spanish kingdoms of Castile and León unite; Ferdinand, count of Castile, becomes King Ferdinand I the Great, of León and Castile, the first king of the Jiménez dynasty.

1039 **Wales** Iago ab Idwal is killed by his own men; Gruffyd ap Llewelyn becomes king. **Germany** Conrad II dies; Henry III continues as sole ruler. **Poland** Casimir I the Restorer, son of Mieszko II, becomes duke of Poland; he reunites the country after the period of turmoil.

1040 **England** Harold I dies; Harthacanute lands at Sandwich and reclaims the English throne; Harold's body is exhumed, beheaded and thrown into a fen bordering the Thames. **Scotland** King Duncan I of Scotland is killed in battle against his cousin and rival, Macbeth, who succeeds him; Macbeth is the son of Findláech mac Ruaidrí, Mormaer of Moray, and his action represents a Celtic rebellion against English influence on Scottish affairs. **Hungary** Stephen I's nephew, Peter Urseolo, becomes king; **Bulgaria** Peter Delyan, claiming to be the son of Tsar Gavril Radomir, leads an uprising against the Byzantine Empire.

1041 **England** Harthacanute's half-brother, Edward the Confessor – they both share the same mother, Emma of Normandy – returns from exile to become the heir to the English throne. **Hungary** Peter of Hungary causes unrest by confiscating the estates of the widow of former King Stephen, by increasing taxes, repressing pagan customs and appointing Germans and Italians to his council at the expense of the Hungarian nobles; he is deposed and flees to Austria; his brother-in-law, Samuel Aba, is proclaimed king. **Bulgaria** Peter Delyan's early successes end when his cousin, Alusian, cuts off his nose and blinds him one night when he is drunk; Alusian is proclaimed emperor, but defects to the Byzantine side; Peter II, although blind, leads his troops into battle, but is captured, taken to Constantinople and probably executed. **Byzantine Empire** Michael IV, second husband of Empress Zoe, dies; Michael V, nephew of Michael IV and adopted son of Empress Zoe, becomes co-emperor with Zoe.

1042 **England** On Harthacanute's death, without an heir, Edward the Confessor, helped by Godwin, earl of Wessex, becomes king of England, the last English king of the House of Wessex; his reign is characterized by conflict between the Norman party at court and the 'National' faction, led by Godwin and his son, Harold Godwinsson, later Harold II. **Denmark** Magnus the Good, king of Norway, also becomes king of Denmark. **Hungary** The former king, Peter of Hungary, allies with Holy Roman Emperor Henry II and attacks Hungary; he fails to gain the support of the Hungarian nobles. **Serbia** Stefan Dobroslav I Vojislav comprehensively defeats Byzantine Emperor Constantine IX; Duklja becomes a leading state in Serbia. **Byzantine Empire** Michael V of Byzantium is deposed by popular revolt; Empress Zoe becomes joint-empress with her sister Theodora; Zoe marries for the third time and elevates her husband to the throne as Constantine IX.

1043 **Venice** Doge Domenico Flabanico dies; Venice has declined during his reign; Domenico Contarini, the first of eight Contarini doges, is elected and revives its fortunes, recapturing lost territories and boosting the economy.

1044 **Hungary** Ex-king Peter again attacks Hungary, supported by troops of the Holy Roman Empire; he defeats King Samuel Aba in the Battle of Ménfő and Samuel Aba dies shortly after; Peter becomes king again, but is subservient to the Holy Roman Empire. **Belarus** Vseslav becomes prince of Polotsk; he is the best-known prince and is also grand prince of Kiev from 1068 until 1069.

1045 **England** Edward the Confessor begins the construction of Westminster Abbey. **Rome** Pope Benedict IX is forced from Rome, although some say he has accepted payment in return for his abdication; Sylvester III is elected pope; in April, Benedict IX forces the expulsion of Sylvester III; Benedict IX resigns in May, possibly to marry, selling the papacy to his godfather, John Gratian, who becomes Pope Gregory VI; Benedict IX returns to the papal throne shortly after, although Gregory continues to be recognized as the true pope.

WESTMINSTER ABBEY
1045–1050

This monument to Edward the Confessor is inside Westminster Abbey. The historic Abbey itself was built by Edward between 1045 and1050 and was consecrated on 28 December 1065. The building came about because Edward failed to keep a promise — to go on a pilgrimage — instead he redeemed himself by constructing this magnificent Abbey.

1046 **Rome** Benedict IX and Sylvester III are deprived of their offices by Holy Roman Emperor Henry III; the German bishop, Suidger, is crowned Clement II. **Holy Roman Empire** Henry III, king of Germany, is crowned Holy Roman Emperor.

1047 **Normandy** William the Conqueror secures control of Normandy. **Rome** Benedict IX seizes the Lateran Palace and becomes pope again. **Denmark** After years of trying, Sweyn II Estridson, nephew of Canute, becomes king when Magnus the Good divides up his empire on his death; he reunites Denmark and repulses the Norwegians. **Norway** The last great Viking king, Harald III Sigurdsson, also known as Harald Hardråde, uncle of Magnus I, takes the throne after sharing power with him for a year. **Hungary** King Peter antagonizes the nobles and clergy and is deposed for a second time; he is captured near Zámoly and is blinded by the rebels and expelled from the country; Hungary favours agnatic seniority for determining succession, and Andrew I, great-grandson of King Stephen's grandfather, returns from 15 years' exile to become king; he follows an anti-pagan policy.

1048 **Rome** Pope Benedict IX resigns; he is the only pope to have served three times and the only man ever to have sold the papacy; Poppo the German, bishop of Brixen, is elected pope as Damasus II; he dies after 21 days, possibly of malaria. **Hungary** King Andrew assigns control of one-third of Hungary to his brother, Duke Béla, as appanage; the two brothers share power.

1049 **Rome** Bruno von Eguisheim-Dagsburg is elected pope, as Leo IX; he becomes the most important German pope of the Middle Ages, renewing the practice of celibacy and introducing many other reforms.

1050 **Portugal** Nuno Mendes becomes 7th count of Portugal; he is the last count of the House of Vímara Peres. **Sweden** Emund the Old, illegitimate son of Olaf Skötkonung and older half-brother of King Anund Jakob, becomes king; he is the last king of the House of

Munsö. **Byzantine Empire** Empress Zoe dies, and her husband and co-emperor, Constantine IX, becomes sole ruler.

1051 **Serbia** Mihailo I becomes grand prince of Duklja.

1054 **Navarre** García Sánchez III dies in the Battle of Atapuerca; he is succeeded by 14-year-old Sancho IV. **Germany** Henry IV becomes king; he is one of the most important figures of the 11th century; he defeats the rebellious Saxons and quarrels with the pope; he faces and defeats three rivals to his throne. **Rome** Pope Leo IX's excommunication of the patriarch of Constantinople, Michael I Cerularius, leads to the split between the Eastern and Western Churches, known as the Great Schism. **Kievan Rus'** Izyaslav I becomes prince of Kiev.

1055 **Wales** Gruffydd ap Llewelyn claims sovereignty over all of Wales, a claim recognized by the English. **Rome** Gebhard, count of Calw, Tollenstein und Hirschberg is elected pope, as Victor II; he strengthens the papacy against the aggressions of the nobles. **Byzantine Empire** On the death of her co-emperor, Constantine IX, Theodora becomes sole ruler.

1056 **León-Castile** Having consolidated his possessions in northern Iberia, Ferdinand I the Great declares himself 'Emperor of Hispania', to the annoyance of Pope Victor II and the Holy Roman Emperor, Henry III. **Byzantine Empire** Empress Theodora dies childless; she recommends the defence minister, Michael VI Bringas, to replace her; he does not receive universal support and conflict breaks out between noble families until around 1081.

1057 **Scotland** King Macbeth is killed in battle against Malcolm III; Macbeth's stepson, Lulach mac Gille Coemgáin, grandson of Kenneth III, is installed as king; he is a weak king, known as 'the Foolish'. **Rome** Frederick of Lorraine is elected pope as Stephen IX. **Hungary** King Andrew I tries to ensure succession by having his son Solomon crowned 'junior' king, angering his brother, Duke Béla. **Byzantine Empire** Michael VI abdicates; Isaac I Komnenos is the first and only emperor of the Komnenid dynasty.

1058 **Scotland** King Lulach is assassinated; Malcolm III Canmore, oldest son of Duncan I, becomes king; his line will rule Scotland for many years. **Poland** Bolesław II the Bold becomes duke of Poland; he is one of the most talented of the rulers of the House of Piast, making alliances with neighbours to fight the threat of Germany and the Holy Roman Empire.

1059 **Rome** Gérard de Bourgogne, bishop of Florence, is elected pope, as Nicholas II; he achieves the subjugation of Milan to Rome and allies with the Normans; he introduces the practice – in place to this day – of popes being elected by the cardinals instead of the Roman aristocracy. **Byzantine Empire** Isaac I abdicates, believing, wrongly, that he is suffering from an incurable disease; Constantine X Doukas becomes the first emperor of the Doukid dynasty; he is unpopular and unsuccessful, losing most of Byzantine Italy to the Normans.

1060 **France** Philippe I succeeds to the throne aged 7; he is ruling in his own right by the age of 14. **Sweden** Stenkil Ragnvaldson becomes king; he is the first king of the House of Stenkil. **Hungary** Duke Béla defeats his brother, Andrew I, to become Béla I; Andrew is captured and dies.

1061 **Rome** Anselmo da Baggio, bishop of Lucca, is elected pope as Alexander II; an antipope, Honorius II, threatens him for some time, but Alexander is confirmed by a council at Mantua.

1063 **Aragón** Sancho Ramírez becomes king. **Hungary** King Béla I dies when his throne's canopy collapses on top of him; Solomon, son of Andrew I, is crowned king for the second time at the age of 9.

1064 **Wales** Gruffydd ap Llewelyn is killed by Cynan ap Iago, whose father, Iago ab Idwal, Gruffydd had put to death in 1039; Bleddyn ap Cyfyn, half-brother of Gruffydd ap Llewelyn, becomes ruler.

1065 **León-Castile** On the death of Ferdinand I of León-Castile, his kingdom is split between his three sons; Sancho II the Strong receives the Kingdom of Castile; Alfonso VI becomes king of León; García becomes king of Galicia and declares the independence of Galicia and Portugal.

1066 **England** Edward the Confessor's heir, Edgar Ætheling, is thought to be too young to become king, aged 15; Edward allegedly nominates Harold Godwinson, earl of Wessex, as his successor; he is the last Anglo-Saxon to be crowned king of England, as Harold II; at the Battle of Stamford Bridge, Harold II defeats Harald III Hardråde, king of Norway, marking the end of the Viking era in England; at the Battle of Hastings, William the Conqueror, duke of Normandy and bastard son of Robert II of Normandy, defeats and kills Harold II, who has reigned for just 10 months; Edgar Ætheling is proclaimed king by the Witan, but never crowned; William I, his claim to the English crown coming through his great-aunt, Emma of Normandy, is crowned king. **Sweden** On the death of Stenkil Ragnvaldsson, an interregnum ensues until 1078. **Norway** Magnus II Haraldsson, son of Harald Hardråde, becomes king.

1067 **France** The Trencavel family comes to power in Carcassonne, in France. **Norway** Olaf III the Peaceful returns from England to claim

WILLIAM THE CONQUEROR
REIGN: 1028–1087

William the Conqueror was the illegitimate son of Robert, Duke of Normandy and Herleva. Despite his somewhat shaky start in life having been dubbed 'William the Bastard', William was supported by the majority of the Norman barons and succeeded his father in 1035.

His early life was fraught with danger due to the fact that he was not a very popular choice of ruler. However, William quickly learned to trust no one, which led to a series of major conflicts. Prepared to fight for his beliefs and his leadership, William soon learned the skills of fighting and became a gifted knight and warrior.

William the Conqueror is best remembered for the famous Battle of Hastings that took place on 14 October 1066. An event so significant, it completely changed the course of English history. At the time there were three potential contenders to the throne: Harald Hardråde, king of Norway, Duke William of Normandy and the Saxon Harold, son of Godwin, Earl of Wessex. These three contenders for the throne of England resulted in conflict which led to the Battle of Hastings. The battle raged on, but by late afternoon the most famous arrow in history hit King Harold in the eye, causing his soldiers to flee the Senlac ridge. The day belonged to Duke William, soon to be dubbed 'The Conqueror'.

William died on the morning of 9 September 1087 following a spell of illness. He was 59 years old and had ruled England for 21 years and Normandy for 31 more.

his share of the Kingdom of his father Harald Hardråde; Magnus II rules the north and Olaf rules the south. **Byzantine Empire** Michael VII becomes emperor, aged 17; his mother, Eudokia, and general Romanos IV Diogenes, rule as regents.

1068 **Kievan Rus'** A popular uprising deposes Izyaslav I; he flees to Poland.

1069 **England** William the Conqueror crushes rebellion in the north of England, burning houses, crops, cattle and land, resulting in the deaths of over 100,000 people, from starvation and winter cold; the action is known as the Harrying of the North. **Norway** Magnus II dies, leaving his brother Olaf as sole ruler. **Kievan Rus'** Izyaslav I retakes Kiev, with the help of the Polish army.

1070 **England** Hereward the Wake begins a Saxon revolt in the Fens of eastern England.

1071 **Spain** García II, as king of Galicia, is the first to use the title king of Portugal, following his defeat of Count Nuno Mendes, last count of Portugal of the House of Vímara Peres, in the Battle of Pedroso. **Italy** The last Byzantine-controlled city in southern Italy, Bari, is captured by Robert Guiscard. **Venice** Domenico Selvo is elected doge; Venice begins a long period of prosperity. **Byzantine Empire** Emperor Michael VII dispatches his mother to a monastery, murders Romanos IV and is crowned senior emperor.

1072 **England** William I invades Scotland; he defeats Hereward the Wake in the Fens. **Ireland** Toirdelbach Ua Briain becomes high king of Ireland; at 15, he is said to have commanded an army of a thousand men. **León-Castile** Sancho the Strong of León reannexes his brother García's Kingdom of Galicia and then forces his brother, Alfonso, into exile, taking control of León; Sancho is assassinated by a Zamoran noble; his brother, Alfonso VI, takes control of his kingdoms and styles himself 'Emperor of all Hispania'. **Bulgaria** Constantin Bodin, seventh son of Michael I of Zeta, assumes the throne as Peter III, following a revolt by Bulgarian noblemen; the Byzantines retaliate and capture Peter, who is taken into captivity in Constantinople; Bulgaria is ruled by the Byzantine Empire until 1186.

1073 **Rome** Hildebrand of Soana is elected pope as Gregory VII; he restricts the use of the title 'Papa' to the bishop of Rome, the pope. **Kievan Rus'** Izyaslav I is ousted again, by his brothers; Sviatoslav II becomes prince of Kiev.

1074 **Denmark** Harald III, the oldest illegitimate son of Sweyn II, is elected king. **Hungary** Solomon is defeated by Béla I's son, Géza I, in the Battle of Mogyoród, and goes into exile, but remains in control of the western part of the country.

1075 **England** The Revolt of the Three Earls, against William the Conqueror, is the last serious act of resistance to the Norman Conquest. **Wales** Bleddyn ap Gyfyn is killed by Rhys ab Owain of Deheubarth and the nobility of Ystrad Tywi in south Wales; Bleddyn's cousin, Trahaern ap Caradog, becomes king of Gwynedd. **Holy Roman Empire** Henry IV, Holy Roman Emperor, subjugates Saxony.

1076 **Aragón and Navarre** Sancho Ramírez is elected king of Navarre after Sancho IV is murdered by his brothers; Sancho Ramírez becomes king of Aragón and Navarre. **Rome** Pope Gregory VII excommunicates the Holy Roman Emperor, Henry IV; he is the first pope to stand up to a king; Henry pleads forgiveness, but conflict between the empire and the papacy continues into the 12th century.

1076 **Kievan Rus'** Vsevolod I becomes prince of Kiev, but cedes the throne to Izyaslav I who has retaken Kiev.

1077 **England** The rebellious Robert Curthose, future duke of Normandy, instigates his first insurrection against his father, William the Conqueror. **Sweden** Halsten Stenkilsson becomes king. **Hungary** Géza I of Hungary dies; his brother, Ladislaus I, becomes king. **Montenegro** The Kingdom of Duklja is founded with the support of Pope Gregory VII; Mihailo I is its first king.

1078 **Wales** Trahaern ap Caradog, king of Gwynedd, defeats Rhys ab Owain in the Battle of Goodwick. **Bulgaria** Constantin Bodin – Peter III of Bulgaria – is freed by Venetian sailors and returns to his homeland of Zeta. **Byzantine Empire** Michael VII resigns and enters a monastery amid widespread dissatisfaction; Nikephoros III Botaneiates, a general and governor, proclaims himself emperor, and bigamously marries the wife of Michael VII. **Kievan Rus'** Izyaslav I dies in a civil war; Vsevolod I is restored to power.

1079 **Poland** Bolesław II the Bold murders the bishop of Kraków and future saint Stanislaus of Szczepanów; nobles and prelates revolt, and Bolesław is forced into exile in Hungary; his brother, Władysław I Herman, becomes duke of Poland.

1080 **England** William I writes to the pope to remind him that the king of England owes him no allegiance. **Sweden** Inge I becomes king, sharing the throne with his brother, Halsten. **Denmark** Canute IV becomes king.

1081 **Wales** Trahaearn ap Caradog, king of Gwynedd, is murdered by one of Gruffydd ap Cynan's men; Gruffydd becomes king of north Wales, but spends the first 12 years of his reign imprisoned in England by William the Conqueror; his successors are styled 'princes', not 'kings'. **Sweden** Blot Sven, brother-in-law of King Inge, overthrows him on a resurgence of pagan feeling against Christianity. **Serbia** Constantin Bodin, Mihailo I's seventh son, becomes king of Duklja; he has been Tsar Peter III of Bulgaria for a short time, in 1072; **Byzantine Empire** Emperor Nikephorus III is overthrown by Alexios I Comnenus, ending the Middle Byzantine period and beginning the Comnenan dynasty; he revives the empire's military, financial and territorial fortunes.

1082 **Holy Roman Empire** Henry IV, Holy Roman Emperor, besieges Rome and gains entry; a synod is agreed upon by the Romans, to rule on the dispute between Henry and Pope Gregory VII.

1083 **Sweden** Inge I kills Blot Sven around this time, and returns to the throne. **Bosnia** is conquered by Duklja. **Hungary** King Stephen is canonized and becomes patron saint of his country.

> ***"I want there to be no peasant in my kingdom so poor that he cannot have a chicken in his pot every Sunday."***

Henry IV

1084 **Venice** Doge Domenico Selvo is heavily defeated at Corfu by Robert Guiscard's Normans; a popular revolt peacefully deposes Selvo; Venetian nobleman Vitale Faliero Dodoni is elected doge. **Holy Roman Empire** Henry IV, king of Germany, is crowned Holy Roman Emperor.

1086 **Rome** Desiderius, the great abbot of Monte Cassino, is elected pope as Victor III. **Denmark** King Canute IV is assassinated in the church of St Alban at Odense; he is made a saint and becomes the patron saint of Denmark; his brother, Oluf I, becomes king.

1087 **England** William the Conqueror dies from injuries received falling from his horse, while besieging Mantes in France; William II Rufus, duke of Normandy, becomes king; Normans in England revolt in favour of his older brother, Robert, but they are suppressed; William is a ruthless and unpopular king. **Germany** Conrad II is elected king and crowned in Aachen. **Hungary** Former King Solomon I is killed in battle near Hadrianopolis, fighting with the Pecheneg tribe against his former kingdom.

1088 **Rome** Urban II is elected pope; he will launch the First Crusade, in 1095, and bring Sicily and Campagna under Catholic control.

1090 **Ireland** Domhnall MacLochlainn becomes high king, following an interregnum. **Spain** García II, former king of Galicia, dies in the monastery to which he was consigned by his brothers, in 1072.

1093 **Scotland** After a reign lasting 35 years, Malcolm III is killed at the Battle of Alnwick, while invading Northumberland; his son, Edward, is also killed; Donald III Bane, second son of Duncan I, becomes king; he expels the English from the Scottish court. **Portugal** Henry of Burgundy, who has fought in the Reconquista against the Moors in the Iberian Peninsula and helped King Alfonso VI of Castile and León conquer part of northern Portugal, is rewarded by marriage to Alfonso's daughter, Theresa, countess of Portugal; he receives the County of Portugal as a dowry. **Norway** Haakon Magnusson, son of King Magnus, becomes king; Magnus Barefoot, son of Olaf III the Peaceful, declares a rival claim to the throne. **Germany** Conrad II betrays his father, Holy Roman Emperor Henry IV, by supporting the reforming Pope Gregory VII in their quarrel about Henry's right to appoint bishops; the pope promises Conrad the imperial crown. **Italy** Conrad II of Germany is crowned king. **Kievan Rus'** Sviatopolk II, illegitimate son of Izyaslav I, becomes prince of Kiev; his reign is characterized by incessant fighting with his cousin, Vladimir Monmakh, son of Vsevolod I.

1094 **Scotland** Donald III Bane is deposed; Duncan II, son of Malcolm III, who has spent his life at the English court under Norman influence, succeeds him; shortly after his accession, he is killed in a revolt against the Norman influence in Scotland; Donald III Bane is restored to the throne. **Aragón and Navarre** Pedro I becomes king following the death of his father, Sancho I, at the Siege of Huesca. **Norway** Haakon Magnusson dies; Magnus Barefoot becomes king; he conquers the Orkney Islands, the Isle of Man, the Hebrides and Dublin.

1095 **Denmark** Eric I, son of Sweyn Edrison, becomes king. **Hungary** Ladislaus I dies preparing to join the First Crusade; he has been one of Hungary's greatest kings, conquering Croatia and enlarging his kingdom; he is canonized; Coloman, son of Géza I by a Greek concubine, becomes king.

1096 **Venice** Vital I Michele is elected the 32nd doge.

1097 **Scotland** Edgar, son of Malcolm III and half-brother of the murdered Duncan II, succeeds Donald III Bane as king.

1098 **Germany** Henry IV deposes his son, Conrad II, replacing him as king with his younger son, Henry V.

1099 **Germany** Henry V becomes the last king of the Salian dynasty. **Rome** Pope Urban II dies 14 days after the capture of Jerusalem by the Crusaders, but before news reaches Italy; the monk, Ranierius, is elected pope as Paschal II; he excommunicates Holy Roman Emperor Henry IV. **Sweden** Halsten dies, leaving his brother Inge as sole ruler.

1100
England William II Rufus is killed by an arrow while hunting – was it an accident or was it murder? Henry I becomes king.

1101 **England** Robert Curthose gives up his claim to the Anglo-Norman throne, therefore confirming Henry I as king of England. **Serbia** Constantin Bodin, king of Duklja, dies, setting off a dynastic struggle; his sons, Mihailo II Vojislav and Dobroslav II, rule jointly. **Belarus** Boris I becomes prince of Polotsk.

1102 **Venice** Ordelafo Faliero, son of previous doge, Vitale Faliero, succeeds him; he wars against Hungary from 1105 to 1115, recapturing Zara and Sebenico, and captures a part of Acre, in Syria. **Poland** Zbigniew and Bolesław III Wrymouth, sons of Władysław I Herman, rule the country jointly on the death of their father. **Serbia** Dobroslav III becomes ruler of Duklja; he is captured, castrated and blinded; Kočapar Branislavljević is brought to power by Grand Prince Vukan of another Serbian state, Rascia.

1103 **Norway** Olaf Magnusson becomes king, aged 4; his older brothers act as regents. **Serbia** Vladimir, oldest brother of King Constantin Bodin, becomes king of Duklja; he brings peace by marrying a daughter of Vukan of Rascia.

1104 **Aragón and Navarre** Alfonso I the Warrior, second son of Sancho Ramírez, becomes king; he reconquers substantial areas held by the Moors. **Denmark** Niels becomes the fifth son of Sweyn Edridson to become king. **Holy Roman Empire** Encouraged by supporters of the pope, Henry V declares that he cannot hold allegiance to an excommunicated emperor, his father, Henry IV; Henry IV is forced to abdicate and is imprisoned.

1106 **England** Henry I defeats his older brother, Robert Curthose, duke of Normandy, at the Battle of Tinchebrai. **Germany** Henry IV escapes from prison, and defeats his son in Lorraine, but dies shortly after. **Belarus** David becomes prince of Polotsk.

1107 **Scotland** On the death of the unmarried King Edgar, his brother, Alexander I, becomes king on condition that he gives his brother, David, an appanage – a title – in southern Scotland, possibly Strathclyde or Cumbria. **Poland** Bolesław III puts his half-brother, Zbigniew, to flight, and becomes sole ruler; Zbigniew joins forces with the Holy Roman Empire against Poland, but is defeated, and Bolesław later captures and blinds him.

1108 **Scotland** Around this time, Alexander I marries Sybilla, illegitimate daughter of Henry I of England. **France** Louis VI the Fat becomes king.

1109 **León-Castile-Galicia** After her only brother is killed in the Battle of Ucles, in 1108, Urraca, Alfonso IV's daughter, becomes queen of Castile, León and Galicia, on her father's death; she marries Alfonso I of Aragón.

1110 **Holy Roman Empire** Henry V invades Italy.

1111 **Holy Roman Empire** Henry V of Germany is crowned emperor after giving up his right to invest bishops; his decision is rejected by German bishops and princes; Henry takes the pope prisoner, forcing him to concede investiture rights; the pope later withdraws his concession and excommunicates Henry.

1112 **Portugal** On the death of his father Henry, 3-year-old Alfonso I Henriques becomes count of Portugal; his mother, Teresa, possibly aged only 18, rules as regent, but styles herself queen of Portugal; she fights to gain a larger share of the Leónese inheritance from her sister, Queen Urraca of Castile, León and Galicia. **Sweden** Philip Halstensson becomes king, he has to share the throne with Inge II.

1113 **Scotland** David, brother of King Alexander I, demands further titles and land; he is known as 'Prince of the Cumbrians'. **Hungary** Coloman imprisons and blinds his brother Almos, legitimate son of Géza I, and his son Béla. **Serbia** Vladimir of Duklja is poisoned under the orders of Queen Jakvinta, King Constantin Bodin's widow; she appoints her son George to the throne. **Kievan Rus'** Vladimir II Monomakh, son of Vsevolod I, becomes prince of Kiev by popular acclaim.

1114 **León-Castile-Galicia** The marriage of Queen Urraca and Alfonso I of Aragón is annulled, due to consanguinity. **Holy Roman Empire** Matilda, daughter of Henry I of England, marries Holy Roman Emperor Henry V.

1115 **Norway** Olaf Magnusson dies; his brothers, Øystein and Sigurd I the Crusader, share the throne.

1116 **Hungary** Coloman dies, having retaken Croatia; Stephen II becomes king of Hungary and Croatia.

1117 **Venice** Doge Ordelafo Faliero is killed in battle against the Hungarians; Domenico Michele is elected doge; he fights successfully in the Holy Land and defeats the Greeks.

1118 **Normandy** A rebellion against Henry I breaks out in Normandy. **Ireland** Tairrdelbach Ua Conchobair becomes high king of Ireland. **Rome** Giovanni Coniulo is elected pope as Gelasius II; Holy Roman Emperor Henry V drives Gelasius from Rome and installs Burdinus, archbishop of Braga, as antipope Gregory VIII; with Norman support, Gelasius returns to the papal throne; he is driven out, once again, and goes to France where he dies. **Sweden** Philip Halstensson dies; Inge II becomes sole ruler. **Serbia** King George's cousin, Prince Grubeša Branislavljević, deposes him as king of Duklja, following his defeat by the Byzantine Empire. **Byzantine Empire** John I Comnenos becomes emperor; during his reign, he attempts to reconquer all of the important Byzantine territory lost to the Arabs, Turks and Christian Crusaders.

1119 **Rome** Guy de Vienne, the son of William I, count of Burgundy and archbishop of Vienne, is elected pope as Calixtus II.

1120 Thomas Becket was born, the son of a prosperous London merchant.

1120
England *The White Ship* sinks in the English Channel; King Henry II's only son, the heir to the throne, William Adelin, is tragically drowned.

1122 **Holy Roman Empire** In the Concordat of Worms, Henry V renounces the right of investiture of bishops; Henry's excommunication is lifted.

1123 **Rome** Pope Calixtus II returns to Rome and ousts antipope Gregory VIII, who is imprisoned. **Norway** On the death of Øystein, Sigurd I becomes sole ruler.

1124 **Scotland** Prince of the Cumbrians, David I, younger brother of Alexander I, becomes king, with the support of Henry I of England. **Rome** Lamberto Scannabecchi, cardinal of Ostia, is elected pope as Honorius II.

1125 **Germany** Lothair, duke of Saxony, is elected king on the death of Henry V, without issue. **Serbia** Former Duklja king, George, defeats and probably kills his usurper, King Grubeša, in Antivari, with Rascian help; George returns to the throne. **Kievan Rus'** Vladimir II dies, following what is regarded as the golden age of the city of Kiev; Mstislav I, son of Vladimir II by his wife Gytha of Wessex, becomes prince of Kiev; his grandfather is Harold II of England.

1126 **León-Castile-Galicia** Queen Urraca dies in childbirth; Alfonso VII, the emperor, whose father is Raymond of Burgundy, is crowned king of Castile, Galicia and León, the first king in Spain from the House of Burgundy.

1127 **Belarus** Boris I becomes prince of Polotsk for a second time.

1128 **Portugal** effectively becomes independent when 19-year-old Alfonso I Henriques, count of Portugal, defeats his mother Teresa, 'Queen of Portugal', at the Battle of São Mamede, winning control of the County of Portugal; he also defeats Alfonso VII of Castile and León, freeing the county from its political dependence on Castile and León; his subjects declare him 'Duke of Portugal'. **Belarus** Sviatopolk of Kiev becomes prince of Polotsk.

1129 **Portugal** Count Afonso Henriques is declared prince of Portugal.

1130 **Sweden** Sverker I the Elder, Blot Sven's grandson, becomes king; he is the first king of the House of Sverker and Eric. **Norway** On the death of Sigurd I, civil war breaks out (until 1217) between two claimants to the throne, Magnus Sigurdsson and Harald IV Gille, son of Magnus Barefoot. **Venice** Pietro Polani is elected doge; there are protests because he is married to the daughter of his predecessor, Domenico Michele, and Venetians fear public positions being passed on through inheritance. **Rome** Cardinal Gregorio Papareschi is elected pope, as Innocent II; a group of cardinals elects antipope Anacletus II; Innocent II flees Rome. **Sicily** Norman nobleman Roger II, count of Sicily, receives royal investiture from Antipope Anacletus II; he becomes King Roger II of Sicily, which comprises Sicily and the southern third of the Italian peninsula.

1131 **Hungary and Croatia** Stephen II dies; Béla II the Blind, son of Almos, blinded by King Coloman in 1113, becomes king. **Serbia** King George dies, imprisoned by the Byzantine Empire, following defeat in the second Duklja–Byzantine war; Gradihna Branislavljević, brother of King Grubeša, becomes a Byzantine puppet king of Duklja. **Belarus** Vasil becomes prince of Polotsk.

1132 **Kievan Rus'** Yaropolk II, another son of Vladimir II Monomakh and Gytha of Wessex, becomes prince of Kiev.

1133 **Holy Roman Empire** Lothair III, elected king of Germany, is crowned Holy Roman Emperor.

1134 **Aragón and Navarre** Alfonso I of Aragón leaves his kingdom to the Knights Templar; the Aragónese ignore his wishes, and Ramiro II the Monk, yet another son of Sancho Ramírez, becomes king; Ramiro is given special dispensation by the pope to temporarily renounce his monastic vows to secure the succession to the Aragónese throne; Navarre becomes independent once more, after 58 years, under García Ramírez, half-brother of Sancho IV, restoring the House of Jiménez. **Denmark** King Niels dies in battle in Schleswig; Eric II, son of Eric I, becomes king. **Norway** Magnus IV Sigurdsson defeats Harald IV at the battle at Färlev.

1135 **England** Henry I dies from food poisoning, after famously eating 'a surfeit of lampreys'; Henry has stipulated that his daughter Matilda should become queen on his death, but her gender, and the fact that she has married into the House of Anjou, sworn enemies of the Normans, turns the barons against her; Henry's nephew, Stephen of Blois, comes to England and claims the crown, signalling a period of unrest known as 'the Anarchy'; Stephen will be the last Norman king of England. **León-Castile-Galicia** Alfonso VII of Castile is crowned 'Emperor of all the Spains'. **Norway** Harald IV captures Magnus IV, blinds him and imprisons him.

1136 **Wales** Owain Gwynedd of Wales defeats the Normans at Crug Mawr. **Norway** Sigurd Slembedjakn, illegitimate son of Magnus Barefoot, murders Harald IV; Sigurd II Munn, son of Harald IV, becomes co-ruler with his brothers, Inge and Øystein; Harald's killer, Sigurd Slembedjakn, makes a rival claim for the throne.

1137 **France** Louis VII the Young becomes king of France; his first wife is Eleanor of Aquitaine, who later marries Henry II of England. **Aragón** Ramiro the Monk abdicates and returns to his monastery; his daughter Peronilla becomes queen. **Germany** Lothair III dies while campaigning in Italy. **Denmark** Eric III, nephew of Eric II, becomes king. **Sicily** Naples is captured and integrated into the Kingdom of Sicily.

1138 **England and Scotland** The English defeat David I of Scotland in the Battle of the Standard. **Germany** Conrad III, grandson of Henry IV and previously a rival king to Lothair III, is elected king; civil war breaks out when he deprives rival Henry the Proud of his lands, the first manifestation of the struggle between the Guelphs and the Ghibellines, rival factions supporting the papacy and the Holy Roman Empire respectively. **Rome** Antipope Anacletus II dies, ending his rivalry with Pope Innocent II. **Poland** Bolesław III divides the country between his five sons, with the most important part being given to the oldest; this will cause fighting and disorder in Poland for 200 years; Władysław II the Exile becomes high duke of Poland.

1139 **Portugal** Following the Battle of Ourique, in which he defeats the Almoravids army, led by Ali ibn Yusuf and four other Emirs, Prince Alonso is declared King Alfonso I of an independent Portugal; he is crowned king in Bragança, the first Portuguese king of the House of Burgundy. **Norway** Pretender to the throne Sigurd Slembedjakn is imprisoned and executed by supporters of Inge I. **Sicily** Pope Innocent II recognizes the Kingdom of Sicily. **Kievan Rus'** Vsevolod II becomes ruler, styling himself grand prince of Kiev.

1141 **Hungary and Croatia** Béla II dies of an over-indulgence in alcohol; Géza II is crowned king, aged 11.

1143 **Portugal** After years of bitter conflict, King Alfonso VII of Castile recognizes Portugal as an independent kingdom by the Treaty of Zamora. **Rome** Guido di Castello is elected pope as Celestine II; during his reign, the Roman people establish a republic to curb the power of the pope. **Byzantine Empire** John II Comnenus dies in a hunting accident, having recovered substantial territories for the empire; Manuel I Comnenus becomes emperor.

1144
France Geoffrey of Anjou, second husband of Empress Matilda, conquers Normandy, bringing it under Angevin control.

1144 **Rome** Gherardo Caccianemici dal Orso is elected pope as Lucius II. **Belarus** Rogneda Borisovich becomes prince of Polotsk.

1145 **Rome** Pope Lucius II is killed by a stone thrown at him as he marches against the Roman Senate; Bernardo dei Paganelli di Montemagno, abbot of a Cistercian monastery near Rome, is elected pope as Eugene III; his pontificate is spent almost entirely outside Rome, after the Romans rebel against papal power.

1146 **Holy Roman Empire** Emperor Conrad III takes part in the Second Crusade. **Poland** Władysław II is driven into exile by his younger brothers; Bolesław IV the Curly, oldest surviving son of Bolesław III, becomes high duke. **Serbia** Radoslav Gradišnić becomes ruler of Duklja, but only with the authority of Byzantine Emperor Manuel I Comnenus; Duklja's power has diminished so much that he may only style himself prince. **Kievan Rus'** Igor II, brother of Vsevolod II, becomes prince of Kiev; within weeks he is deposed by his cousin, Iziaslav Msistislavich, who becomes Iziaslav II.

1147 **Portugal** King Afonso I and the Crusaders capture Lisbon from the Moors, following a siege. **Germany** Conrad III has his son, Henry Berengar, elected king – to rule while he is away on the Second Crusade and to ensure the succession for his family in the event of his death in battle.

1148 **Aragón** On the death of her husband, Raymond Berenguer IV, count of Barcelona, Queen Petronella abdicates in favour of her son Ramon, who becomes Alfonso II; he is the first ruler of both Aragón and Catalonia, his realms stretching as far as Provence; the union of Aragón and Catalonia lasts until the crown of Aragón is dissolved in 1707. **Navarre** Sancho VI becomes king; his reign sees numerous clashes with Aragón and Castile. **Portugal** King Afonso I takes Abrantes from the Moors. **Denmark** Eric III abandons the throne and retires to a monastery; the son of Eric II, Sweyn III, becomes king, but is challenged by Canute V and Valdemar 'the Great'; he kills Canute but is himself killed by Valdemar, who becomes king in 1157. **Venice** Domenico Morosini is elected doge; he reconciles warring factions in Venetian patrician families and defeats the Normans. **Kievan Rus'** Yuri I Dolgoruki, sixth son of Vladimir II Monomakh, becomes grand prince of Kiev.

1150 **Germany** King Henry Berengar dies; the succession is thrown wide open.

1151 **Belarus** Rostislav of Minsk becomes prince of Polotsk. **Kievan Rus'** Prince Yuri I is driven from Kiev by his nephew Iziaslav III.

1152 **Germany** Conrad III dies never having been crowned Holy Roman Emperor; Frederick I Barbarossa, nephew of Conrad III, is elected king, the first king of Germany of the Hohenstaufen dynasty; he attempts to establish German dominance in Europe.

1153 **Scotland** King David I dies, having brought great change to Scotland, including the foundation of burghs, implementation of the ideals of Gregorian Reform, foundation of monasteries, Normanisation of the Scottish government and the introduction of feudalism through immigrant French and Anglo-French knights; his grandson, 11-year-old Malcolm IV, becomes king. **France** The Angevin dynasty takes control of Gascony and Guyenne. **Rome** The Roman, Corrado di Suburra, cardinal bishop of Sabina, is elected pope as Anastasius IV.

1154 **England** The Treaty of Winchester ends the period in England known as 'the Anarchy' and allows Empress Matilda's son, Henry of Anjou, to become King Henry II of England, the first Plantagenet king. **Italy** Frederick I Barbarossa is crowned king. **Rome** Cardinal Nicholas of Albano, born Nicholas Breakspear, is elected pope as Adrian IV; he is the only Englishman to become pope. **Sicily** Having made his kingdom one of the greatest in Europe, Roger II dies; William I the Bad, fourth son of Roger, becomes king; he goes to war with Greece until 1158. **Kievan Rus'** Rostislav I, son of Mstislav I, becomes grand prince for one week, before Iziaslav III drives him out and returns to power.

1155 **Norway** Sigurd II is murdered by his brother and co-ruler Inge I. **Holy Roman Empire** Frederick I Barbarossa of Germany is crowned Holy Roman Emperor. **Kievan Rus'** Yuri I retakes Kiev.

1156 **Ireland** Muirchertach MacLochlainn, King MacLochlainn's grandson, becomes high king. **Sweden** Sverker I is shockingly murdered on his way to church on Christmas day, probably by the pretender to the throne, Magnus Henriksson; Erik IX the Saint becomes king;

he consolidates Christianity in the kingdom and codifies Sweden's laws. **Venice** Vitale II Michele is elected doge.

1157 **León-Castile-Galicia** On the death of King Alfonso VII, his kingdom is split between his sons; Ferdinand receives León and Galicia; Sancho becomes king of Castile and Toledo. **Denmark** Valdemar the Great becomes king after 10 years of unrest. **Norway** Inge I fights his other brother Øystein near Moster; Øystein is forced to flee and is captured and killed; Inge, the last remaining brother, becomes sole ruler, but faces opposition in an ongoing civil war from Haakon the Broadshouldered, son of Sigurd II, whose supporters are calling him king. **Russia** The beginning of the Golden Age of the city of Vladimir, east of Moscow; Andrei Bogolyubsky becomes Prince Andrei I of Vladimir-Suzdal. **Kievan Rus'** On Yuri I's death, Iziaslav III is restored to the throne.

1158 **León-Castile-Galicia** Alfonso VIII becomes king of Castile, aged 3.

1159 **Rome** Cardinal Orlando Bandinelli is elected pope as Alexander III; he introduces the law whereby a pope must obtain the votes of two-thirds of the cardinals to be elected. **Belarus** Rogneda Borisovich becomes prince of Polotsk for a second time. **Kievan Rus'** Rostislav I becomes grand prince for the second time.

1160 **Sweden** Erik IX is murdered, either by Emund Ulvbane, an assassin hired by people working for the Sverker dynasty, or Swedish rebels; Erik is later canonised and becomes Sweden's patron saint; Magnus II, whose mother is the granddaughter of Inge I, becomes the last king of the House of Stenkil. **Sicily** William I defeats a revolt, but his son Roger is killed.

1161 **Sweden** Karl VIII, son of Sverker I, becomes king. **Norway** Haakon II the Broadshouldered defeats and kills Inge I, in battle near Oslo; to his supporters, Haakon II succeeds Øystein as king; the civil war continues with two parties, known as Bagler and Birkebeiner, constantly uniting behind a royal son to oppose the rule of a king from the other party; Magnus Erlingsson is elected king by one party. **Hungary and Croatia** Stephen III becomes king.

1162 **Norway** Haakon II the Broadshouldered is killed by nobleman Erling Skaake; Haakon's supporters name his half-brother, Sigurd Markusfostre king. **Serbia** Mihailo III Vojislav becomes the last ruler of Duklja. **Belarus** Vseslav Vasilkovich becomes prince of Polotsk.

1163 **Wales** Owain Gwynedd is recognized as ruler. **Norway** Aged 7, Magnus V Erlingsson is the first Norwegian king to be crowned; Erling Skaake kills the pretender Sigurd Markusfostre.

1165 **Scotland** Malcolm IV dies unmarried, aged 24; William I the Lion, Malcolm's brother, succeeds him; his standard, a red lion rampant with a forked tail on a yellow background, goes on to become the Royal Standard of Scotland.

1166 **Ireland** Ruaidrí Ua Conchobair, son of King Tairrdelbach Ua Conchobair, is the last 'High King of all Ireland'; his persecution of Dermot MacMurrough of Leinster gives Henry II of England a pretext for invading. **Sicily** Aged 11, William II becomes king; his mother, Margaret of Navarre, acts as regent.

1167 **Sweden** Canute I Ericson, son of Eric the Saint, kills Karl VII to take the throne. **Belarus** Volodar of Minsk becomes prince of Polotsk. **Kievan Rus'** Mstislav II, son of Iziaslav II, becomes grand prince.

1168 **England** Prince Richard, later King Richard I the Lionheart of England, becomes duke of Aquitaine.

1169 **England** Eleanor of Aquitaine leaves England to establish her great court in Poitiers. **Portugal** Disabled by a fall from his horse during a battle near Badajoz, King Afonso is taken prisoner by soldiers of King Alfonso VIII of Castile and Leon; in return for his freedom, Portugal is forced to return all its recent Galician conquests. **Germany** Henry VI is elected king.

ASSASSINATION OF THOMAS BECKET
1170

Henry II (1154–89) was the son of Queen Maud and Geoffrey of Anjou. Although he was a good ruler, he suffered from a quick temper and paid the consequences. His chief administrator was a man called Thomas Becket. When the See of Canterbury fell empty in 1162, Henry talked a very reluctant Becket into becoming the new Archbishop. Henry foolishly believed that Becket would be sympathetic to the royal cause in the escalating battle between the Church and the state — he wasn't! Becket was ostentatiously severe in his adherence to the laws of the Church and argued bitterly with Henry II. Becket eventually infuriated Henry to the point that the king flew into one of his famous rages. Four knights — Hugh de Merville, William de Tracy, Reginald Fitzurse and Richard le Breton — perhaps seeking to curry favour with the king, rode from Westminster to Canterbury Cathedral and killed Becket in front of the main altar.

Henry was full of remorse following the murder of Becket, and asked the Pope to impose penance. He walked to Canterbury Cathedral wearing a sackcloth and ashes and allowed himself to be flogged by monks.

1170 **Ireland** Henry II sponsors the Norman invasion of Ireland, sparking eight centuries of conflict and war between Ireland and England. **Kievan Rus'** Gleb, son of Yuri I, becomes grand prince.

1171 **Wales** Rhys ap Gruffydd agrees to negotiate with Henry II of England. **Sicily** William II is declared old enough to rule. **Kievan Rus'** Vladimir II, son of Mstislav I, is briefly grand prince; Roman I, son of Rostislav I, succeeds him.

1172 **England** The Council of Avranches absolves Henry of the assassination of Thomas Becket. **Ireland** Henry II conquers Ireland and is confirmed as lord of Ireland by the pope. **Venice** Sebastiano Ziani, one of the city's greatest planners, is elected doge. **Hungary and Croatia** Stephen III dies, having dispensed with two pretenders, Ladislaus II and Stephen IV, both sons of King Béla II, and having been deposed twice; Béla III, Stephen's younger brother, becomes king; he marries the sister of Philippe II of France, and becomes one of the wealthiest monarchs in Europe.

1173 **England** Eleanor of Aquitaine and her sons rebel, unsuccessfully, against her husband Henry II in the Revolt of 1173–1174. **Poland** Mieszko III 'the Old', fifth son of Bolesław III, becomes high duke. **Kievan Rus** Vsevolod the Big Nest, future grand prince of Vladimir, is briefly installed on the Kievan throne, before being taken prisoner by two princes of Smolensk for a year; Rurik, son of Rostislav, becomes grand prince; he will occupy the Kievan throne seven times.

1174 **Scotland** William I is captured by Henry II of England and taken to Normandy; Henry occupies Scotland. **Norway** In the ongoing civil war, Øystein Meyla, son of Øystein II, is declared king by his supporters. **Russia** Discontented Vladimir nobles assassinate Prince Andrei I Bogolyubsky; his half-brother Mikhail becomes prince of Vladimir-Suzdal. **Kievan Rus'** Iaroslav II, son of Iziaslav II, is manoeuvred onto the Kievan throne by relatives.

1175 **Scotland** In order to regain his kingdom, William the Lion has to acknowledge Henry II of England as his feudal superior and agree to pay for the cost of the English army's occupation of Scotland by taxing the Scots; William signs the Treaty of Falaise, agreeing to this, and is allowed to return to Scotland. **Ireland** Ruaidri Ua Conchobair, the last high king, submits to Henry II with the Treaty of Windsor.

1177 **Norway** Øystein Meyla, pretender to the throne, is killed in the Battle of Re. **Sicily** William II marries Joan, daughter of Henry II of England. **Poland** A rebellion by the barons of Lesser Poland leads to the expulsion of Mieszko III; his younger brother, Casimir II the Just, is elevated to high duke; Mieszko never abdicates or renounces the throne and returns several times to claim it. **Russia** Vsevolod the Big Nest becomes grand prince of Vladimir; Vladimir is at the height of its power during his reign. **Kievan Rus'** Sviatoslav III, son of Vsevolod II, deposes Iaroslav II.

1178 **Venice** Orio Mastropiero is elected doge.

1179 **Portugal** Privileges and favours given to the Catholic Church during Alfonso's reign, as well as the churches and monasteries he has constructed, result in a papal bull, *Manifestis Probatum*, in which Pope Alexander III acknowledges Afonso as king of an independent Portugal. **Rome** Pope Alexander III is forced to leave Rome by the Roman republic; Innocent III, the antipope, is installed.

1180 **France** Philippe II Augustus becomes king, conquering Normandy, Anjou, Maine, Poitou and Lorraine. **Rome** Antipope Innocent III is deposed by Pope Alexander III. **Poland** Casimir II eases taxes on the clergy and gives land back to the Church in order to ensure that hereditary rights to the high dukedom of Poland fall to his line, that of Krakow, of which he is duke; nonetheless, it will be more than a century before the Polish kingship is restored. **Byzantine Empire** Manuel I Comnenus dies, having pursued an aggressive foreign policy, attempting to recreate a new Roman Empire; Alexios II Comnenus becomes emperor. **Kievan Rus'** Rurik returns to power.

1181 **Rome** Cardinal Ubaldo Allucingoli is elected pope, as Lucius III; in 1184 he will launch the Inquisition.

1182 **Denmark** Canute VI, who has been co-ruler with his father, Valdemar the Great, becomes sole ruler on Valdemar's death. **Kievan Rus'** Sviatoslav III becomes grand prince for the third time, ruling alongside Rurik.

1183 **Byzantine Empire** Alexios II, having lost substantial parts of the empire, is strangled with a bow string on the orders of Andronikos Comnenos, his co-emperor and cousin of his father; Andronikos becomes sole emperor.

1184 **Norway** Sverre Sigurdsson, leader of the Birkebeiners, takes the throne as sole ruler after the death of his rival, former King Magnus V, in the Battle of Firmreite.

1185 **Scotland** Richard the Lionheart, in need of funds for the Third Crusade, terminates the Treaty of Falaise in return for 10,000 silver marks. **Portugal** King Alfonso Henriques I, recognized as the founder of the Portuguese nation, dies; his son, Sancho I, becomes king. **Norway** Jon Kuvlung, son of Inge I, becomes pretender to the throne. **Rome** Lucius III dies during preparations for the Third Crusade; the cardinal of Milan, Uberto Crivelli, is elected pope, as Urban III. **Bulgaria** The Asen brothers revolt against Byzantium, winning independence; Ivan Asen I is proclaimed king of Bulgaria along with his brothers, Teodor I and Peter IV, launching the Second Bulgarian Empire. **Byzantine Empire** Isaac II Angelus deposes, tortures and executes Andronikos I Comnenus, and takes the throne as the first emperor of the Angelid dynasty; during his reign, the empire will lose Bulgaria, Lefkada, Kefallonia, Zakynthos, Cilicia and Cyprus.

1186 **Serbia** Grand prince of Rascia and duke of all Serbia, Stefan Nemanja conquers the state of Duklja; he unifies Duklja and Rascia into a single state.

1187 **Rome** Pope Urban III is reported to die of grief upon hearing news of the Crusader defeat in the Battle of Hattin; Cistercian monk Alberto di Morra is elected pope as Gregory VIII, but dies two months later; cardinal bishop of Palestrina, Paulino Scolari, is elected pope as Clement III.

1188 **León-Castile-Galicia** Alfonso IX, son of Ferdinand I of León, becomes king of León and Galicia; he is nicknamed 'the Slobberer', as he had a habit of foaming at the mouth when angry; he foams at the mouth a great deal during his reign, as he argues incessantly with the pope over his marriages; he is the first western European monarch to summon his citizens to a parliament – the Cortes. **Norway** Pretender Jon Kuvlung is killed by King Sverre.

1189 **England** Richard the Lionheart allies with Philippe II of France against his father, Henry II of England, and is crowned king; forever crusading or held prisoner by Duke Leopold in Austria, he will spend only a few weeks of his reign in his kingdom. **Holy Roman Empire** Frederick I Barbarossa leads the Third Crusade against Saladin. **Sicily** William II dies childless; his nephew Tancred, illegitimate son of Roger III, duke of Apulia, seizes power and is crowned king.

1190 **England** Richard I threatens war against Tancred of Sicily, and captures Messina. **Holy Roman Empire** Frederick I Barbarossa drowns in the Saleph river while leading an army to Jerusalem. **Poland** Mieszko II the Old returns to power as high duke, but only for a short time, until Casimir II is restored. **Albania** Progon becomes prince of Albania and founder of the Progon dynasty.

1191 **Rome** Giacinto Bobone, 85 years old and a mere deacon, is elected pope, as Celestine III. **Holy Roman Empire** Henry VI of Germany is crowned Holy Roman Emperor.

1192 **England** A truce between Richard I and Saladin ends the Third Crusade; Richard is taken hostage by Leopold V of Austria. **Venice** The blind Enrico Dandolo, son of a prominent family, is elected doge; he plays a crucial role in the Fourth Crusade, which captures Constantinople; Venice captures almost half of the Byzantine Empire, which never really recovers. **Belarus** Ginwill becomes prince of Polotsk.

1193 **Norway** Sigurd Magnusson, illegitimate son of Magnus Erlingsson, becomes pretender to the throne.

1194 **England** Richard I is ransomed from Henry VI, Holy Roman Emperor. **Norway** King Sverre Sigurdsson is excommunicated by the Norwegian Church; civil war breaks out again with the Baglers;

he kills the pretender to the throne, Sigurd Magnusson. **Navarre** Sancho VII the Strong becomes king; he is the last legitimate male-line descendant of the Houses of Íñiguez and Jiménez, the first two dynasties of kings of Navarre; his sister is married to English king, Richard the Lionheart. **Sicily** King Tancred dies just a few days after the death of his son and co-king, Roger III; William III becomes king under the regency of his mother, Sibylla of Acerra; Holy Roman Emperor Henry VI invades and captures the kingdom, taking Tancred's family prisoner; William III is castrated and blinded, dying in Germany in 1198, the last of the Norman kings of Sicily; Constance, daughter of King Roger II and wife of the Holy Roman Emperor, becomes queen jointly with her husband. **Poland** Casimir II dies unexpectedly, probably poisoned, at a banquet; Leszek I the White becomes high duke. **Kievan Rus'** Rurik becomes sole ruler on the death of Sviatoslav III.

1195 **Byzantine Empire** While he is absent on a hunting expedition, Isaac II's older brother, Alexios Angelos, proclaims himself emperor as Alexios III; Isaac is blinded and imprisoned.

1196 **Aragón** Pedro II becomes king, the first king of Aragón to be crowned by the pope. **Norway** Inge Magnusson, another illegitimate son of Magnus Erlingsson, becomes Bagler pretender to the throne. **Germany** Frederick II is elected king of Germany, disputed by Philip of Swabia and Otto of Brunswick. **Sweden** Canute I dies, leaving children too young to become rulers; Sverker II the Younger, son of Karl VII, is elected king. **Hungary and Croatia** Emeric becomes king. **Serbia** Grand Prince Stefan Namanja abdicates in favour of his son Stefan, and retires to a monastery; his other son, Vukan II Nemanjić, rules over Zeta until 1208. **Bulgaria** Following the assassinations of his older brothers, Peter IV and Ivan Asen I, Kaloyan, younger brother of the Asen brothers, becomes tsar.

1197 **Holy Roman Empire** Henry VI dies of malaria while preparing for a crusade.

1198 **Germany** Philip of Swabia is elected king; disputed by Otto IV of Brunswick, duke of Swabia, who is a grandson of English king Henry II, and fifth and youngest son of Frederick I; he is elected as rival king and crowned by the archbishop of Cologne; civil war ensues. **Rome** Cardinal Deacon Lotario de' Conti di Segni is elected pope, as Innocent III; he reasserts papal power and becomes the most prominent political figure in Europe. **Sicily** Frederick I becomes the first king of the Hohenstaufen dynasty; he is known as 'Stupor Mundi' (Wonder of the World), is a patron of the arts and science and can speak six languages. **Bohemia** Following a period of anarchy, Ottokar I, of the Premyslid dynasty, becomes king. **Bulgaria** King Peter is murdered by his own nobles, probably with the encouragement of his younger brother Kalojan, who becomes king. **Poland** Leszek I the White is replaced as high duke by Mieszko III the Old, who returns to power for the third time. **Albania** Gjin Progon becomes sovereign prince.

1199 **England** King Richard I is killed at the siege of Châlus and John 'Lackland' becomes king; his reign is disastrous, but he does sign the *Magna Carta* in 1215. **Poland** Leszek I the White ousts Mieszko the Old, and is restored as high duke. **Belarus** Boris II becomes prince of Polotsk.

1202 **Denmark** Canute VI's brother, Valdemar II the Conqueror, becomes king; he extends his kingdom to Estonia, but, captured by the Germans, gives up his conquests in return for freedom. **Norway**

King Sverre dies; his son, Haakon III, is pronounced king; he makes a settlement with the Church; Inge Magnusson, Bagler pretender to the throne, dies; the Bagler party is dissolved. **Poland** Mieszko the Old replaces Leszek the White as high duke; it is the fourth time he has been ruler; his return is shortlived, as he dies and is succeeded by Władysław III Spindleshanks. **Kievan Rus'** Ingvar I briefly rules as grand prince before Rurik regains the throne for the fourth time; Roman II the Great is a powerful rival.

1203 **France** Philippe II of France enters Rouen, leading to the eventual unification of Normandy and France. **Sweden** The late Canute I's four sons claim the throne, but Sverker II exiles them. **Byzantine Empire** Alexios III flees, following the arrival of the armies of the Fourth Crusade; Isaac II returns to the throne after eight years of imprisonment; his son, Alexios IV, is co-emperor, but he actually rules. **Thessalonica** Boniface of Montferrat, a leader of the Fourth Crusade, founds the Kingdom of Thessalonica.

1204 **Norway** Haakon III dies, unmarried and without a legitimate heir; his 4-year-old nephew, grandson of King Sverre, Guttrum Sigurdsson, is named king; the second Bagler war begins when pretender Erling Steinvegg arrives in Viken, supported by King Valdemar II of Denmark; on the death of King Guttrum, Inge II Baardsson, grandson of Sigurd II, is chosen by the Birkebeiner as king; intense fighting begins with the Baglers. **Hungary and Croatia** Ladislaus III is crowned king, aged 5. **Bulgaria** Kalojan proclaims himself tsar. **Byzantine Empire** Emperor Alexios IV is overthrown in a revolution; Nicolas Canabus is elected emperor by an assembly of the senate and priests, but refuses to accept the throne; influential court official Alexios Doukas Murzuphlus has Canabus and Alexios IV strangled on the same day, and is proclaimed emperor as Alexios V; he loses in battle to the Crusaders and flees to Thrace; Constantine Laskaris is proclaimed emperor, but remains uncrowned; Constantinople comes under the control of what, for the next 57 years, would be the Latin Empire. **Latin Empire** Baldwin, count of Flanders, is crowned emperor of the Latin Empire, a Crusader state founded by the leaders of the Fourth Crusade, on lands captured from the Byzantine Empire. **Kievan Rus'** Rostislav II becomes grand prince.

1205 **Sweden** Canute I's four sons, supported by the Norwegians, lose to Sverker II at the Battle of Älgarås; three of them die. **Venice** Pietro Ziani is elected doge. **Latin Empire** Henry of Flanders is crowned emperor. **Hungary and Croatia** Five-year-old Ladislaus III dies, probably murdered by his uncle, Andrew, after just six months on the throne; Andrew, brother of King Emeric, becomes king as Andrew II.

1206 **Poland** Władysław III is deposed; Leszek I the White is restored to the throne. **Kievan Rus'** Rurik briefly seizes power for the fifth time; Vsevolod IV deposes him to become grand prince.

1207 **Norway** Bagler pretender Erling Steinvegg dies; they name Philip Simonsson as new Bagler pretender. **Germany** King Philip's triumphant entry into Cologne brings the civil war to an end. **Bulgaria** Tsar Kaloyan is murdered by his own military commander, in a plot possibly engineered by his wife; his nephew Boril becomes tsar. **Albania** Gjin Progoni's brother, Dhimitër Progoni, becomes the third and last sovereign prince of Albania from the Progon dynasty.

1208 **Sweden** The only surviving son of Canute I defeats Sverker II at the Battle of Lena, and drives him into exile in Denmark; he takes the throne as Erik X, and is the first Swedish king to be crowned. **Germany** Philip of Swabia is murdered by Otto of Wittelsbach; Philip had refused to let him marry one of his daughters; Otto IV becomes sole, undisputed ruler, gaining the support of all the electoral princes. **Kievan Rus'** Rurik briefly seizes power, for the sixth time.

1209 **Holy Roman Empire** Otto IV is crowned emperor.

1210 **Poland** Mieszko I Tanglefoot, second son of Władysław II, becomes high duke. **Kievan Rus'** Vsevolod IV concludes an alliance with Vsevolod the Big Nest, grand prince of Vladimir, and seizes Kiev.

1211 **Portugal** Afonso II becomes king. **Germany** While Otto IV is campaigning in southern Italy, Frederick Roger, king of Sicily and son of Henry VI, becomes king as Frederick II. **Poland** Mieszko II dies; Leszek I the White is restored for the fourth and final time.

1212 **Sicily** Henry, son of Frederick II, becomes king. **Russia** Yuri III becomes grand prince of Vladimir-Suzdal.

1213 **Aragón** Pedro II dies fighting the Crusader army of Simon de Montfort, at the Battle of Muret; James I the Conqueror becomes king and expands Aragón as far south as Valencia and into Languedoc in the north; he makes Catalan the official language of his territories.

1214 **Scotland** William the Lion dies after the second-longest reign – 49 years – of a Scottish monarch before the Act of Union in 1707; Alexander II succeeds him; he supports the English barons against King John, invading England. **France** Philippe II defeats John of England. **Kievan Rus'** Mstislav III the Bold expels Vsevolod IV from Kiev to succeed him as grand prince.

1215 **England** King John seals the *Magna Carta*, giving more power to the barons.

THE MAGNA CARTA
1215

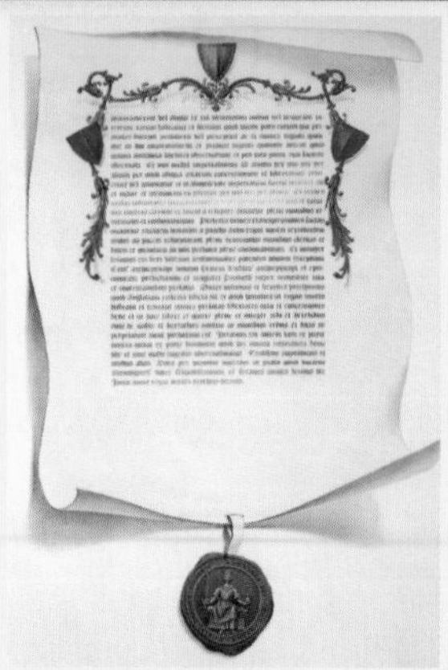

The Magna Carta is one of the most celebrated documents in English history, but its real significance is often misunderstood.

In January 1215, a group of barons demanded a charter of liberties to safeguard against the king's despotic behaviour. They took up arms against King John and captured London in May 1215. Both parties met to negotiate on 10 June at a place called Runnymede — a meadow by the River Thames. The concessions made by John were outlined in a document known as 'The Articles of the Barons', to which the king attached his great seal. At the same time the royal chancery also produced a formal royal grant, which was based on the agreements reached at Runnymede. This later became known as Magna Carta (Latin for 'Great Charter'). Four copies of the original grant still survive. Two are held at the British Library, while others can be seen in the archives at Lincoln and Salisbury cathedrals.

1215 **Spain** Henry I, son of Alfonso VIII, becomes king of Castile; Pedro II of Aragón, helping the Albigensians, is killed in battle against Simon de Montfort's Crusaders; James the Conqueror becomes king; he conquers Valencia, Murcia and the Balearics.

1216 **England** On the death of King John, Prince Louis of France is offered the crown by English barons; he invades England and the First Barons' War begins; 9-year-old Henry III becomes king under the regency of William Marshal and then Hubert de Burgh. **Rome** Cardinal Priest Cencio, former Camerlengo and treasurer of the Catholic Church, as well as tutor of future Holy Roman Emperor, Frederick II, is elected pope as Honorius III; he endorses the Fifth Crusade. **Sweden** Johan I Sverkersson, son of Sverker II, becomes king, aged 15. **Albania** Dhimitër Progoni dies without issue; his wife Komnena marries nobleman Grigor Kamona, who becomes sovereign prince. **Latin Empire** Pierre II de Courtenay, younger son of Louis VI of France and brother-in-law of previous emperor Henry, becomes emperor; he leaves France and is consecrated as emperor in Rome; he is kidnapped by the despot of Epirus en route to claim his empire. **Russia** Yuri II's brother, Konstantin I, defeats him and other brothers to seize the Grand-Principality of Vladimir-Suzdal; Yuri is sent into exile.

1217 **England** Prince Louis of France renounces his claim to the English throne in the Treaty of Lambeth, which ends the First Barons' War. **Castile** Henry I of Castile is killed by a falling roof tile; his cousin, Ferdinand III, succeeds him. **Norway** Inge Baardsson dies, having failed to achieve overall control of his kingdom; 13-year-old Haakon IV, illegitimate son of King Sverre, succeeds him as king. **Serbia** The Kingdom of Serbia is founded; Stefan II becomes its first king. **Latin Empire** Pierre II de Courtenay dies while being held prisoner; he never governs his empire; his wife Yolanda takes power.

1218 **Bulgaria** Ivan Asen I's son, also Ivan Asen, captures and blinds Tsar Boril, who is sent into exile; Ivan Asen II becomes tsar, and adds Macedonia, Epirus and much of Albania to his kingdom. **Russia** On the death of his brother Konstantin, Yuri II returns to the throne.

1219 **Latin Empire** Robert de Courtenay, son of Pierre de Courtenay and his wife Yolanda, becomes emperor after his brother Philip renounces the succession.

1220 **Holy Roman Empire** Frederick II is crowned emperor.

1222 **Sweden** Johan I is deposed; Erik XI, 5-year-old son of Erik X, becomes king. **Germany** Henry (VII) is crowned co-king with his father, Frederick II.

1223 **France** Louis VIII the Lion becomes king. **Portugal** Afonso II dies, leaving his country embroiled in a diplomatic conflict with the Catholic Church; he had been excommunicated by Pope Honorius III for trying to reduce the Church's power; Sancho II the Pious becomes king. **Kievan Rus'** Vladimir III, son of Rurik, becomes grand prince.

1226 **France** Louis IX the Saint becomes king; France enjoys something of a golden age during his reign.

1227 **England** Henry III comes of age and assumes government. **Rome** Cardinal bishop of Ostia, Ugolino di Conti, is elected pope as Gregory IX; he excommunicates Emperor Frederick II for not carrying out the Sixth Crusade. **Poland** Leszek I the White is assassinated; Władysław III Spindleshanks returns to power. **Serbia** Stefan Radoslav becomes king of Serbia.

1228 **Latin Empire** Emperor Robert de Courtenay dies, having been driven from Constantinople; 11-year-old Baldwin II becomes the last emperor of the Latin Empire; the empire consists of little more than Constantinople, which has a population of only around 35,000; John of Brienne rules as regent.

1229 **Sweden** Canute II, who has been acting as regent for Erik XI and then joint ruler, exiles Erik to Denmark and seizes the throne. **Poland** Konrad I of Masovia, son of Casimir II and brother of Leszek I the White, becomes high duke. **Venice** Jacopo Tiepolo is elected doge.

1230 **León-Castile-Galicia** Ferdinand III, already king of Castile, becomes king of León, permanently uniting the two kingdoms; he will spend much of his reign fighting the Moors, reconquering all Andalusia except Granada, and expanding his power over the Iberian Peninsula; he is later canonized. **Bohemia** Wenceslaus I, son of Ottokar I, becomes king. **Bulgaria** becomes the dominant power in the Balkans, when Ivan Asen II captures land from the Black Sea in the east to the Adriatic in the west.

1231 **Majorca** King James I the Conqueror of Aragón conquers Majorca and becomes king.

1232 **Poland** Henry I the Bearded, duke of Silesia, becomes ruler.

1233 **Serbia** Stefan Radoslav is deposed by his brother, Stefan Vladislav I, with the support of his father-in-law, Ivan Asen II, king of Bulgaria.

1234 **Sweden** On the death of Canute II, Erik XI returns from exile to take the throne. **Navarre** Sancho VII's will names James I of Aragón as his heir, but the Navarrese elect, instead, Theobald I the Posthumous, count of Champagne and nephew of Sancho VII, as king; in previous years, he has tried to poison French king, Louis VIII, and has had an affair with his wife, Queen Blanche, regent for Louis IX. **Germany** Frederick II outlaws his son, Prince Henry.

1235 **Germany** Prince Henry is tried by his father, Frederick II, and dethroned. **Hungary and Croatia** Andrew II dies, having weakened the throne; Béla IV becomes king; he becomes known as the country's 'second founder', after his programme of reconstruction following the invasion by Mongol troops, during which half the population of Hungary has perishes. **Lithuania** Mindaugas is the first-known grand duke of Lithuania. **Kievan Rus'** Iziaslav IV becomes grand prince.

1237 **England and Scotland** The Treaty of York defines the boundary between the two kingdoms as running between the Solway Firth in the west, and the mouth of the river Tweed in the east. **Germany** Conrad IV, son of Frederick II, is elected king. **Kievan Rus'** Iaroslav II, fourth son of Vsevolod the Big Nest, becomes grand prince; he restores the territory after the Mongol invasion.

1238 **Poland** Henry II the Pious becomes high duke. **Russia** Iaroslav II, grand prince of Novgorod and Kiev, becomes grand prince of Vladimir. **Kievan Rus'** Mikhail II, son of Vsevolod IV, becomes grand prince.

1239 **Norway** Skule Baardson, half-brother of King Inge II, is declared king by his supporters, and raises an army to fight King Haakon IV. **Kievan Rus'** Rostislav III becomes grand prince.

1240 **Norway** Skule Baardson is defeated and killed by Haakon IV; the civil war era in Norway comes to an end. **Kievan Rus'** Around this time, the Mongols destroy Kiev because of its princes' refusal to submit to them; the state is controlled, for the next 142 years, by the Mongol Horde.

1241 **Rome** Cardinal bishop of Sabina, Goffredo da Castiglione, reigns as Pope Celestine IV for just 17 days. **Denmark** Eric IV, son of Valdemar II, becomes king. **Bulgaria** Aged 7, Kaliman Asen I becomes tsar; Bulgaria loses much of its power during his reign. **Poland** High Duke Henry I dies fighting the Mongols at the Battle of Legnica; the thousands of dead are beheaded and mutilated, but he is identified because of his 11 toes; Konrad of Masovia becomes high duke for the second time.

1243 **Rome** Cardinal priest Sinibaldo Fieschi is elected pope as Innocent IV. **Poland** Bolesław V the Chaste, son of Leszek the White, becomes high duke of a fragmented country. **Serbia** Stefan Uroš overthrows his brother, Stefan Vladislav, to become king; during his reign, Serbia becomes a prosperous and influential power in the area.

1245 **Russia** Iaroslav II, grand prince of Vladimir, is poisoned by the khan's wife while visiting him in Karakorum, and dies a week after returning home; Sviatoslav III, sixth son of Vsevolod the Big Nest, becomes grand prince of Vladimir.

1246 **Germany** Henry Raspe is elected antiking (until 1247), following Pope Innocent IV's excommunication of Frederick II and his declaration that Conrad IV is deposed; he defeats Conrad in battle at Nidda, but dies a few months later; William of Holland is elected antiking. **Bulgaria** Kaliman I dies, aged 12, possibly of poisoning; his brother, Michael Asen I, also a child, becomes tsar, with his mother Eirene as regent; with a second successive underage tsar, a great deal of territory is lost.

1248 **León** Fernando III of León takes Seville from the Moors. **Portugal** Following a formal complaint from the archbishop of Porto, the pope orders the Portuguese to select a new king; increasingly discontented nobles invite Sancho II's brother, Afonso, then count of Boulogne, to usurp the throne; he marches into Portugal, and Sancho II is removed from the throne; Sancho goes into exile and Afonso III becomes king. **Russia** Mikhail Khorobrit of Moscow, nephew of Sviatoslav III, defies the traditional succession system when he seizes the city of Vladimir and ousts the grand prince; Mikhail Khorobrit is killed several months later, in battle with the Lithuanians.

1249 **Scotland** Aged 8, Alexander III becomes king of Scots. **Venice** Marino Morosini is elected 44th doge. **Russia** Mikhail Khorobrit's brother, Andrei II, third son of Iaroslav II, becomes grand prince of Vladimir.

1250 **Sweden** Eric XI dies without issue, and the crown passes to his 12-year-old nephew, Valdemar I Birgersson; his father, the great statesman and founder of Stockholm, Birger Jarl, acts as regent. **Denmark** Abel, third son of Valdemar II, kills his brother, King Eric IV, and assumes the throne. **Germany** Frederick II defeats William of Holland and his supporters, but dies shortly after; Conrad IV becomes sole ruler. **Sicily** Conrad of Germany becomes king as Conrad I; he wages war with the Papal States.

1251 **France** The First Shepherds' Crusade is launched, a French peasants' crusade, to rescue Louis IX from captivity in Egypt. **Lithuania** Mindaugas, grand duke, is acknowledged as king by Pope Innocent IV, the only man to be king of Lithuania; he converts to Christianity to discourage attacks by the Livonian Order and Teutonic Knights.

1252 **León-Castile-Galicia** Alfonso X 'the Wise' becomes king. **Denmark** King Abel is killed in battle; his younger brother is elected King Christopher I. **Venice** Reniero Zeno, formerly a diplomat in France and Italy, is elected doge. **Russia** The Mongols eject Andrei II from Vladimir; the great military commander and politician Alexander Nevsky, fourth son of Iaroslav II, becomes grand prince.

1253 **Navarre** Theobald II becomes king. **Bohemia** Ottokar II becomes king; he becomes the greatest Bohemian monarch and, for some time, the most powerful prince in the Holy Roman Empire. **Albania** Around this date, Grigor Kamona dies, and is succeeded by his son-in-law, Gulam.

1254 **England** Lesser barons are replaced on the King's Council by elected representatives from the shires and cities. **France** King Louis IX expels all Jews from France. **Portugal** To placate the middle classes, King Afonso III holds the first session of the Cortes, Portugal's general assembly. **Germany and The Holy Roman Empire** The Great Interregnum begins, lasting until 1273. **Rome** Rinaldo di Jenne, dean of the Sacred College of Cardinals, is elected pope as Alexander IV. **Sicily** Aged 2, Conrad II, commonly known as Conradin, becomes king; the pope declares Sicily a papal possession and installs Edmund Crouchback, son of Henry III of England, as a rival king; Edmund fails to secure the kingdom. **Albania** Gulam, prince of Albania, dies.

1256 **Bulgaria** Tsar Michael Asen I is murdered by his cousin, Kaliman Asen II, while hunting.

1257 **Germany** Alfonso X, king of León, Castile and Galicia, is elected king of the Germans, but holds no authority over the country and is never crowned; among other contenders is Richard of Cornwall, second son of England's King John. **Bulgaria** Kaliman II flees, and Mitso Asen, grandson of Ivan Asen II, briefly becomes tsar, but loses control; the nobles replace him with Constantine Tikh, son of a Bulgarian noble.

1258 **England** King Henry III is forced to accept the Provisions of Oxford, requiring the summoning of a parliament and the end of absolute monarchy in England. **Wales** Llywelyn the Last is the final ruler of an independent Wales. **Sicily** Manfred, illegitimate son of Frederick I (Holy Roman Emperor as Frederick II), becomes king.

1259
England The Treaty of Paris is signed between Kings Henry III of England and Louis IX of France.

1259 **Denmark** Christopher I is deposed by nobles loyal to his son, who becomes king as Eric V.

1261 **Rome** Patriarch of Jerusalem Jacques Pantaléon is elected pope as Urban IV. **Byzantine Empire** Constantinople is recaptured by Nicaean forces, led by Michael VIII, re-establishing the Byzantine Empire; Michael is the great-grandson of Emperor Alexios III Angelos.

1262 **England** King Henry III obtains a papal bull from Pope Alexander IV, releasing him from the Provisions of Oxford, setting the scene for the Second Barons' War. **Norway** Iceland and Greenland come under Norwegian rule. **Sicily** The pope grants the Kingdom of Sicily, which he has claimed as a papal possession, to Charles I of Anjou, youngest son of Louis VIII of France and the first Sicilian king of the Angevin dynasty.

1263 **Scotland** Alexander III defeats the Norwegians, led by Haakon IV, in the Battle of Largs. **Norway** King Haakon IV dies in the Orkney Islands; his youngest son, Magnus VI the Law-Mender, is crowned king; he will modernize Norwegian law and make peace abroad. **Lithuania** Grand Duke Mindaugas and his two sons are murdered by his nephew Treniota; a war between the nobles erupts; Treniota becomes ruler.

1264 **England** Civil war breaks out with the Second Barons' War. **Ireland** The first definitively known meeting of the Irish legislature takes place at Castledermot in County Kildare. **Germany** The war of the Thuringian Succession ends; the western half becomes independent, under the name of Hesse; most of the remainder comes under the rule of the Wettin dynasty of the nearby Margraviate of Meissen and will form the nucleus of the later Electorate and Kingdom of Saxony. **Lithuania** Vaišvilkas, prince of Black Ruthenia and younger son of Mindaugas, deposes Treniota and seizes power; Treniota is murdered by his father's servants. **Russia** The great Alexander Nevsky dies; Iaroslav III, son of Iaroslav II, becomes grand prince of Vladimir.

1265 **England** In Westminster, the first elected English parliament (De Montfort's Parliament) takes place; the Battle of Evesham is fought in the Second Barons' War, with Edward's army defeating Simon de Montfort and killing him. **Rome** Cardinal Gui Faucoi le Gros is elected pope as Clement IV.

1266 **Scotland** The war between Scotland and Norway ends with Magnus VI of Norway ceding the Western Isles and the Isle of Man to Scotland in exchange for a large monetary payment. **Sicily** King Manfred is killed in the Battle of Benevento against Charles of Anjou, leading the pope's army; Charles of Anjou becomes king as Charles I.

1267 **Wales** Henry III acknowledges Llywelyn ap Gruffydd's title of prince of Wales in the Treaty of Montgomery. **Lithuania** Grand Duke Vaišvilkas becomes a monk, passing his title to his brother-in-law, Shvarn, prince of Kholm and knyaz of Galicia.

1268 **France** The House of Bourbon first rises to prominence when Robert, count of Clermont, sixth son of King Louis IX of France, marries Beatrix of Bourbon, heiress to the lordship of Bourbon. **Rome** Pope Clement IV dies; divisions among the cardinals lead to the papal throne remaining unoccupied for three years. **Holy Roman Empire** Aged 16, Conradin, the last legitimate male heir of the Hohenstaufen dynasty of the kings of Germany and Holy Roman Emperors, is captured and beheaded by Charles of Anjou, a political rival and ally to the hostile Roman Catholic Church. **Venice** Lorenzo Tiepolo, son of former doge Jacopo Tiepolo, is elected doge; during his reign, Venetian pre-eminence in the Adriatic is confirmed; Marco Polo begins his journey to China. **Rome** Papal Interregnum begins (until 1271).

1269 **Bohemia** King Otakar II inherits Carinthia and part of Carniola, making him the most powerful prince in the Holy Roman Empire.

Lithuania Traidenis becomes grand duke, ending the unrest following the assassination of King Mindaugas and establishing the country as a pagan state for the next hundred years.

1270 **France** Louis IX dies of the plague while besieging Tunis; Philippe III 'the Bold' becomes king of France, adding Toulouse to his country. **Hungary and Croatia** Stephen V becomes king.

1271 **Rome** Deadlock in the election of a new pope is broken when the inhabitants of Viterbo remove the roof of the building in which the cardinals are assembled and lock them in with only bread and water; after three days, Cardinal Tebaldo Visconti is elected pope as Gregory X.

1272 **England** Henry III dies, leaving Westminster as his memorial; Edward I Longshanks becomes king; he conquers Wales and tries, and fails, to conquer Scotland, but becomes known as 'the Hammer of the Scots'; he is the fourth Edward to be an English king, but is known as Edward I. **Navarre** Theobald II dies on the Eighth Crusade, while besieging Tunis; his brother, Henry I the Fat, becomes king. **Hungary and Croatia** Stephen V dies, possibly murdered, while searching for his kidnapped infant son Ladislaus; Ladislaus IV becomes king, and his reign is filled with unrest. **Albania** Charles I of Anjou occupies Durres and establishes an Albanian kingdom with himself as king; he is the first Albanian ruler of the Angevin dynasty. **Russia** Vasily of Kostroma, youngest son of Iaroslav II, becomes grand prince of Vladimir; he never leaves his home town of Kostroma.

1273 **Germany** Rudolph I is elected king; the first Habsburg ruler of Germany, he attempts to increase the power of the monarchy by restoring all the lands and rights usurped by the princes since 1245.

1274 **England** King Edward I returns from the Ninth Crusade to be crowned king. **Navarre** Henry the Fat dies, reportedly suffocated by his own fat; his son and heir has died in a fall from a battlement; Henry is the last in the male line of the House of Champagne; his daughter Joanna I becomes queen, aged 3.

1275 **Sweden** Valdemar I's brother, Magnus III Ladulås, deposes him, with Danish help, to become king. **Venice** Jacopo Contarini is elected doge.

1276 **Germany** Rudolf forces Otakar II of Bohemia to cede to him Austria, Styria, Carinthia and Carniola; Austria will eventually become the seat of Habsburg power. **Rome** Pierre de Tarentaise reigns as Pope Innocent V for just five months; under the influence of the Sicilian king, Charles of Anjou, Cardinal deacon Ottobuono Fieschi, a Genoese nobleman, is elected pope as Adrian V; he dies a month later, never having been ordained to the priesthood; he never becomes bishop of Rome, but is traditionally counted in the papal succession; the Portuguese Pedro Julião is elected Pope John XXI. **Aragón** Pedro III becomes king; he conquers Sicily, is also king of Valencia and Majorca and becomes known as Pedro the Great. **Majorca** James II becomes king; his other territories include Ibiza, Formentera, the counties of Roussillon and Cerdanya, the dominion of Montpellier and others; he is a vassal to his brother in Aragón, even though Majorca is larger than Aragón. **Serbia** King Stefan Uroš I is forced to abdicate by his son, Stefan Dragutin, who becomes king. **Russia** Dmitry of Pereslavl, second son of Alexander Nevsky, becomes grand prince of Vladimir after fighting for a decade against the previous two grand princes.

1277 **Rome** The roof of a new wing of Pope John XXI's palace, at Viterbo, collapses on top of him while he is sleeping; he dies eight days later, possibly the only pope to die in an accident; Giovanni Gaetano Orsini, cardinal deacon and inquisitor general, is elected pope as Nicholas III. **Bulgaria** Tsar Constantine Tikh dies fighting the usurper Ivailo; Ivailo had started life as a goatherd; in the next three years, another two usurpers, Ivan Asen III and another Ivailo, briefly occupy the Bulgarian throne.

1278 **Holy Roman Empire** Rudolph I of Germany and Ladislaus IV of Hungary defeat and kill Ottakar II of Bohemia in the Battle of Marchfield, the largest battle of knights of the Middle Ages; the Habsburgs will continue to rule Austria and other captured territories until the end of the First World War, in 1918. **Bohemia** Wenceslaus II becomes king.

1279 **Portugal** Denis, 'the Farmer King', becomes king of Portugal and the newly added Algarve; he effectively founds the Portuguese navy. **Poland** Leszek the Black becomes ruler.

1280 **Norway** Twelve-year-old Erik II Magnusson becomes king. **Venice** Giovanni Dandolo, from the prominent Dandolo family, is elected doge; he introduces the Venetian Ducat, a coin that is valid in every state with which Venice trades. **Bulgaria** George Terter becomes the first Terter tsar as George I.

1281 **Rome** The French cardinal Simon de Brion, former chancellor of France, is elected pope as Martin IV. **Norway** Erik II marries Princess Margaret of Scotland. **Byzantine Empire** Michael IX Palaiologos, son of Andronikos II, is named as co-emperor. **Belarus** Gleb and Iziaslav have both been princes of Polotsk at unknown dates; Daumantas becomes prince of Polotsk.

1282 **Spain** Alfonso X of Castile and León is unseated by his son, Sancho IV the Brave, in a bitter civil war. **Norway** Queen Margaret dies giving birth to Margaret, Maid of Norway, who will later become queen of Scots. **Sicily** The Sicilian rebellion known as the Sicilian Vespers begins against the rule of Angevin King Charles I; Charles is deposed from rule of the island of Sicily but retains the throne of mainland Sicily, informally known as the Kingdom of Naples; he is replaced by Pedro III of Aragón, husband of Constance, daughter of King Manfred of Sicily; son of James I of Aragón, he is also king of Valencia and Majorca, as well as count of Barcelona. **Lithuania** Traidenis is the first Lithuanian grand duke to die of natural causes; Daumantas becomes grand duke. **Serbia** King Stefan Dragutin breaks his leg while hunting and becomes ill; he gives the throne to his younger brother, who becomes Stefan Uroš II Milutin, retaining for himself several parts of the country; he becomes king of Srem; Stefan Uroš II Milutin conquers large parts of Macedonia and makes Skopje his capital. **Byzantine Empire** Andronikos II Palaiologos becomes emperor, having been co-emperor since 1261.

1283 **England** Death by drawing and quartering is first used as a form of execution by King Edward I in the execution of Dafydd ap Gruffydd, the last ruler of an independent Wales.

1284 **Wales** The creation of the Statute of Rhuddlan, formally incorporating Wales into England in the entity England and Wales. **León-Castile-Galicia** Alfonso X dies defeated and unpopular; his second son, Sancho IV the Brave, becomes king against his wishes. **Navarre** Queen Joanna marries Prince Philippe, future king of France.

1285 **France** Philippe III dies in battle in Aragón; Philippe IV the Fair becomes king; he determines to strengthen the monarchy. **Navarre**

Queen Joanna I becomes queen of France; King Philippe III of France becomes Felipe I of Navarre, the first king of the House of Capet in Navarre; the crowns of France and Navarre are united until 1328. **Majorca** Alfonso III, king of Aragón, annexes Majorca and the Balearic Islands after defeating his uncle, James II, at the Battle of Les Formigues. **Rome** Giacomo Savelli, protodeacon of the College of Cardinals, is elected pope as Honorius IV; he is the last pope to be married before taking holy orders. **Aragón** Alfonso III the Liberal becomes king; he reconquers Majorca and Ibiza from his uncle, James II of Majorca; during his reign, he quarrels with the nobles and Aragón comes close to anarchy. **Naples** Charles II becomes king. **Sicily** James I becomes king; Charles II of Anjou continues to claim the kingdom. **Albania** Charles II of Anjou succeeds his father as king. **Lithuania** Butigeidis becomes grand duke; he is the first grand duke of the House of Gediminaičiai, which will rule the country until the 16th century; another branch of this powerful dynasty, the Jagiellons, will also reign in Poland, Hungary and Bohemia; he builds a castle system along the Neman river to discourage raids by the Livonian Order and Teutonic Knights.

1286 **Scotland** Alexander III dies in a fall from his horse, initiating the First War of Scottish Independence; his granddaughter Margaret, Maid of Norway, becomes queen. **Denmark** Eric V is assassinated by his followers; he is succeeded by his son, Eric VI.

1287 **Spain** King Alfonso III of Aragón conquers the island of Minorca from the Moors.

1288 **Sicily** Edward I of England obtains the release of Charles II from captivity, on condition that he rules only Naples, leaving Sicily to the Aragónese. **Rome** Girolamo Masci, cardinal bishop of Palestrina, is elected pope as Nicholas IV; he proclaims a crusade against King Ladislaus IV of Hungary. **Poland** Henryk IV Probus becomes high duke.

1289 **Venice** Pietro Gradenigo is elected doge. **Sicily** The pope absolves Charles II of his promises to the Aragónese, and he is crowned king of Sicily.

1290 **Scotland** Three-year-old Queen Margaret dies, uncrowned, on her way to Scotland to marry Edward, prince of Wales. **Sweden** Birger Magnusson becomes king. **Hungary and Croatia** Stephen V is murdered by assassins of the nomadic Turkic people, the Cumans; he dies without an heir, and Andrew III, grandson of Andrew II, becomes the last king of the Árpád line. **Poland** Premislas II, son of the duke of Greater Poland, becomes high duke.

1291 **Scotland** Scottish nobles recognize the authority of Edward I of England in mediating a resolution of the succession crisis created by the death of Alexander III. **Germany** In an attempt to limit the increasing power of the Habsburgs, the princes refuse to elect Rudolf I's son, Albert, as co-king. **Aragón and Sicily** James II becomes king; he resigns as king of Sicily. **Switzerland** Three Swiss cantons join together to begin a struggle for independence from the Habsburgs. **Italy** The independence of San Marino is confirmed by a papal bull. **Lithuania** Butvydas, brother of Butigeidis, becomes grand duke.

1292 **Scotland** Six years of interregnum, when the country is governed by the Guardians of Scotland, ends when John Balliol, great-great-great-grandson of King David I, through his mother, Dervorguilla of Galloway, is elected as king; his rival is Robert Bruce, 5th lord of Annandale, grandfather of the future Robert the Bruce. **Rome**

Pope Nicholas IV dies; a papal interregnum begins (until 1294). **Germany** Adolf of Nassau, a minor German noble, is elected king; he is elected because the princes want a weak emperor. **Bulgaria** George I flees and is replaced by two usurpers – Smilitz, a Mongol puppet monarch, until 1298, and George's son-in-law, Caka, who is tsar for only a few months.

1293 **Norway** Eric II marries Isabel Bruce, sister of Robert the Bruce, King Robert I of Scotland.

1294 **Scotland** John Balliol negotiates the Auld Alliance with France and Norway. **Rome** Benedictine hermit Pietro Angelerio is surprisingly elected pope as Celestine V; he abdicates after five months and eight days; cardinal priest Benedetto Caetani is elected pope, as Boniface VIII; he is the last pope to challenge the growing power of European nation-states and their rulers. **Albania** Charles II surrenders his rights to Albania to his son Philip II, who rules as lord of the Kingdom of Albania. **Russia** Andrey III Alexandrovich, son of Alexander Nevsky, ousts his brother Dmitri from Vladimir, with the help of the Mongols, and becomes grand prince.

1295 **England** Edward I summons the Model Parliament. **Aragón** With the Treaty of Anagni, James II returns the Balearics to James II of Majorca. **León-Castile-Galicia** Nine-year-old Ferdinand IV the Summoned becomes king of Castile and León; his mother's bravery during her regency saves him from the violence of competitors and nobles. **Poland** Premislas II, already high duke, is crowned king of Poland; the Polish Kingdom will survive for 500 years. **Lithuania** Vytenis becomes grand duke; his reign is marked by constant warfare; he makes an alliance with Riga and defeats the Livonian Order in the Battle of Turaida.

1296
King John Balliol abdicates and is imprisoned in the Tower of London until 1299, when he is released and goes into exile in France; there is an interregnum until 1306.

1296 **England and Scotland** Edward I storms Berwick-upon-Tweed, slaughtering the inhabitants; he defeats the Scots at the Battle of Dunbar. **Sicily** James II, also king of Aragón, agrees with Charles II, king of Naples, to give up Sicily, but the Sicilians install James's brother, Frederick II, as king. **Poland** King Premislas II is kidnapped and murdered by representatives of the electors of Brandenberg and Polish nobles; Wenceslaus II, king of Bohemia and son of Bohemian King Ottokar II the Great, also becomes High Duke Wenceslaus II of Poland; he is the first ruler for almost 500 years not to be a member of the Piast family.

1297 **Scotland** William Wallace begins his revolt against the English, defeating them at the Battle of Stirling Bridge. **France** Louis IX is canonized as St Louis. **Monaco** gains independence from Genoa when it is captured by François Grimaldi; the Grimaldi family still rule the principality today.

1298 **England** Edward I defeats William Wallace in the Battle of Falkirk, reconquering Scotland. **Germany** The princes tire of Adolf of Nassau and elect Albrecht I, son of Rudolf I, as king; Adolf of Nassau dies in battle against Albert, never having been crowned Holy Roman Emperor. **Bulgaria** Ivan II succeeds his father Smilitz as tsar; he is still a child and a regent rules on his behalf.

1299 **Norway** Erik II dies without sons; his brother is crowned King Haakon V; he is the last king of the Fairhair dynasty, which has ruled for more than 400 years. **Bulgaria** Chaka, son of Mongol leader Nogai Khan, forces Ivan II and his regency to flee, and he becomes tsar.

1300 **Poland** High Duke Wenceslaus I is crowned king. **Bulgaria** Teodor Svetoslav, son of George I, deposes Tsar Chaka and becomes tsar; Chaka is strangled and beheaded in prison; Teodor stabilizes the country and ends Mongol involvement in its affairs.

1301 **Wales** Edward of Caernarvon (later King Edward II) becomes the first prince of Wales. **Scotland** Robert I makes peace with Edward I of England. **Monaco** The Genoese regain control; the Grimaldis go into exile. **Hungary and Croatia** On the death of Andrew III, the succession moves briefly to the Premyslid line, when Wenceslaus of Bohemia becomes king.

1302 **Italy** The war of the Sicilian Vespers over the rule of the Angevin king, Charles I, ends.

1303 **Rome** Niccolò Boccasini is elected pope as Benedict XI.

1304 **England** Edward I takes Stirling Castle, the last rebel stronghold in the war of Scottish Independence. **Rome** Pope Benedict XI dies after reigning for eight months. **Russia** Michael of Tver, second son of Iaroslav III, becomes grand prince of Vladimir.

1305 **Navarre** Joanna I dies; Louis I, who will be Louis X of France from 1314, becomes king. **Rome** After a year's interregnum, caused by divisions between Italian and French cardinals, Raymond Bertrand de Got, archbishop of Bordeaux, is elected pope as Clement V. **Poland** Wenceslaus III, also king of Bohemia and king of Hungary, becomes king of Poland.

1306 **Scotland** Robert the Bruce becomes king and begins the fight for Scottish independence from English rule; the earl of Pembroke defeats Bruce's Scottish rebels at the Battle of Methven. **Austria** Rudolf III declares himself king and then ensures the election of his son-in-law, Henry V of Carinthia, but Henry is deposed. **Poland, Bohemia, Hungary and Croatia** Wenceslaus III, king of Hungary and Croatia, becomes king of Bohemia and renounces the Hungarian throne in favour of Otto, duke of Lower Bavaria, a member of the House of Wittelsbach and descendant of Stephen V; he is not universally accepted as king; Wenceslaus III is assassinated in Poland; Władysław I the Short becomes high duke of Poland.

1307 **England** Edward I dies en route to fight Robert Bruce; Edward II becomes king.

> ## "Try, try, try again."
>
> Robert the Bruce

1308 **Rome** The papal court moves to Avignon; the Great Schism follows. **Hungary and Croatia** Otto abdicates; Charles I becomes king, marking the beginning of the reign of the Angevin dynasty in Hungary. **Germany** Albrecht I is murdered by his nephew, Johann Parricida; Albrecht had deprived him of his inheritance; Henry VII becomes king.

1309 **Monaco** Rainier I, lord of Cagnes, son-in-law of François Grimaldi, becomes the first sovereign ruler; he builds Château Grimaldi. **Rome** Pope Clement V settles the papal seat in Avignon; the Papal States are entrusted to three cardinals, but Rome, at this time, is ungovernable. **Sicily** Robert the Wise becomes king. **Hungary and Croatia** Otto is replaced as king by Robert of Anjou, great-grandson of Stephen V, as Charles I; he is also king of Naples and Sicily.

1310 **Venice** A failed rebellion against the doge and the Grand Council of Venice burns down the Rialto Bridge. **Bohemia** John the Blind becomes the first member of the House of Luxembourg to be elected king, assuming the throne in the right of his wife Eliška, sister of Wenceslaus III. **Wallachia** Basarab I is the first non-legendary ruler of the Principality of Wallachia.

1311 **England** A committee of 21 English barons draws up a series of ordinances, which replace the king with ordainers as the effective government of the country. **Majorca** James II's oldest son, also called James, renounces his claim to the throne to become a monk; Sancho I, his second son, becomes king. **Venice** Marino Zorzi, considered a saint in his own lifetime, is elected as the 50th doge.

1312 **León-Castile-Galicia** Alfonso XI the Just becomes king of Castile and León. **Venice** Giovanni Soranzo is elected doge. **Holy Roman Empire** Henry VII is crowned emperor, the first to be crowned since Frederick II in 1220.

1313 **Germany** On the death of Henry VII, two rivals emerge for the German crown – Ludwig of Bavaria of the House of Wittelsbach, grandson of Rudolf I, and Frederick I the Fair of the House of Habsburg, king of Austria.

1314 **Scotland** Robert the Bruce routs the English at the Battle of Bannockburn, and Scotland regains its independence. **France** Louis X the Quarreller becomes king. **Germany** Ludwig IV is elected king, but Frederick the Fair remains a rival. **Rome** Clement V dies; a two-year papal interregnum ensues.

1315 **Belarus** Vainus, brother of Gaediminas, grand prince of Lithuania, becomes prince of Polotsk.

1316 **Ireland** The Second Battle of Athenry results in over 5,000 dead, and ends the power of the Ua Conchobair (O'Connor's) as kings of Connacht. **France** Louis X dies of dehydration, or possibly poisoning; newborn John I the Posthumous becomes king, but dies five days later; Philippe V the Tall, Louis X's uncle, succeeds him; barring the claims to the throne of Louis X's daughter, Jeanne, he effectively establishes that, unlike other European monarchies, no woman could ever reign in France. **Navarre** John the Posthumous, king of France, is king for the five days he lives; Philippe V of France becomes King Felipe II of Navarre. **Rome** Frenchman Jacques Duèze is elected pope as John XXII; he continues the Avignon papacy. **Lithuania** Vytenis dies without an heir; his younger brother, Gediminas, becomes one of the nation's greatest grand dukes, inheriting a huge territory including Lithuania, Samogitia, Red Russia, Polotsk and Minsk. **Byzantine Empire** Andronikos III becomes co-emperor.

1318 **Scotland** The Scots capture Berwick-upon-Tweed from the English. **Russia** Grand Prince Michael of Vladimir is executed by the Mongol khan; the unpopular Yuri of Moscow becomes grand prince.

1319 **Norway and Sweden** Haakon V of Norway dies and is succeeded by his grandson, the Swedish Prince Magnus – his daughter having married a son of Magnus I of Sweden; the two countries are united by Magnus.

1320 **Scotland** The Scots reaffirm their independence by signing the Declaration of Arbroath.

Declaration of Arbroath
1320

The Declaration of Arbroath is undoubtedly the most famous document in the history of Scotland. To a certain degree, the American Declaration of Independence was based on it and it is seen by many as the founding document of the Scottish nation. It was written, in Latin, on 6 April 1320, in the form of a letter. Once completed, the Declaration was sent to Pope John XXII in May of the same year and is believed to have been scribed in the scriptorium of Arbroath Abbey by Abbot Bernard. The Abbot was chosen to act on behalf of the nobles and barons of Scotland.

The Declaration of Arbroath just one of three letters sent to the Pope residing in Avignon, France. The other two letters were sent by King Robert the Bruce and four Scottish bishops, who were trying to appease the hostility shown towards the papacy. The Declaration was first sealed by 51 magnates and Scottish barons and then delivered to the papal court in Avignon by Sir Adam Gordon. The Declaration of Arbroath is the only letter to have survived of the original three.

> “*It is in truth not for glory, nor riches, nor honours that we are fighting, but for freedom – for that alone, which no honest man gives up but life itself.*”

Extract from the Declaration of Arbroath

1320 **Denmark** Following the death of Eric VI, violent civil war and a year-long interregnum, Christopher II, son of Eric V, becomes king in exchange for agreeing to the demands of the nobles; Denmark is virtually bankrupt and mortgaged to German and Danish nobles. **Poland** Władysław I the Short, already high duke, is crowned king. **Byzantine Empire** Co-emperor Michael IX Palaiologos dies after hearing that his son, Andronikos III, has killed another of his sons, Palaiologos.

1321 **Serbia** A short civil war follows the death of Stefan Uroš II Milutin; Stefan Uroš III Dečanski becomes king. **Byzantine Empire** Andronikos III, son of Michael IX Palaiologos, becomes a rival emperor to Andronikos II.

1322 **France** Philippe V dies without a male heir; his younger brother, Charles IV the Fair, becomes the last Capet king.

1322 **Navarre** Charles I of France becomes Charles I of Navarre.

1322 **Germany** Ludwig of Bavaria defeats Frederick the Fair at the Battle of Mühldorf – often called the last battle of knights – to become undisputed king as Ludwig IV. **Bulgaria** George Terter II becomes the last Terter tsar. **Russia** Grand Prince Yuri of Vladimir is killed by Dmitri the Terrible Eyes, son of the executed Michael of Tver; Dmitri takes his place.

1323 **Bulgaria** George II dies of natural causes, without issue; Michael Šišman becomes the first king of the Šišmanovich dynasty. **Denmark** Christopher II is overthrown by Danish nobles and forced into exile; Duke Valdemar of South Jutland becomes puppet king.

1324 **Majorca** Sancho I dies without a legitimate heir; he wills the throne to his nephew, James III, to prevent it falling into the hands of the king of Aragón.

1325 **Portugal** King Dinis dies, having established Portugal on equal footing with the other Iberian kingdoms; Afonso IV becomes king; his rival for the throne, his half-brother Afonso Sanches, is stripped of all his lands and fiefdoms and sent into exile.

1326 **England** Isabella, Edward II's wife, invades England with her lover, Roger Mortimer, capturing the king. **Russia** Grand Prince Dmitri the Terrible Eyes is executed on the orders of the Mongol Uzbeg Khan for the murder, four years earlier, of Grand Prince Yuri; Dmitri dies childless and Grand Prince Michael's second son, Alexander, takes the throne.

1327 **England** Edward II abdicates and is then savagely murdered by agents of his wife Isabella, and her lover Roger Mortimer, earl of March; Edward III becomes king, the first king to speak English as his chosen language. **Aragón** Alfonso IV the Kind becomes king.

THE 'SHE-WOLF' OF FRANCE

1292-1358

Isabella of France, dubbed the 'She-Wolf of France', was the Queen consort of Edward II of England and mother of Edward III. By the 1320s, Isabella and Edward were at loggerheads and they spent more and more time apart. It is believed that Edward had a homosexual affair with Piers Gaveston, while Isabella took her own lover, Roger Mortimer. Sick of Edward's weak and foolish rule, the English people welcomed the rebel army that Queen Isabella and Mortimer led from France. Between them they arranged for the murder of Edward II in 1327, leaving Isabella's son, Edward III, free to be crowned king of England.

When Edward III turned 18, he had both Isabella and Mortimer taken prisoner. Despite his mother's pleas to save her beloved Mortimer, he was executed for treason in November 1330. Isabella, however, was spared the death sentence and allowed to retire to Castle Rising in Norfolk where she remained for the rest of her life.

1328 **France** Charles IV dies without a male heir; Philippe VI the Fortunate, nephew of Philippe IV, becomes the first king of France from the House of Valois. **Navarre** Joanna II, only daughter of Louis I of Navarre, denied the throne of France in 1316 because of her gender, becomes queen. **Holy Roman Empire** Ludwig IV is crowned Holy Roman Emperor. **Byzantine Empire** Andronikos III becomes emperor, following an eight-year civil war against his grandfather, Andronikos II. **Russia** Ivan Kalita of Moscow leads an army against Grand Prince Alexander; Alexander flees and Ivan becomes Grand Prince Ivan I, nicknamed 'the Moneybag' because he is given the right, by the khan, to collect taxes from all Russian lands.

1329 **Scotland** England recognizes Scotland as an independent nation; King Robert the Bruce dies and is succeeded by his 5-year-old son, David II. **Navarre** Queen Joanna II marries Philippe of Évreux, who becomes *de jure uxoris* King Felipe III of Navarre, first Navarrese king of the House of Évreux. **Denmark** Christopher II is restored to the throne, but without much power. **Venice** Francesco Dandolo is elected doge; he institutes a policy of expanding Venetian territory on the mainland.

1330 **Bulgaria** The Bulgars, under Michael III, are beaten by the Serbs, led by Stephen Urosh, at the Battle of Velbuzhd; Michael III Šišman is killed; large parts of Bulgaria fall to Serbia; the balance of power shifts in the Balkans; Michael III's son, Ivan Stephen, becomes tsar for only a few months. **Wallachia** Prince Basarab I defeats his Hungarian overlord, Charles I of Anjou, at the Battle of Posada, gaining independence for Wallachia.

1331 **Monaco** After 30 years of Genoese control, Charles I Grimaldi retakes the Rock of Monaco. **Serbia** Stefan Uroš III is imprisoned by his son, Dušan, and strangled; Dušan becomes Stefan Uroš IV Dušan, known as Dušan the Mighty; he is, perhaps, the greatest of all Serbian leaders, with the Serbian Empire growing to be one of the largest states in Europe during his reign. **Bulgaria** Ivan Alexander becomes tsar, sharing his throne with his son for part of his reign.

1332 **England** The first record of the division of the English parliament into two houses. **Scotland** Edward Balliol is crowned king of Scots by the English and his own supporters, but later flees to England. **Denmark** An interregnum begins. **Bulgaria** Ivan Alexander begins the process of splitting the country up between his sons, leaving it weak and divided in the face of the imminent Ottoman conquest. **Albania** Robert of Taranto succeeds Philip II; he swaps the Kingdom of Achaea with his uncle, John, count of Gravina, in exchange for 5,000 ounces of gold and the rights to the Kingdom of Albania; John styles himself duke of Durazzo.

1333 **Scotland** Edward III of England and Edward Balliol, son of John Balliol, beat the Scots at Halidon Hill; David II and his queen, Joan of the Tower, are sent to France for safety. **Poland** Casimir III the Great becomes king; during his reign, he doubles the size of the country and restores its prosperity.

1334 **Rome** Cardinal Jacques Fournier is elected pope as Benedict XII.

1336 **Aragón** Pedro IV, a stickler for etiquette, becomes king. **Albania** Charles becomes duke of Durazzo, ruler of Albania.

1337 **England** Edward III claims the French throne and the Hundred Years' War (1337–1453) begins. **Sweden and Norway** Magnus IV is crowned joint ruler in Stockholm, causing resentment among Norwegian nobles wanting a separate Norwegian coronation. **Sicily** Peter II becomes king.

1339 **Venice** Bartolomeo Gradenigo is elected doge.

1340 **England** Edward III is declared king of France. **Denmark** Valdemar III becomes king and ends the country's eight-year interregnum and its internal conflicts; Denmark becomes the leading Baltic state during his reign.

1341 **Scotland** King David II returns from France. **Lithuania** Jaunutis, Gediminas's middle son, becomes grand duke. **Byzantine Empire** John V Palaiologos becomes emperor under the regency of his mother, Anna of Savoy; a civil war breaks out with administrative leader John Kantakouzenos, lasting until 1347.

1342 **Rome** Cardinal Pierre Roger is elected pope as Clement VI. **Sicily** 5-year-old Louis the Child becomes king, his mother and uncle act as regents. **Hungary and Croatia** Louis I the Great becomes king; he extends his kingdom to the Adriatic, securing Dalmatia and taking part of Bosnia and Bulgaria; much of his reign is spent in wars with the Republic of Venice and in competition for the throne of Naples. **Belarus** Narimont has been prince of Polotsk at an unknown date; Prince Lubart dies; Wigund becomes prince of Polotsk. **Russia** Simeon of Moscow, son of Ivan Kalita, becomes grand prince of Vladimir.

1343 **Navarre** Charles II the Bad becomes king, allying himself with England and trying to enlarge his kingdom; he is deeply untrustworthy. **Norway** Three-year-old Haakon VI takes the throne, with his father, King Magnus IV, acting as regent. **Venice** Law professor Andrea Dandolo is elected doge. **Sicily** Robert the Wise dies; he has been nicknamed 'the peacemaker of Italy' and has been a notable patron of the arts; Joan I, daughter of Charles, duke of Calabria, eldest son of King Robert, becomes queen.

1344 **Aragón** Pedro IV captures Majorca from James III.

1345 **Lithuania** Jaunutis is overthrown by his brothers, Algirdas and Kęstutis; Algirdas becomes grand duke, while Kęstutis rules in the west of the country; Algirdas makes Lithuania Europe's largest state and one of its most powerful.

1346
The English defeat Philippe VI of France at the Battle of Crécy.

1346 **Scotland** King David II is taken prisoner by the English at the Battle of Neville's Cross; he remains a prisoner for 11 years. **Germany** Charles IV, son of John the Blind of Bohemia and Poland, is elected king, in opposition to Ludwig IV. **Bohemia** John the Blind, who has spent most of his reign fighting abroad, is killed at the Battle of Crécy; Charles IV becomes king. **Serbia** Dušan the Mighty is crowned emperor and Autocrat of Serbs and Greeks; he is the most powerful medieval Serbian ruler, and possibly the most powerful ruler in Europe, during the 14th century.

1347 **England** The English defeat the French at the Battle of Croytoye. **Bohemia** Charles IV of Germany becomes king; he makes Prague one of Europe's leading cities. **Byzantine Empire** John VI Kantakouzenas wins the civil war, becoming senior emperor; the previous emperor, John V Palaiologos, is demoted to co-emperor.

1348 **England and France** A truce is signed between England and France; it lasts until 1352. **Spain** Pedro IV of Aragón defeats his own nobles at Epila. **Albania** Joanna becomes duchess of Durazzo, ruler of Albania.

1349 **Majorca** James III is driven out and killed at the Battle of Llucmajor by Pedro IV's invading forces; Majorca becomes part of Aragón until the Nueva Planta decrees of 1707; James IV becomes pretender to the throne of Majorca; he is kept in close confinement in Barcelona until 1362 and marries Joan I of Naples, taking the title duke of Calabria. **Germany** Charles IV is again elected king, following the death of Ludwig IV in 1347.

1350 **England** An English fleet, personally commanded by King Edward III, defeats a Spanish fleet in the battle of Les Espagnols sur Mer. **France** John II the Good becomes king. **León-Castile-Galicia** Alfonso XI is the only European monarch to die during the Black Death; Pedro the Cruel, a vicious monster, succeeds him, and years of civil war ensue.

1352 **Monaco** Charles I, lord of Monaco, introduces a co-rulership with his own sons, Rainier II and Gabriel, and his uncle, Antonio. **Rome** Cardinal Étienne Aubert is elected pope as Innocent VI. **Wallachia** Nicolae Alexandru comes to power as prince; he yields to Louis I, king of Hungary, in 1354. **Byzantine Empire** Civil war breaks out again.

1353 **Byzantine Empire** Matthew Kantakouzenos, son of John VI Kantakouzenos, becomes co-emperor in recognition of his support for his father, during his struggle against John V Palaiologos. **Russia** Ivan II the Fair, second son of Ivan Kalita, becomes grand prince of Vladimir.

1354 **Venice** Marino Faliero is elected doge. **Byzantine Empire** John V Palaiologos becomes emperor again; Matthew Kantakouzenos becomes rival emperor.

1355 **Portugal** Inês de Castro is killed and then posthumously declared to be the lawful wife of heir to the throne, Prince Pedro; civil war breaks out between Pedro and Afonso IV. **Norway** Haakon VI, son of Magnus IV of Sweden, reaches his majority and becomes king of Norway, temporarily splitting the union between Norway and Sweden. **Venice** Doge Marino Faliero stages a *coup d'état,* aimed at establishing himself as prince; he is found guilty of treason and beheaded; Giovanni Gradenigo is elected doge. **Italy** Charles IV is crowned king. **Sicily** King Louis dies of plague, aged 17; Frederick III, second son of Peter II, becomes king. **Holy Roman Empire** Charles IV is crowned emperor; he is now the personal ruler of every kingdom in the empire. **Serbia** Tsar Dušan dies, possibly poisoned by Hungarians wary of Serbian power; his empire immediately begins to disintegrate.

1356 **England** England's Black Prince defeats the French at Poitiers, capturing King John II of France. **Scotland** Edward Balliol surrenders his claim to the title of king of Scotland to Edward III of England. **Sweden** Erik XII becomes joint ruler of Sweden until 1359. **Venice**

Giovanni Gradenigo is elected doge; Giovanni Dolfin is elected doge. **Serbia** The king of Raška, Stefan Dušan, is proclaimed 'Tsar of all Serbs', Arbanasses and Greeks. **Zeta** Territories that encompass the present-day Republic of Montenegro are ruled by Balša I; he is the first ruler of the House of Balšić. **Bulgaria** Ivan Alexander crowns a son of his second marriage, Ivan Šišman, co-tsar, upsetting his older son from his first marriage, Ivan Stratsimir.

1357 **Scotland** King David II is ransomed for 100,000 marks and returns to Scotland; the country fails to raise the ransom money and David tries, unsuccessfully, to make a secret agreement with English King Edward III to make Edward's son Lionel, duke of Clarence, heir to the Scottish throne. **Monaco** On the death of Charles I, Monaco is captured again by the Genoese. **Portugal** Pedro I, the third, but only surviving son of Afonso IV, becomes king; Pedro's revolt against his father, following the murder by his father of his mistress, Inês, has carried on since 1355.

1359 **Russia** Dmitry of Suzdal, a descendent of Vsevolod the Big Nest, becomes grand prince of Vladimir.

1360 **France** John II is allowed to return to France from captivity in England to raise his ransom money; the substitute hostage, his son, Louis, escapes, but John, a man of his word, returns to England, where he will die in 1364. **Sweden** Erik XII, son of Magnus IV, becomes joint ruler of Sweden with his father, until 1359. Erik XII dies of plague, as do his wife and two sons.

1361 **Venice** Lorenzo Celsi is elected doge.

1362 **Norway** Haakon VI of Norway is elected king of Sweden. **Hungary and Croatia** Louis I conquers northern Bulgaria. **Rome** Guillaume Grimoard, abbot of Saint-Victor in Marseille, is elected pope as Urban V. **Sweden** Haakon VI of Norway becomes joint ruler of Sweden with his father, Magnus IV, until 1364. **Zeta** Đurađ I becomes ruler. **Byzantine Empire** is reduced to the city of Constantinople.

1363 **Sweden** Albrecht von Mecklenberg, a northern German feudal lord and nephew of Magnus IV, is invited to be king of Sweden by rebel members of the Swedish Council of Aristocracy. **Russia** Grand Prince Dmitry of Suzdal is deposed from the throne of Vladimir; Dmitry Donskoi replaces him and is the first grand prince to challenge Tatar control of Russia.

1364 **France** Charles V the Wise becomes king and recovers the territory his father lost to the English. **Navarre** Charles II is heavily defeated in battle by French military commander Bertrand du Guesclin, and loses his French territories and his claim to the duchy of Burgundy. **Sweden** Albrecht von Mecklenberg invades and is crowned king; eight years of civil war ensue between Albrecht and Magnus. **Wallachia** Vladislav I becomes prince, recognizing King Louis I of Hungary as his overlord.

1365 **Sweden** King Magnus is taken prisoner by King Albrecht's forces. **Venice** Marco Cornaro is elected doge.

1366 **Spain** Pedro I is unseated from the throne of Castile by his illegitimate brother, Henry of Trastámara, the first king of the House of Trastámara, which will rule Spain until 1504. **Albania** Louis of Évreux, youngest son of Philippe III of Navarre, marries Joanna, duchess of Durazzo; the marriage brings him the rights to Durazzo and the Kingdom of Albania.

1367 **France** Charles V creates the first royal library. **Spain** Pedro the Cruel of Castile is restored to the throne with the help of Edward the Black Prince and the French. **Portugal** Pedro I dies and Henry of Trastámara, his illegitimate brother, claims the crown; Ferdinand, son of Pedro, is the legitimate candidate, but other rivals include the kings of Aragón and Navarre, as well as John of Gaunt; Pope Gregory XI mediates and gives the crown to Ferdinand, who becomes king as Ferdinand I. **Venice** Andrea Contarini is elected doge; there is war against the Republic of Genoa during his reign. **Rome** Pope Urban V returns the papacy to Rome from Avignon after 59 years, but soon returns to Avignon, following instability in the Papal States. **Albania** Karlo Thopia, grandson of Robert of Taranto, captures Durazzo and becomes prince of Albania.

The Black Prince
1330–1376

Edward Prince of Wales was otherwise known as the Black Prince due to the black armour that he wore. Edward died before his father, Edward III, and therefore never became king. Despite this fact he is remembered as a great military hero, with many victories against the French during the Hundred Years War.

Edward was made Prince of Wales in 1343 and quickly showed military brilliance. He played a key role in the defeat of the French army at the Battle of Crécy when he was still only 16 years old.

Edward married Joan of Kent in 1362 and was appointed the title Prince of Acquitaine and Gascony by his father. Edward led an expedition to Spain in 1367, but made himself unpopular when he levied taxes to pay for this mission. The nobility rose up in revolt against him and in 1370 Edward besieged the city of Limoges where 3,000 of its inhabitants were massacred. Edward died on 8 June 1376 at the age of 45, and was buried in great splendour in Canterbury Cathedral.

1369 **England** war breaks out with France; the French recapture most of Aquitaine. **León-Castile-Galicia** Henry II the Bastard, illegitimate son of Alfonso XI, kills Pedro the Cruel, the last king of the House of Burgundy, and seizes the throne; he is the first king of the House of Trastámara; throughout his reign he has to fight the efforts of John of Gaunt, son of Edward III of England, to obtain the throne for his wife, who is the daughter of Pedro the Cruel.

1370 **Rome** Pierre Roger de Beaufort is elected pope as Gregory XI. **Poland** Casimir the Great dies, the last king from the House of Piast. Louis I the Great of Hungary and Croatia is elected king.

1371 **Scotland** David II dies, the last male of the House of Bruce; Robert II, grandson of Robert I, becomes the first king of the House of Stewart, later spelt 'Stuart'. **Norway** A peace agreement allows King Magnus to return to Norway, where he lives the remainder of his life; Albrecht is confirmed as king. **Bulgaria** Ivan Šišman becomes co-tsar with his brother, Ivan Stratsimir.

1373 **Byzantine Empire** A failed revolt by John V's son, Andronikos, results in him being blinded in one eye and imprisoned.

1375 **Majorca** James IV, pretender to the throne of Majorca, dies, possibly poisoned; his claim passes to his sister Isabella, who styles herself Elizabeth I. **Denmark** Aged 5, Oluf II becomes king; his mother,

Queen Margaret, is regent. Norway and Denmark are united in a personal union with the same king; the two countries will have the same king, with the exception of brief interregnums, until Norway's independence in 1814.

1376 **England** The Good Parliament is held; it attempts to reform the corrupt Royal Council; the Black Prince dies. **Germany** Wenceslaus the Drunkard is elected king. **Bosnia and Serbia** Stephen Tvrtko, of the House of Kotromanić, is crowned king. **Byzantine Empire** With the help of the Republic of Genoa, Andronikos IV Palaiologos deposes his father John V to become emperor; he is opposed during his short reign by the Republic of Venice and Murad I.

1377
England Edward III dies; he has reigned for 50 years and is one of the most successful English monarchs of the Middle Ages; Richard II, son of the Black Prince, becomes king.

1377 **Sicily** Mary, daughter of Frederick III, becomes queen. **Lithuania** Jogaila becomes the last pagan grand duke of Lithuania. **Wallachia** Radu I becomes prince of Wallachia.

1378 **Rome** The Western Schism occurs, following the death of Pope Gregory XI – a split in the Catholic Church, with one pope in Rome and one in Avignon; Archbishop Bartolomeo Prignano is elected pope as Urban VI, the last to be elected from outside the College of Cardinals; the French cardinals declare his election invalid, electing antipope Robert of Geneva as Clement VII; the papacy will be divided for 40 years. **Bohemia** Wenceslaus IV the Drunkard, already king of Germany, becomes king.

1379 **León-Castile-Galicia** Henry II is poisoned by a monk; John I becomes king. **Zeta** Đurađ I's younger brother, Balša II, becomes ruler. **Byzantine Empire** Andronikos IV is deposed but allowed to retain the title of co-emperor; John V Palaiologos returns to power as senior emperor.

1380 **France** Charles VI becomes king; France is riven with civil war during his reign.

1381 **Naples** Charles III is the first king of Naples from the House of Durazzo.

1382 **Venice** Michele Morosini is elected doge; Antonio Venier is elected doge. **Hungary and Croatia** Ten-year-old Mary, daughter of Louis I, becomes queen. **Albania** Balsh II becomes ruler. **Poland** Jadwiga, the younger sister of Mary of Hungary and Croatia, is chosen as queen, ending the link with Hungary.

1383 **Portugal** Ferdinand I dies without male issue, rendering extinct the Burgundian line that has been on the throne since around 1112; a period of civil war and anarchy, known as the 1383–1385 Crisis, begins; Ferdinand's daughter Beatrice claims the throne, but as she is married to King Juan I of Castile, there are concerns that Portugal will simply be merged into Castile; there is an interregnum until 1385. **Wallachia** Dan I becomes prince.

1385 **Portugal** The Cortes selects João I, illegitimate son of Pedro I, as the first king of the House of Aviz or Joannine dynasty; Castile's Juan I invades but João's army deals it a crushing defeat; João makes Philippa of Lancaster, daughter of John of Gaunt, his queen. **Hungary and Croatia** Queen Mary is deposed for several months by Charles III, king of Naples; she is restored to the throne. **Albania** Karlo Thopia returns to power as prince of Albania. **Zeta** Đurađ II Stracimirović becomes ruler; he is ruler of several Serbian and Albanian territories. **Albania** is conquered by the Ottomans, beginning 80 years of resistance to Turkish rule.

1386 **Switzerland** Winning the Battle of Sempach, the Swiss safeguard their independence from Habsburg rule. **Naples** Charles III is assassinated on the orders of Dowager Queen Elisabeth of Hungary, Queen Mary's mother; Ladislaus becomes king. **Lithuania and Poland** Grand Duke Jogaila of Lithuania converts to Catholicism, marries 11-year-old Queen Jadwiga of Poland and becomes King Władysław II Jagiełło of Poland; he rules Poland jointly with Jadwiga. **Wallachia** Prince Dan I dies in battle against the Bulgarian army of Tsar Ivan Šišman; Mircea I the Great, father of Vlad II Dracul and Vlad Tepes the Impaler, the character on whom Bram Stoker's Dracula is based, becomes prince of Wallachia; his reign brings stability to the principality and expands it to its largest area.

1387 **Aragón** John I becomes king. **Navarre** Charles II dies horrifically when he is accidentally burned alive during medical treatment; Charles II the Noble becomes king and mends relations with France. **Denmark and Norway** Oluf of Norway dies without issue; his mother, Margaret I, is elected regent in both countries; she rules as queen but does not use the title. **Hungary and Croatia** Dowager Queen Elisabeth is strangled in front of her daughter, Queen Mary, on the anniversary of the murder of Charles III of Naples, possibly by Mary's husband, Sigismund; Mary and Sigismund, son of Holy Roman Emperor Charles IV, rule Hungary jointly. **Albania** Gjergj Thopia becomes prince of Albania. **Belarus** Skirgaila becomes prince of Polotsk; the title is from this date held by the grand duke of Lithuania.

1388 **Bulgaria** Tsar Ivan Stratsimir is forced to accept Ottoman overlordship, following an invasion.

1389 **England and France** sign a truce in the Hundred Years' War. **Rome** Pietro Tomacelli is elected second Roman pope of the Western Schism as Boniface IX; Clement VII remains antipope in Avignon. **Sweden** Queen Margaret of Norway and Denmark is asked by Swedish nobles to depose Albrecht I; she defeats him at the Battle of Åsle; he is imprisoned and Margaret becomes queen; she declares her great-nephew, 7-year-old Eric of Pomerania, descendant of Magnus I of Sweden, Haakon V of Norway and Valdemar IV of Denmark, king of Norway, but she acts as regent; he will, in time, become king of all three Scandinavian countries, but she will retain de facto power until her death in 1412. **Russia** Dmitri Donskoi is the first grand prince for centuries to bequeath the throne of Vladimir to his son without consulting the Mongol Khan; Vasli I becomes grand prince of Vladimir-Moscow; he continues the unification of the Russian lands.

1390 **Scotland** John, son of Robert II, becomes king, changing his name to Robert to avoid any link to John Balliol that might weaken his family's claim to the throne; he is crowned Robert III; in reality, power lies in the hands of his brother, the earl of Fife. **León-Castile-Galicia** John I dies when his horse falls on him during an equestrian performance; Henry III the Infirm becomes king; dynastic conflicts have been ended by Henry's marriage to John of Gaunt's daughter, Katherine of Lancaster. **Bosnia and Serbia** King Stephen Tvrtko assumes the title of 'Bosnian King of Rascia, Bosnia, Dalmatia, Croatia and the Seacoast'. **Byzantine Empire** John VII Palaiologos deposes John V Palaiologos to become emperor, but John V Palaiologos is restored through the auspices of Venice and the Ottoman Empire; he dies shortly after.

1391 **Bosnia and Serbia** Stephen Dabiša becomes king and loses Croatia and Dalmatia to King Sigismund of Hungary. **Byzantine Empire** Manuel II Palaiologos, second son of John V Palaiologos, becomes emperor.

1392 **Scotland** The earl of Orkney takes control of the Shetland Islands and the Faroe Islands. **France** Charles VI becomes insane; in one incident, he kills six knights; he believes, at one time, he is made of glass and will break if moved; he roams the corridors of his palaces howling like a wolf; Philippe the Bold, Charles's uncle, becomes regent, beginning a feud that will divide the kings of France and the dukes of Burgundy for 85 years. **Lithuania** Vytautas the Great, son of Kęstutis, becomes grand duke; he expands the empire until it stretches from the Black Sea to the Baltic Sea.

THE OTTOMAN EMPIRE
1299–1923

Othman or Osman I (1259–1326) was the founder of the Ottoman empire. The Ottomans are considered to be one of the greatest and most powerful civilisations of the modern period. The empire that they built became the largest and most influential of all the Muslim empires. The Ottoman empire lasted until the 20th century and did not really end until the secularisation of Turkey after the Second World War.

Perhaps the greatest figure associated with Ottoman history is Sultan Suleiman 'the Magnificent' (left), a poet and accomplished goldsmith. He ruled the Ottoman empire for 46 years between 1520 and 1566 and was responsible for helping it reach a peak of grandeur and prosperity which was never afterwards surpassed.

1393 **Bulgaria** King Ivan Šišman dies in battle against the Turks.

1394 **Rome** Antipope Clement VII dies in Avignon; French cardinals replace him, with Cardinal Pedro de Luna as Benedict XIII.

1395 **Monaco** Louis is briefly lord of Monaco, ruling jointly with Jean I; they are ousted when the Genoese take control again. **Aragón and Sicily** Martin becomes king; Queen Mary of Sicily marries Martin; they rule jointly. **Hungary and Croatia** Queen Mary dies under suspicious circumstances while pregnant; her husband Sigismund, Holy Roman Emperor, becomes an unpopular sole ruler. **Bosnia and Serbia** Helena, widow of Stephen Dabiša, becomes queen on behalf of Stephen Tvrtko's illegitimate son, underage Stephen Ostoja.

1396 **Aragón** John I dies without issue; his brother, Martin I, succeeds him. **Bulgaria** The defeat of Ivan Stratsimir by the Ottoman Turks at Vidin, ends Bulgaria's independence until 1878.

1397 **Scandinavia** Denmark, Norway (with Iceland, Greenland, the Faroe Islands, Shetland and Orkney) and Sweden (including some of Finland) are united – with some interruptions – under a single monarch by the Kalmar Agreement, devised by Queen Margaret, until 1523. **Bulgaria** Tsar Ivan Stratsimir is taken prisoner by the Ottoman Sultan Bayezit I and conveyed to Turkey; he is never heard of again; his son, Constantine II, becomes tsar.

1398 **Bosnia and Serbia** Stephen Ostoja, nephew of Stephen Dabiša, becomes king and organizes an ultimately unsuccessful revolt against the Ottomans in the north-west of the country, with support from Serbia and Wallachia; Constantine spends much of his reign in Hungary and Serbia.

1399 **England** Henry Bolingbroke, son of John of Gaunt, Edward III's only surviving son, deposes Richard II and takes the throne as Henry IV; he is the first English king of the House of Lancaster. **Poland** Queen Jadwiga dies in childbirth; Władysław II Jagiełło becomes sole ruler.

RENAISSANCE MONARCHS

1400–1599

1400 **England** Former king Richard II is murdered or starved to death in Pontefract Castle. **Wales** Owen Glendower declares himself prince of Wales, and starts a rebellion. **Germany and the Holy Roman Empire** Wenceslaus, who has not visited Germany for 10 years, is deposed because of his drunkenness and incompetence; Ruprecht, elector of Palatinate, becomes king of Germany; Wenceslaus refuses to recognize him. **Venice** Michele Steno is elected doge.

1401 **Sicily** On the death of Queen Mary, Martin I becomes sole ruler.

1402 **Wales** Henry IV fights Owen Glendower. **Scotland** David Stewart, duke of Rothesay, the heir to the throne, dies while being kept prisoner by his uncle, Robert Stewart, the 1st duke of Albany. **Monaco** Louis is briefly Lord again, but Genoa recaptures Monaco. **Germany** Wenceslaus is temporarily imprisoned, and deposed by his younger brother Sigismund.

1403 **England** Henry IV defeats Harry 'Hotspur' Percy at the Battle of Shrewsbury. **Zeta** Đurađ II Stracimirović dies of injuries received in the Battle of Gračanica; aged 16, Balša III becomes ruler; his chief adviser is his mother Jelena, a sister of the ruler of Serbia at the time, Stefan Lazarević; Balša goes to war with Venice for 10 years.

1404 **Rome** Cardinal Cosimo de' Migliorati is elected pope, as Innocent VII. **Bosnia and Serbia** Stephen Tvrtko II, legitimate son of Stephen Tvrtko I, deposes Stephen Ostoja to become king. **Zeta** Stefan Lazarević accepts vasselage to King Sigismund of Hungary; he is rewarded with Belgrade, which becomes capital of Serbia for the first time.

1405 **Wales** French troops arrive in Wales to support Owen Glendower against Henry IV.

1406 **Scotland** Robert III's only surviving son, 11-year-old James, is imprisoned on the Bass Rock for a month, after trying to sail for France; he is captured by the English and held prisoner for 18 years; his father reputedly dies of grief, and the imprisoned boy becomes king of Scots as James I; Robert Stewart, duke of Albany, becomes regent in James's absence. **Wales** Henry, prince of Wales, defeats Owen Glyndower. **León-Castile-Galicia** John II becomes king; he is weak and ineffectual. **Majorca** Isabella of Majorca dies, having reigned as Elizabeth I; her descendents renounce their claim to the crown of Majorca. **Rome** Angelo Correr is elected pope as Gregory XII; negotiations begin for both pontiffs to renounce their claims and a fresh pope to be elected; they fail.

1408 **Bosnia and Serbia** Stephen Ostoja regains the Bosnian throne from Stephen Tvrtko II.

1409 **Rome** The Council of Pisa tries to resolve the 30-year Great Schism, deposing both popes and electing Cretan Peter Phillarges, antipope, as Alexander V. **Sicily** Martin II becomes king, and the kingdom comes under direct rule from Aragón.

1410 **Rome** Antipope Alexander V dies; John XXII, backed by the Medici family, is elected antipope. **Germany** Ruprecht dies; both Jobst of Moravia and Wenceslaus's brother, Sigismund of Hungary, are elected king; meanwhile, Wenceslaus persists with his claim that he is king; Sigismund of Hungary, son of Charles IV, is finally elected king. **Poland** In the Battle of Tannenberg, Ladislaus II beats the Teutonic Knights. **Aragón and Sicily** King Martin dies – apparently of a combination of chronic indigestion and a fit of uncontrollable laughter – without leaving heirs or a will; there is a two-year interregnum.

1411 **Germany** Jobst of Moravia dies, and Wenceslaus gives up his claim in return for being permitted to keep Bohemia. **Holy Roman**

Empire Sigismund of Hungary is elected Holy Roman Emperor.

1412 **Aragón, Valencia, Majorca, Sardinia, Corsica and Sicily** By the Compromise of Caspe, Martin II's nephew, Ferdinand, son of John of Castile, becomes king. **Scandinavia** Dowager Queen Margaret, regent of Sweden, Denmark and Norway, dies; Eric VII of Pomerania, great-grandson of Valdemar III and already king of Norway, is elected king of both Denmark and Sweden.

1413 **England** Henry V becomes king. **Venice** Tommaso Mocenigo is elected doge; during his reign, Venice acquires Aquileia, Friuli and Dalmatia.

1414 **England** Henry V adopts the claims of Edward II to the French crown. **Naples** King Ladislaus dies, possibly poisoned; his sister, Joan II, succeeds him.

1415 **England** Henry V comprehensively defeats Charles VI at Agincourt, mainly thanks to the longbow. **Rome** Pope Gregory XII, already deposed, formally resigns; a two-year papal interregnum begins.

1416 **Wales** Owen Glendower dies. **Aragón, Valencia, Majorca, Sardinia, Corsica and Sicily** Alfonso V becomes king; he is one of the most prominent figures of the Renaissance.

1417
Rome The Great Schism in the Catholic Church finally comes to an end; a single pope is elected when Cardinal Oddone Colonna becomes Pope Martin V.

1418 **Bosnia and Serbia** Ostojic, son of Stephen Ostoja, becomes king. **Wallachia** Mihail I becomes prince.

1419 **Monaco** Amboise of Menton recaptures Monaco from the Genoese, sharing power with Antonie of Roquebrune and Jean I, who is Lord for the third time. **Bohemia** King Wenceslaus dies of a heart attack while hunting; Sigismund, Holy Roman Emperor and king of Hungary and Germany, succeeds him; 20 years of violent warfare follow in the Hussite wars.

1420 **England** The Treaty of Troyes acknowledges Henry V as heir to the French throne. **Wallachia** Dan II becomes prince; he will rule five times, on four of those occasions being succeeded by his rival, Radu II Chelul.

1421 **Bosnia and Serbia** Stephen Tvrtko II returns to the Bosnian throne. **Zeta** Balša III dies while seeking help against the Venetians from his uncle, Stefan Lazarević, the Serbian despot; Stefan Lazarević, a poet and a modernizer, becomes despot of Zeta. **Wallachia** Dan II is deposed by Radu II, but regains the throne.

1422 **England** Henry VI becomes king. **France** On the death of Charles VI, both his grandson, Henry VI of England, and son, Charles VII, are proclaimed king; with Joan of Arc's support, Charles becomes king. **Bulgaria** Constantine II dies; he is the last tsar of Bulgaria; the Ottoman Turks rule until 1878.

1423 **Scotland** James I returns from imprisonment in England, to a country in chaos. **Venice** Francesco Foscari is elected doge; he leads Venice in long and costly wars against Milan. **Wallachia** Radu II deposes Dan II for a second time; Dan II regains the throne.

1424 **Wallachia** Radu II again overthrows Dan II to become prince.

1425 **Navarre** Charles III dies, having outlived his sons; his daughter, Blanche I, becomes queen, ruling with her husband, John II, the first Navarrese king of the House of Trastámara – already in power in Aragón. **Russia** Vasili II becomes grand prince of Vladimir-Moscow, aged 10; his mother acts as regent; his reign is marked by a long and damaging civil war, when his uncle, Yuri of Zvenigorod, and his two sons, Vasili the Cross-eyed and Dmitry Shemyaka, make claims on the throne. **Byzantine Empire** John VIII Palaiologos becomes emperor.

1426 **Wallachia** Dan II returns to the throne for the fourth time.

1427 **Monaco** Jean I becomes sole ruler. **Zeta** Despot Stefan Lazarević dies and is eventually canonized; his nephew, Durad Brankovic, a baron of the Kingdom of Hungary, becomes despot; he is the richest monarch in Europe; his annual income is about 200,000 Venetian ducats, gained from gold and silver mines in Kosovo and possessions in Hungary. **Wallachia** Radu II deposes Dan II once more to seize power; Dan II regains the throne for the fifth and final time.

1428
France Joan of Arc leads the French against England; the English begin the siege of Orléans.

1429 **France** Joan of Arc raises the Siege of Orléans; she defeats the English at the Battle of Patay, forcing them to leave the Loire Valley; Charles VII is finally crowned king.

1430 **France** Joan of Arc is taken prisoner. **Lithuania** Vytautas dies a few days before being crowned king of Lithuania; Švitrigaila, son of Algirdas and brother of Jogaila, becomes grand duke, and declares full independence from Poland.

1431 **France** Joan of Arc is burnt at the stake by the English; she is 19. Henry VI of England is crowned king of France in Paris. **Rome**

Cardinal Gabriele Condulmer, nephew of Gregory XII, is elected pope as Eugene IV.

1432 **Wallachia** Dan II dies in battle against a large Ottoman army; Alexandru I Aldea, son of Mircea I, becomes prince; the throne of Wallachia will change hands, violently, 15 times in the 15th century.

1433 **Portugal** João I dies of plague, just as his wife, Philppa of Lancaster, had in 1415; his son, Duarte, great-grandson of England's Edward III through his mother, becomes king; he finances his brother, Prince Henry the Navigator, initiator of many important seafaring expeditions. **Holy Roman Empire** Sigismund, king of Germany, Bohemia and Hungary, becomes the last Holy Roman Emperor of the House of Luxembourg. **Russia** Yuri of Zvenigorod claims the Vladimir-Moscow throne after defeating and capturing Grand Prince Vasili.

"I am not afraid . . . I was born to do this."

Joan of Arc

1434 **Italy** Cosimo de Medici becomes ruler of Florence. **Russia** Grand Prince Vasili II ousts the usurper Yuri of Zvenigorod; Yuri dies and his son, Vasili the Cross-eyed, takes Moscow and the throne of Vladimir-Moscow.

1435 **Naples** Queen Joan II dies, bringing to an end the House of Anjou-Durazzo and the entire senior Angevin line of Naples; René, from the House of Valois-Anjou, becomes king; his house has provided rival claimants to the throne since 1382. **Lithuania** Švitrigaila's forces are routed in the Battle of Pabaiskas by rival for the Grand Duchy, Žygimantas, son of Kęstutis and brother of Vytautas; Švitrigaila goes into exile and reportedly becomes a shepherd; Žygimantas becomes grand duke. **Russia** Vasili the Cross-eyed is ousted by Grand Prince Vasili the Blind, in alliance with Dmitri Shemyaka.

1436 **Wallachia** On the death of Alexandru I, his half-brother Vlad Dracul succeeds him.

1437 **Scotland** James I is assassinated by Sir Robert Graham and others; James II becomes king, aged 7. **Portugal** Prince Fernando, heir to the throne, is captured and dies during an unsuccessful attack on Tangiers. **Hungary, Croatia and Bohemia** Sigismund dies, the longest-reigning king of Hungary, at 50 years; Albert I of Habsburg becomes king of Hungary and of Bohemia on Sigismund's death; his father is Albert IV, duke of Austria.

1438 **Portugal** Like his father and mother, King Duarte dies of plague; his 6-year-old son, Afonso V, becomes king; his mother, Leanor of Aragón, as both a foreigner and a woman, is an unpopular choice as regent. **Germany** Sigismund's son-in-law Albrecht, already king of Bohemia and of Hungary, becomes Albrecht II of Germany; he is never crowned Holy Roman Emperor. **Denmark** Eric VII is deposed, and a two-year interregnum follows.

1439 **Portugal** The Cortes replaces Queen Leanor as regent with Pedro, duke of Coimbra, the young King Afonso's eldest uncle. **Scandinavia** Erik XIII is deposed in Denmark and Sweden; he refuses an offer to remain king of Norway only. **Germany** Albrecht

II dies. **Bohemia, Hungary and Croatia** Władysław III, Jagiellon of Poland, is chosen as king of Hungary; there is an interregnum in Bohemia. **Zeta** The capital Smederevno, is captured by the Ottoman Turks; Despot Đurađ Branković flees to Hungary.

1440 **Germany** Frederick IV, son of Duke Ernest the Iron, from the Leopoldinian line of the Habsburg family ruling Inner Austria, is elected king. **Denmark** Christopher III, Eric III's nephew, is chosen as king; he is the last direct descendant of Gorm to be king of Denmark. **Lithuania** 13-year-old Casimir IV Jagiellon becomes grand duke; Poland, unhappy with this appointment, makes warlike noises.

1441 **Navarre** Queen Blanche I dies; her husband, John II, remains king, denying the throne to Blanche's rightful heir, Charles of Viana. **Sweden** Christopher of Bavaria, king of Denmark, becomes king.

1442 **Norway** Christopher of Bavaria, already king of Sweden and Denmark, becomes king. **Naples** Alfonso V of Aragón deposes King René and adds Naples to his southern-Italian kingdom – Sicily. **Wallachia** While his father, Vlad II Dracul, is away at the Ottoman court, his son Mircea II rules in his place.

1443 **Bohemia** Ladislaus V, son of Albert II king of Germany, becomes king. **Bosnia and Serbia** Stephen Thomas Ostojich, illegitimate son of Stephen Postoja, becomes king.

1444 **Hungary** The Ottomans conquer Hungary at the Black Sea, opening their route to Constantinople. **Poland, Hungary and Croatia** Władysław III, king of Poland and Hungary, is killed fighting the Turks at the Battle of Varna; he dies without an heir, and there is a three-year interregnum in Poland; in Hungary and Croatia, Ladislaus V, known as 'the Posthumous' because he was born after his father's death, becomes king; he is already king of Bohemia. **Albania** Gjergj Kastrioti Skanderbeg, of the Kastrioti family, becomes prince of Albania; he becomes the national hero as the dragon of Albania; he keeps the Ottoman Turks at bay for two decades. **Zeta** Đurađ Branković is restored as despot.

1446 **Hungary and Croatia** János Hunyadi becomes regent on behalf of Ladislaus V, until 1453; he fights successfully against the Ottomans. **Russia** Dmitri Shemyaka seizes Moscow and has Grand Prince Vasili blinded; he becomes known as Vasili the Blind.

1447 **Rome** Cardinal Tommaso Parentucelli is elected pope, as Nicholas V. **Poland and Lithuania** Following the death of his brother, Władysław III, and an interregnum of three years, Grand Duke Casimir IV Jagiellon becomes king, uniting the Polish Kingdom with the Grand Duchy of Lithuania. **Wallachia** John Hunyadi's troops capture Mircea II, blinding him with a red-hot poker and burying him alive; Vlad Dracul is also killed; Vlad III Tepes, the Impaler, son of Vlad Dracul, is put on the throne by the Ottomans, but ousted by Hungarian regent, John Hunyadi; Vlad flees to Moldavia; Hunyadi puts Vladislav II, son of Dan II, on the throne.

1448 **Portugal** King Afonso V comes of age and nullifies all laws and edicts introduced during the regency of his uncle, the duke of Coimbra. **Sweden** On the death of King Christopher, without issue, Swedish nobleman Charles VIII is elected king. **Denmark** The dynasty of Gorm the Old, begun in 960, comes to an end; Christian I becomes the first Oldenburg king, and the Oldenburg family still rules the country today; he takes Schleswig and Holstein for Denmark. **Russia** Vasili II the Blind finally defeats and poisons Dmitri Shemyaka.

1449 **Portugal** Afonso V declares his former regent, the duke of Coimbra, a rebel, and defeats his army at the Battle of Alfarrobeira; the duke is killed in the battle. **Norway** Karl VIII of Sweden is elected Karl I of Norway. **Byzantine Empire** Constantine XI becomes emperor.

1450 **Norway** Karl I is forced to cede Norway to Christian I, king of Denmark.

1451 **Zeta** Stefan I Crnojević, third son of Despot Đurađ Branković, becomes ruler; he is the first ruler from the House of Crnojević; Zeta gradually comes to be known as Montenegro.

1452 **Holy Roman Empire** German King Frederick IV becomes Holy Roman Emperor as Frederick III; he is the last to be crowned by the pope in Rome.

1453 **England** Henry VI becomes insane; Richard Duke of York becomes regent. **France** The Hundred Years' War ends; the English are expelled from France, retaining only Calais. **Byzantine Empire** Constantine XI dies fighting the Ottomans; Constantinople falls and the Byzantine Empire comes to an end.

1454 **Monaco** Catalan becomes lord of Monaco. **León-Castile-Galicia** Henry IV the Impotent becomes the last of the weak late medieval Spanish kings; during his reign, the nobles gain more power.

1455
England The Wars of the Roses begin between the houses of York and Lancaster.

1455 **Rome** Cardinal Alfonso de Borgia is elected pope as Calixtus III; he issues a papal bull authorising Portugal to enslave non-Christian people, giving permission for the transatlantic slave trade.

1456 **Hungary and Croatia** The Hungarians, under nobleman John Hunyadi, storm Belgrade and drive out the Turks. **Wallachia** Vlad III the Impaler invades and seizes power; he uses extreme violence to control the country, including impaling some 20,000 Turkish prisoners on stakes.

1457 **Monaco** Claudine becomes ruler, jointly with Pomelline Fregoso. **Sweden** Charles VIII is deposed; Christian I takes the throne. **Venice** Doge Francesco Foscari is forced to withdraw from government, following the death of his son Jacopo, who had been tried and banished for corruption; Pasquale Malipiero is elected doge. **Aragón, Navarre, Valencia, Majorca, Sardinia, Corsica and Sicily** John II becomes king. **Bohemia** Ladislaus V's death is followed by a brief interregnum.

1458 **Monaco** The Grimaldi control of Monaco is confirmed when Lambert Grimaldi marries his cousin Claudine, as the state's constitution stipulates that the inheritance of Monaco can only be passed to male heirs; he spends his reign fighting to preserve Monaco's independence. **Aragón, Navarre and Sicily** On the death of Alfonso V of Aragón and Sicily, his younger brother, King John of Navarre, becomes king of all three states. **Rome** Bishop Enea Silvio Piccolomini, former poet laureate of the Holy Roman Empire, is elected pope as Pius II. **Naples** Ferdinand I becomes king. **Hungary and Croatia** Matthias Corvinus the Great, son of John Hunyadi, is elected king; he extends his kingdom and introduces the Renaissance into Central Europe. **Bohemia** George of Poděbrady becomes king as George I.

1459
Serbia is taken by the Ottoman Turks.

1460 **England** The earl of Warwick and Edward, earl of March, eldest son of the duke of York, seize London; at the Battle of Northampton, they defeat a Lancastrian army and capture King Henry; York becomes Henry's heir, but dies in the Battle of Wakefield. **Scotland** James II is accidentally killed by an exploding cannon, during the siege of Roxburgh Castle; James III succeeds him as king of Scots.

1461 **England** Henry VI is deposed and Edward IV becomes the first king from the House of York. **France** Louis XI the Prudent becomes king, establishing an absolute monarchy; he wears ordinary clothes and mixes with the people. **Bosnia and Serbia** Stephen Tomašević becomes king.

1462 **Venice** Cristoforo Moro is elected doge, the 11th person of his family to hold the position; his reign is characterized by wars with the Turks as well as threats from northern Italian cities. **Wallachia** Vlad III the Impaler is ousted by the Ottomans, who place his brother Radu cel Frumos on the throne. **Russia** Ivan III the Great becomes grand prince of Vladimir-Moscow; he is the first ruler to adopt the title 'Grand Duke of all the Russias'; he is effectively the first sovereign of all of Russia.

1463 **Bosnia and Serbia** King Stephen Tomašević is executed by Mehmet II of Turkey, who seizes control of his kingdom; the Ottoman Empire rules Bosnia until 1875.

1464 **Rome** Cardinal Pietro Barbo is elected pope as Paul II. **Sweden** Christian I is deposed; Charles VIII is restored to the throne. **Zeta/Montenegro** Ivan Crnojević the Black becomes ruler and the first lord of the Principality of Montenegro.

1465 **England** Henry VI is imprisoned by Edward IV. **Sweden** Charles VIII is deposed again and exiled; the country is governed by regents until 1467. **Byzantine Empire** Thomas Palaiologos, brother of Constantine XI and claimant to the Byzantine throne, dies in exile in Rome; Andrew Palaiologos, his son, is next in line; he sells his titles to King Ferdinand II of Aragón and Queen Isabella of Castile.

1467 **Sweden** Charles VIII is restored to the throne for the final time.

1468 **Sicily** Ferdinand II of Aragón becomes king.

1469 **Bohemia** Matthias Corvinus, king of Hungary, is elected king by dissident Catholic nobles, but never crowned.

1470 **England** Henry VI is restored to the English throne, but is deposed once more by Edward IV. **Sweden** On the death of Charles VIII, Sten Sture the Elder becomes regent.

1471 **England** Henry VI dies, probably murdered, in the Tower of London. **Venice** Nicolo Tron is elected doge. **Rome** Cardinal Francesco della Rovere is elected pope as Sixtus IV; he founds the Sistine Chapel. **Bohemia** King George of Poděbrady dies suddenly as Bohemian Catholics revolt against him; Ladislaus Jagiellon, nephew of Ladislaus V and first ruler of Bohemia from the Jagiellon dynasty that rules Poland and Lithuania, becomes king.

1473 **Venice** Nicolo Marcello is elected doge. **Wallachia** Basarab Laiotă the Elder, son of Dan II, is elected prince; he will rule on four separate occasions; Radu cel Frumos returns to the throne for the second time.

1474 **France** Louis XI declares war on Charles the Bold, duke of Burgundy. **León-Castile-Galicia** Henry IV dies and a power struggle ensues between supporters of his half-sister Isabella and his daughter, Juana; Henry names Isabella as his successor; her marriage to Ferdinand of Aragón lays the foundations for a united Spain; Ferdinand also becomes king of Valencia, Sardinia and Navarre. **Venice** Pietro Mocenigo, one of Venice's greatest admirals, is elected as Venice's 70th doge. **Wallachia** Basarab Laiotă the Elder regains the throne, but loses it again to Radu cel Frumos.

1475 **England** Edward IV invades France; the peace of Piquigny is agreed between England and France. **Wallachia** Basarab Laiotă the Elder returns to power for the fourth time.

1476 **Venice** Andrea Vendramin is elected doge. **Wallachia** Vlad III the Impaler returns to the throne briefly; Basarab Laiotă the Elder regains power for the fifth time.

1477 **France** Charles the Bold, duke of Burgundy, is defeated and killed by the Swiss. **Portugal** Afonso V retires to a monastery; João II succeeds him. **Austria** The marriage of Maximillian of Austria to Mary of Burgundy makes the Habsburgs heirs to one of the most powerful European states. **Wallachia** Basarab Ţepeluş the Younger seizes power.

1478 **Venice** Giovanni Mocenigo, brother of the previous ruler, Pietro, is elected doge. **Hungary and Croatia** gain Moravia and Silesia. **Albania** is captured by the Turks.

1479 **Spain** is united, with the exception of Navarre, under Ferdinand II and Isabella. **Navarre** Eleanor, daughter of John II, is crowned queen on 28 January and dies on 12 February; aged 10, Francis Phoebus of Foix becomes King Francis I, the first king of the House of Foix; his mother, Magdalena de Valois, acts as regent. **Bohemia** Matthias Corvinus, antiking, agrees to limit his rule to Moravia, Silesia and Lusatia, while retaining his title.

1480 **Russia** Tsar Ivan III stops paying tribute to the Mongols.

1481 **Portugal** Afonso V abdicates; João II formally becomes king. **Denmark** Hans, son of Christian I, becomes king. **Albania** comes under Ottoman rule until 1912. **Zeta/Montenegro** Ivan I Crnojević regains control of Montenegro from occupying Ottoman Turks; he tries to maintain good relations with Venice and the Turks. **Wallachia** Mircea rules for less than a year; Vlad Călugărul the Monk, son of Vlad II Dracul, seizes power before being ousted by Basarab Ţepeluş the Younger.

1482 **Scotland** James III is briefly deposed and imprisoned by the duke of Albany, but is restored to the throne.

1483 **England** Edward IV dies; he is succeeded by Edward V; Richard III deposes Edward, imprisons him in the Tower of London where he dies, and becomes king. **France** Louis XI dies after becoming obsessively fearful of death; he is said to have drunk the warm blood of infants to ward it off; Charles VIII becomes king. **Navarre** Francis I dies; his sister Catherine becomes queen. **Portugal** João II begins to rule through fear; he has the powerful duke of Braganza executed.

1484 **Navarre** Queen Catherine marries John III d'Albret, duke of Gause; they rule jointly. **Portugal** João II personally stabs to death his cousin and brother-in-law, the duke of Viseu; countless others are executed or murdered. **Rome** Cardinal Giovanni Battista Cybo is elected pope as Innocent VIII.

1485 **England** Henry VII becomes the first Tudor king of England and Wales after the defeat and death of the last Plantagenet king, Richard III, at the Battle of Bosworth Field; the Wars of the Roses end. **Venice** Marco Barbarigo is elected doge. **Hungary and Croatia** captures Vienna and Lower Austria, making it the most powerful state in Central Europe.

1486 **Germany** Maximilian I is elected co-king of Germany; through war and marriage, he will extend the influence of the Habsburg family across Europe. **Venice** Agostino Barbarigo succeeds his brother Marco in being elected doge; he forms an Italian coalition that expels the French of Charles VIII from Italy, and Venice annexes Cyprus and strongholds in Romagna; he loses important Mediterranean bases, however.

1488 **Scotland** James III is defeated and killed by an army of disaffected nobles at the Battle of Sauchieburn; James IV, who had fought against his father, becomes king; he is recognized as the most successful of the Scottish Stewart monarchs.

1490 **Hungary** King of Bohemia, Ladislaus Jagiellon, becomes Ulászló II of Hungary. **Zeta/Montenegro** Ivan I Crnojević dies, having become one of the greatest Montenegrin and Serbian leaders; his son, Đurađ IV Crnojević, becomes ruler, calling himself 'Duke of Zeta'.

1491 **Portugal** João II's only son Afonso, also heir to the throne of Castile, dies in a mysterious fall from a horse; the succession to the throne is now in question; Manuel, duque de Beja and brother of Queen Leonor, is next in line.

1492 **Spain** The Spanish capture Granada from the Muslims, ending Muslim influence in Spain. **Rome** Cardinal Rodrigo de Lanzòl-Borgia, nephew of Pope Innocent VIII, is elected pope as Alexander VI; he is said to have bought the papacy; his reign became a byword for the debased standards of the papacy at that time. **Poland** Jan I Olbracht, third son of Casimir IV Jagiellon, becomes king. **Lithuania** Alexander Jagiellon, fourth son of Casimir IV Jagiellon, becomes grand duke.

1493 **Holy Roman Empire** Emperor Frederick dies while having his leg amputated.

1494 **France** Charles VIII invades Italy. **Monaco** Jean II becomes lord of Monaco. **Naples** Alfonso, duke of Calabria, becomes king as Alfonso II.

1495 **France** Charles VIII is defeated by the Holy League. **Portugal** João II dies, possibly poisoned; during his reign, Portuguese explorers have opened up the world; Manuell I, his first cousin and brother-in-law, becomes the first king of the House of Aviz-Beja; he continues the Portuguese exploration of the Atlantic, started by his predecessor, making Portugal a rich and powerful nation. **Naples** Alfonso II, facing invasion by France, abdicates in favour of his son Ferdinand II. **Wallachia** Radu the Great becomes prince.

1496 **Naples** The French capture Naples; Ferdinand II flees, but when the French leave is welcomed back by the citizens; he dies without an heir; his uncle, Frederick IV, becomes king. **Zeta/Montenegro** Đurađ IV Crnojević is forced into exile by the Ottoman Turks; Stefan II Crnojević becomes ruler.

1497 **Sweden** King Hans of Denmark and Norway conquers Sweden; he becomes John II; Scandinavia is united again in the Kalmar Union.

1498 **France** Louis XII, great-grandson of Charles V, becomes king, first king of the Valois-Orléans dynasty; he invades Italy and conquers Milan. **Portugal** Isabella of Aragón, heiress to the throne of the future united Spain, and wife of Manuel I, dies in childbirth, ending Manuel's ambitions to be king of Spain as well as Portugal. **Zeta/ Montenegro** Ivan II Crnojević becomes ruler.

1501 **Sweden** renounces John II (Hans of Denmark and Norway) as king, following a damaging defeat in northern Germany; regents rule the country until 1513.**Venice** Leonardo Loredan is elected doge; Venice is excommunicated for capturing territories in the northern Papal States; Pope Julius II allies with France and the Holy Roman Empire against the republic; Venice is defeated and humiliated. **Naples** France conquers Naples; King Frederick is taken as a prisoner to France, where he dies in 1504; Louis, king of France, becomes king. **Zeta/Montenegro** Đurađ V Crnojević becomes ruler. **Poland** Alexander Jagiellon, grand duke of Lithuania, becomes king on the sudden death of his brother Jan I Olbracht.

1503
Scotland James IV (left) marries Henry's daughter Margaret Tudor in August 1503. This union of the Thistle and the Rose, however, did very little to improve the Anglo-Scottish relations.

1503 **Rome** Cardinal Francesco Todeschini Piccolomini is elected pope as Pius III, after Cesare Borgia is persuaded to leave Rome so that he could not influence the conclave; Pius III dies, possibly poisoned, after a papacy lasting just 26 days; Cardinal Giuliano della Rovere is elected pope as Julius II, and is the first pope to take control of the entire Papal States; he is a patron of Raphael and Michelangelo. **Bohemia** Louis Jagiellon, also Louis II of Hungary, becomes king.

1504 **León-Castile-Galicia** Joanna the Mad, daughter of Queen Isabella, becomes queen; regents take advantage of her mental illness to control the kingdom. **Naples** Ferdinand II of Aragón takes Naples from the French and becomes king as Ferdinand III.

1505 **France** In the Treaty of Blois, France keeps Milan but gives Naples to Spain. **Monaco** Jean II, whose marriage is childless, is murdered by his brother Lucien, who becomes lord of Monaco. **Russia** Vasili III becomes grand prince of Vladimir-Moscow; he consolidates the achievements of his father Ivan the Great, annexing the remaining autonomous provinces for Russia.

1506 **Poland and Lithuania** Alexander Jagiellon dies; he is the last-known ruler of the House of Gediminaičiai to speak the family's ancestral Lithuanian language; following his death, Polish becomes the family language, thus fully Polonizing the Jagiellon family; Sigismund the Old, son of Casimir IV Jagiellon, becomes king of Poland and grand duke of Lithuania.

1508 **Holy Roman Empire** With the approval of Pope Pius III, Maximillian I, often referred to as 'the Last Knight', adopts the title *Erwählter Römischer Kaiser* – Elected Roman Emperor – thereby bringing to an end the custom by which the Holy Roman Emperor had to be crowned by the pope to become emperor. **Wallachia** Mihnea the Great becomes prince.

1509 **England** Henry VIII becomes king; he will reign for 38 years; he marries the Infanta Catalina de Aragón y Castilla, daughter of Ferdinand II of Aragon and Isabella I of Castile, popularly known as Catherine of Aragon. **Wallachia** Mircea III Dracul becomes prince.

> ***“To wish myself (specially an evening) in my sweetheart's arms, whose pretty ducks [breasts] I trust shortly to kiss.”***

Henry VIII — taken from a letter to Anne Boleyn

1510 **Wallachia** Vlad cel Tânăr becomes prince.

1512 **France** The French are driven out of Milan. **Navarre** Pamplona is occupied by the duke of Alba; Queen Catherine and her family flee to France; the Cortes of Navarre declares King Ferdinand of Spain 'King of Navarre' and Upper Navarre becomes part of Spain; Catherine and John reign only in Baja Navarra, north of the Pyrenees, in modern-day France. **Wallachia** Neagoe Basarab becomes prince.

1513 **Scotland** James IV is killed by the English at the Battle of Flodden Field. **Rome** Cardinal Giovanni di Lorenzo de' Medici, second son of Lorenzo de' Medici, ruler of Florence, is elected pope as Leo X; during his pontificate, the Protestant schism begins. **Denmark, Norway and Sweden** Christian II is crowned king of all three countries on the same day.

1515 **France** François I, brother of Louis XII, becomes king; he leads France in a cultural renaissance and captures Burgundy.

1516 **Spain** Charles I, son of Joanna the Mad, becomes king of Spain; already Holy Roman Emperor as Charles V, he rules vast areas of Europe and becomes the most powerful man on the continent; he occupies the thrones of Castile and Leon, Aragón, Navarre, Majorca, Germany, Austria, Sicily and Naples. **Hungary and Bohemia** Ten-year-old Louis II becomes king of both countries. **Zeta/Montenegro** Đurađ V Crnojević retires to Venice; he hands power to Vavila, the vladika or prince-bishop – the local ecclesiastical authority; Zeta/Montenegro becomes a theocracy, and prince-bishops rule Montenegro, as it is now known, until 1918.

1517 **Navarre** Queen Catherine dies in exile; her son, Henry II, becomes king; his throne is disputed by Ferdinand II of Aragón, but Henry enjoys the protection of King François I of France.

1519 **Germany and Holy Roman Empire** Charles I of Spain, grandson of Maximilian I, is elected king of Germany and Holy Roman Emperor, as Charles V; he will fight throughout his reign with France and with the sultan of the Ottoman Empire, Suleiman the Magnificent.

1520 **England and France** François I of France and Henry VIII of England meet on the Field of Cloth of Gold; they fail to form an alliance. **Sweden** Christian II, son of Hans of Denmark and already king of Norway and Denmark, becomes king; the murder of 82 notable people in Stockholm, known as the Stockholm Bloodbath, earns him the nickname 'Christian the Tyrant'. **Montenegro** German II becomes prince-bishop.

1521 **Navarre** French troops seize Navarre in an effort to make Henry II de facto sovereign, but are expelled by the Spanish. **Portugal** João III becomes king; Portugal is at the height of its mercantile and colonial power; during his reign, Portuguese possessions extend into Asia and Brazil in the New World; Lisbon becomes one of the most commercially important cities in the world. **Sweden** Gustav Vasa leads a revolt against Danish rule; Christian the Tyrant is deposed and Gustav becomes regent. **Venice** Antonio Grimani is elected doge. **Wallachia** Teodosie becomes prince; there are 10 rulers in the next eight years.

1522 **France** Charles V drives the French out of Milan. **Rome** Dutch Cardinal Adriaan Florenszoon Boeyens is elected pope, as Adrian VI; he is the last non-Italian pope until Pope John Paul II, 456 years later.

1523 **Monaco** Honoré I, youngest child of Lucien Grimaldi, becomes lord of Monaco, aged 9 months, on the assassination of his father; his uncle, Augustine Grimaldi, rules as regent; he severs the relationship with France and allies Monaco with Spain, which lasts until 1641. **Sweden** The Kalmar Union is effectively ended when Sweden leaves it; Gustav Vasa, related to the influential Sture family, is elected king of Sweden as Gustav I, first monarch of the House of Vasa; he becomes known as the father of modern Sweden. **Norway and Denmark** remain together and will stay united for two centuries; Christian II, as unpopular in Denmark and Norway as in Sweden, is deposed, imprisoned for 27 years and replaced by his son, Frederick I. **Venice** Andrea Gritti, a distinguished diplomat and military man, is elected doge. **Rome** Cardinal Giulio di Giuliano de' Medici, cousin of Leo X, is elected pope. as Clement VII; there is chaos in Rome during his reign.

1524 **France** recaptures Milan.

1526 **Hungary and Bohemia** Louis II is defeated and killed by the Turks, in the Battle of Mohács; Ferdinand I becomes king of Bohemia;

John Zápolya, Hungary's most prominent aristocrat, is elected king by the Hungarians, but is a puppet of the Turks; the succession is disputed by Louis II's sister Anne and her husband Archduke Ferdinand of Austria.

1527 **France** Charles de Bourbon, the Constable of France, dies; he is the last of the Bourbon line. **Rome** Charles V's troops sack Rome and capture Pope Clement VII.

1529 **England** Cardinal Wolsey is dismissed for failing to obtain a divorce for Henry VIII; Sir Thomas More becomes lord chancellor; Henry begins to cut ties with the Church of Rome. **France** renounces its claims to Italy in the Peace of Cambrai. **Wallachia** Moise becomes prince.

1530 **Italy** Charles V is crowned king of Italy. **Montenegro** Pavle becomes prince-bishop. **Wallachia** Moise is killed; Vlad the Drowned becomes prince.

1532 **England** Sir Thomas More resigns over Henry's divorce. **Wallachia** Vlad the Drowned is so named after he gets drunk and rides into the Dâmboviţa river, where he drowns; Vlad Vintilă de la Slatina becomes prince.

1533 **England** Henry VIII's 24-year marriage to Catherine of Aragón is annulled; he marries Anne Boleyn and is excommunicated by Pope Clement VII, an action that leads to the English Reformation; Thomas Cranmer becomes Archbishop of Canterbury. **Denmark and Norway** Christian III, son of Christian I, becomes king; a Protestant, he founds the Lutheran Church in 1536. **Montenegro** Vasilije I becomes prince-bishop.

1534 **England** Henry VIII breaks with Rome; he declares himself head of the English Church. **Rome** Pope Clement VII dies, having ordered Michelangelo to paint *The Last Judgement,* on the ceiling of the Sistine Chapel, a few days before his death; Cardinal Alessandro Farnese is elected pope as Paul III; he fails in his attempts to stem the tide of Reformation in Europe.

1535 **England** Sir Thomas More is executed. **Wallachia** Radu Paisie becomes prince.

1536 **England** Henry VIII's second wife, Anne Boleyn, is executed on the grounds of adultery, incest and high treason; Henry VIII marries Jane Seymour.

1537 **England** Jane Seymour dies after giving birth to the future Edward VI.

1538 **Venice** Pietro Lando is elected doge; he is forced to cede Venice's remaining possessions in the Peloponnese to the Ottoman Empire.

1540 **England** Henry VIII marries Anne of Cleves, divorces her and marries Catherine Howard. **Montenegro** Nikodim becomes prince-bishop and dies soon after; Romil succeeds him.

1541 **Hungary** The Ottoman Turks conquer Hungary.

1542 **England** Henry VIII has his fifth wife, Catherine Howard, executed after less than two years of marriage, on the grounds of treason in the form of adultery. **Scotland** James V dies after the Battle of Solway Moss; his daughter, 6-day-old Mary I, Mary Queen of Scots, succeeds him as queen; she adopts the French spelling of 'Stuart' for her surname. **Ireland** enters into personal union with England when the Protestant Ascendancy that dominates the Irish parliament passes the Crown of Ireland Act 1542, proclaiming Henry VIII of England as king of Ireland.

1543 **England** Henry VIII marries Catherine Parr; his daughter, Elizabeth, is deemed illegitimate, making Mary Queen of Scots the true heir to the English throne; Henry's will stipulates, however, that Stewarts may never rule England; this is formalized by the Third Act of Succession.

1544 **England** The Act of Succession restores Elizabeth to the line of succession to the throne of England. **Sweden** Succession is tied to the male line.

1545 **Venice** Francesco Donato is elected doge. **Wallachia** The Ottoman Turks replace Radu Paisie with his stepbrother, Mircea V Ciobanul, as prince.

1547 **England** Henry VIII dies; aged 56, Edward VI becomes king. **France** Henri II of the House of Valois becomes king; his reign is marked by wars with Austria and the persecution of the Protestant Huguenots. **Russia** Ivan the Terrible, grand-prince of Moscow since 1533, is crowned the first 'Tsar of all Russia'.

1548 **Scotland** Mary Queen of Scots is sent to France after a treaty promises her in marriage to the dauphin, François; she remains there for 13 years. **The Holy Roman Empire** annexes the Netherlands. **Poland and Lithuania** Sigismund II August becomes king of Poland and grand duke of Lithuania; he is the last ruler from the Jagiellon dynasty.

1549 **Russia** Ivan IV creates Russia's first national assembly.

1550 **Rome** Cardinal Giovanni Maria Ciocchi del Monte is elected pope as Julius III.

1552 **Wallachia** Mircea V Ciobanul puts to death 47 nobles and then flees after losing in battle to Radu Ilie, who becomes prince.

1553 **England** Edward VI dies, aged 15; Lady Jane Grey, grand-niece of Henry VIII, is declared queen of England; her reign lasts nine days, before she is deposed and the rabidly Catholic Mary I becomes queen. **Venice** Marcantonio Trivisan is elected Venice's 80th doge. **Wallachia** Mircea Ciobanul retakes his throne.

THE 'NINE DAYS' QUEEN

REIGN: 10–19 JULY 1553

Lady Jane Grey (1537–1554) had the shortest reign in royal history — it lasted just nine days!

Lady Jane Grey was the eldest daughter of Henry Grey, the duke of Suffolk. She was proclaimed queen after the death of her cousin, King Edward VI. Mary Tudor, who should have been the next in line, was disregarded due to the fact that she was Catholic and Edward wanted to keep England firmly Protestant. Lady Jane ascended to the throne on 6 July 1553 at the tender age of 16.

Her reign was cut short when the country rose up in favour of the true royal line and proclaimed Mary Tudor queen just nine days later. Lady Jane, along with her husband Lord Dudley, were taken to the Tower of London and then beheaded on Tower Green on 12 February 1554.

1554 **England** Lady Jane Grey is executed; Mary I marries Philip, heir to the Spanish throne. **Venice** Francesco Venier is elected doge. **Wallachia** Pătraşcu the Kind replaces Radu Ilie as prince.

1555 **Spain** Having spent only 17 of his 40-year reign in Spain, Charles I abdicates and enters a monastery; his son Philip II, king of

Portugal, becomes king and leads Spain's global exploration; he is the husband of Mary Tudor, queen of England; Charles I awards his non-Spanish territories to his other son, Ferdinand I. **Navarre** Joanna III becomes queen, ruling with her husband Antoine de Bourbon; she declares Calvinism the official religion of Navarre, and becomes the acknowledged political and spiritual leader of the French Huguenot movement. **Rome** Cardinal Marcello Cervini is elected pope as Marcellus II, the last pope to use his own name; he dies after just 22 days; Cardinal Giovanni Pietro Carafa is elected pope as Paul IV.

1556 **Spain, Germany, Bohemia, Naples and the Holy Roman Empire** Charles V abdicates, giving Spain, the Netherlands and Naples to his son Philip II; his brother Ferdinand I, king of Bohemia, becomes king of Germany and the Holy Roman Emperor. **Venice** Lorenzo Priuli is elected doge.

1557 **Portugal** João III dies of apoplexy; his grandson, Sebastião I, becomes king, aged 3; his paternal grandmother, Catherine of Habsburg, becomes regent, and then his great uncle, Henry of Évora, takes over.

1558 **England** Mary I's half-sister Elizabeth I, daughter of Henry VIII and Anne Boleyn, becomes queen of England and reigns for 45 years; Catholic legislation is repealed; Spain's naval power is destroyed. **Scotland** Mary Queen of Scots marries François, heir to the French throne; he adopts the title 'King Consort of Scots'. **Holy Roman Empire** Charles V's brother, Ferdinand I, becomes emperor; he is also archduke of Austria and king of Bohemia as well as Hungary. **Wallachia** Mircea V Ciobanul returns to power for the third time.

1559 **France** The Dauphin François marries Mary Queen of Scots, when he is 14 and she is 15; Henri II is accidentally killed in a jousting match by Gabriel, Comte de Montgomery of France's Scots Guards; François II becomes king; Mary Queen of Scots becomes queen consort of France. **Spain** now controls almost all of Italy. **Venice** Girolamo Priuli is elected doge. **Rome** Cardinal Giovanni Angelo Medici is elected pope as Pius IV. **Denmark and Norway** Frederick II becomes king, and he emerges as one of the best-loved Danish monarchs. **Montenegro** Makarije becomes prince-bishop. **Wallachia** Petru the Younger becomes prince.

"In my end is my beginning."

Mary Queen of Scots

1560 **England and Scotland** The Treaty of Berwick is signed between England and the Scottish reformers; it is agreed that the two countries act jointly to expel the French from Scotland. **France** King François II dies, aged 15, when an ear infection causes an abscess in his brain; the mentally and physically weak Charles IX becomes king, and his mother, Catherine de' Medici, effectively rules until 1574; the French wars of religion begin (until the 1590s); the Protestant minority is in conflict with the Catholic majority, as nobles fight for power under the weak Valois kings. **Sweden** Erik XIV becomes king; he has unsuccessfully wooed Princess Elizabeth Tudor, later Elizabeth I of England.

1561 **Scotland** Mary Queen of Scots returns to Scotland a widow, following the death of François II. **Montenegro** Ruvim I becomes prince-bishop.

1562 **Germany** Maximilian II is elected co-king with his father, Ferdinand I.

1563 **Hungary** Maximilian II is crowned king of Hungary.

1564 **Holy Roman Empire** Maximilian II, already crowned king of Bohemia and Hungary, becomes emperor.

1565 **Scotland** Mary Queen of Scots marries her cousin Henry Stuart, Lord Darnley; the marriage is a disaster.

1566 **Scotland** Lord Darnley, consort of Mary Queen of Scots, brutally murders her secretary, David Rizzio, suspecting he and Mary were having an affair. **Rome** Bishop Michele Ghislieri is elected pope as Pius V.

1567 **Scotland** Mary's suitor, the earl of Bothwell, is implicated in the murder of her husband Lord Darnley; Mary marries Bothwell, is imprisoned and forced to abdicate; she flees to England looking for sanctuary; her son by Darnley, James VI, becomes king at the age of 1. **Venice** Pietro Loredan is elected doge.

1568
Scotland Mary Queen of Scots is imprisoned by Elizabeth I in England.

1568 **Netherlands** A Dutch campaign for independence from Spanish rule begins; it is finally achieved in 1648. **Sweden** Erik XIV becomes insane and is replaced on the throne by his brother John III; it is thought that John later orders Erik's murder by poisoning. **Wallachia** Alexandru II Mircea becomes prince.

1569 **Polish-Lithuanian Commonwealth** The Union of Lublin formalizes the union of Poland and Lithuania in the Polish-Lithuanian Commonwealth, and introduces an elective monarchy to determine the succession; until this time, the Lithuanian Grand Duchy has always been hereditary. **Montenegro** Pahomije II Komanin becomes prince-bishop.

1570 **Venice** Alvise I Mocenigo is elected doge; Cyprus is lost to the Turks during his reign.

1572 **Navarre** Henry III becomes king. **Rome** Cardinal Ugo Boncompagni is elected pope as Gregory XIII; he creates the Gregorian calendar. **Poland and Lithuania** Sigismund II August dies childless, despite three marriages; Henri of Valois, brother of Charles IX of France, is elected King Henry III of Poland and grand duke of Lithuania.

1574 **France** Henri of Valois, king of Poland, secretly returns to France, on the death of his brother Charles IX, to be crowned Henri III of France.

1575 **Germany** Rudolf II is elected co-king. **Montenegro** Gerasim becomes prince-bishop.

1576 **Germany and Holy Roman Empire** Maximilian II dies while preparing to invade Poland; Rudolf II, also king of Bohemia and Hungary, becomes king and emperor; his poor decisions will lead to the Thirty Years' War. **Polish-Lithuanian Commonwealth** Anna Jagiellon, daughter of Sigismund I, is elected queen; her husband Stephen Báthory, a prince of Transylvania in Romania, becomes king consort of Poland and duke consort of Lithuania; he is crowned king and grand duke, and will become one of the greatest elected rulers of Poland and Lithuania; a skilled politician, he strengthens royal authority.

1577 **Venice** Sebastiano Venier is elected doge. **Wallachia** Mihnea the Turned-Turk becomes prince.

1578 **Portugal** Sebastião I dies in the Battle of Alcácer Quibir in Morocco, trying to help Abu Abdallah Mohammed II Saadi regain his crown; unmarried and without male issue, Cardinal-King Henry, younger brother of João III, becomes king. **Venice** Doge Sebastiano Venier allegedly dies of a broken heart after the Doge's Palace (Palazzo Ducale) is badly damaged by fire; Nicolò da Ponte is elected to succeed him.

1579 **England** forms an alliance with the Netherlands against Spain. **Netherlands** The Dutch northern provinces form the Union of Utrecht.

1580 **Portugal** Cardinal-King Henry dies without issue and without appointing a council of regency to choose a successor; King Philip II of Spain, a claimant to the Portuguese throne, invades and captures Lisbon; Philip is elected king of Portugal on condition that neither it nor its overseas possessions would become Spanish provinces; he is the first Portuguese king from the House of Habsburg, also known as the Philippine dynasty.

1581
Russia Ivan the Terrible kills his son, Ivan, during an argument.

1581 **Monaco** Charles II becomes lord of Monaco. **Netherlands** The Union of Utrecht declares independence from Spain, calls itself the Dutch Republic and elects William of Orange, known as William the Silent, leader of the revolt that sets off the 80 years' war for independence from Spain William becomes the first ruler of the House of Orange-Nassau.

1582 **Montenegro** Venijamin becomes prince-bishop.

1583 **Wallachia** Petru Cercel becomes prince.

1584 **Netherlands** Prince William of Orange, of the Dutch Republic, is assassinated by a supporter of the Spanish. **Russia** On the death of Ivan the Terrible, probably from poisoning, Fyodor I becomes tsar; Fyodor is probably mentally retarded, and his brother-in-law, Boris Godunov, actually governs the country.

1585 **Venice** Pasqual Cicogna is elected doge. **Rome** Cardinal Felice Peretti is elected pope as Sixtus V. **Wallachia** Petru Cercel, facing hostility from nobles and aggression from his rival, Mihnea, flees; Mihnea the Turned-Turk returns to the throne.

1586 **England** Mary Queen of Scots is implicated in a conspiracy against Elizabeth I, led by Anthony Babington; she is tried and sentenced to death. **Polish-Lithuanian Commonwealth** Stephen Báthory dies, and an interregnum of one year ensues.

1587 **England** Mary Queen of Scots is executed; Elizabeth I is furious, and she claims she has not ordered the execution, even though she has signed the death warrant. **Polish-Lithuanian Commonwealth** Sigismund III Vasa, son of John III of Sweden and grandson of Sigismund the Old, is elected king of Poland and grand duke of Lithuania; trying to regain the Swedish throne, he instigates a series of wars with Sweden that continue until the 1660s; as a condition of his election, he agrees to a reduction in power in favour of the Sejm, the Commonwealth's parliament.

1588 **England** Francis Drake, leading the English fleet, defeats the Spanish Armada off the south coast of England; Spanish power declines. **France** Henri of Guise, leader of the Catholic League that has been formed to keep the Protestant Henry of Navarre off the throne, is murdered on the orders of King Henri III; there is outrage, and the king has to take refuge with Henry of Navarre. **Denmark and Norway** Aged 11, Christian IV succeeds his father Frederick II; a council of regents rules; he creates one of Europe's most splendid courts.

“There is plenty of time to win this game, and to thrash the Spaniards, too.”

Catherine II of Russia.

1589 **France** Henri III of France, the last of the Valois kings, is assassinated by a monk, Jacques Clément, while besieging Paris; the Protestant Henri, king of Navarre, succeeds him as Henri IV, the first king of the House of Bourbon. **Navarre** The crown of Navarre is held by the kings of France from this date. **Monaco** Charles II dies without issue; his younger brother, Hercule, becomes ruler.

1590 **Rome** Cardinal Giovanni Battista Castagna is elected pope as Urban VII; he reigns for just 13 days, making him the shortest-reigning pope; Cardinal Niccolò Sfondrati is elected pope as Gregory XIV.

1591 **Rome** Titular Archbishop of Jerusalem, Giovanni Antonio Facchinetti, is elected pope as Innocent IX. **Montenegro** Nikanor and Stefan rule jointly as prince-bishop. **Wallachia** Ştefan Surdul becomes prince.

1592 **Rome** Cardinal Ippolito Aldobrandini is elected pope as Clement VIII. **Sweden** On his father John III's death, Sigismund, already king of the Polish-Lithuanian Commonwealth, becomes king of Sweden. **Wallachia** Alexander the Wrongdoer, already ruler of Moldavia, becomes prince.

1593 **France** Henry IV, the first Bourbon king of France, converts to Catholicism, ending the French religious wars. **Germany and the Holy Roman Empire** Emperor Rudolf II starts a long and destructive war against the Ottoman Turks. **Montenegro** Ruvim II Boljević-Njegos becomes prince-bishop. **Wallachia** Mihail the Brave becomes prince, uniting Wallachia with Transylvania and Moldavia – he is already ruler of both countries.

1595 **Sweden** gains Estonia in the Treaty of Teusina, with Russia. **Venice** Tommaso Mocenigo is elected doge. Marino Grimani becomes doge.

1597 **Ireland** A rebellion against the English is led by Hugh O'Neill, earl of Tyrone.

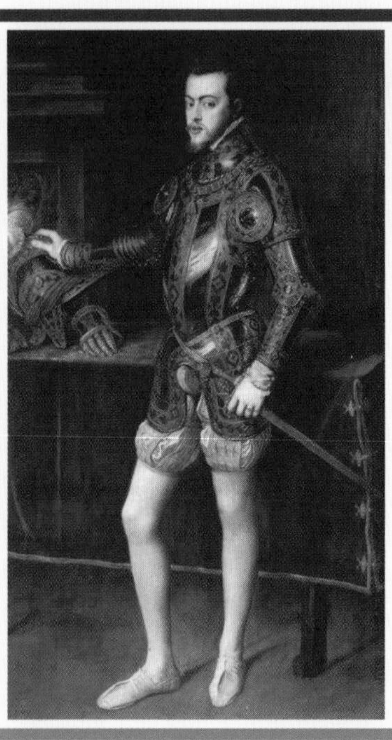

1598
Spain and Portugal Philip II dies, having almost bankrupt Spain with global exploration and colonial expansion; Philip III succeeds him as king of Spain and Portugal; during his reign, the Moors are finally expelled from the Spanish peninsula.

1598 **Russia** Fyodor I dies childless; regent Boris Godunov seizes the throne.

1599 **Sweden** Sigismund's Catholicism leads to him being deposed by his father's brother, the warrior-king Charles IX; during his reign, Charles takes his army as far as Moscow and attacks Poland, Denmark and Finland.

RISE OF EMPIRE

1600–1799

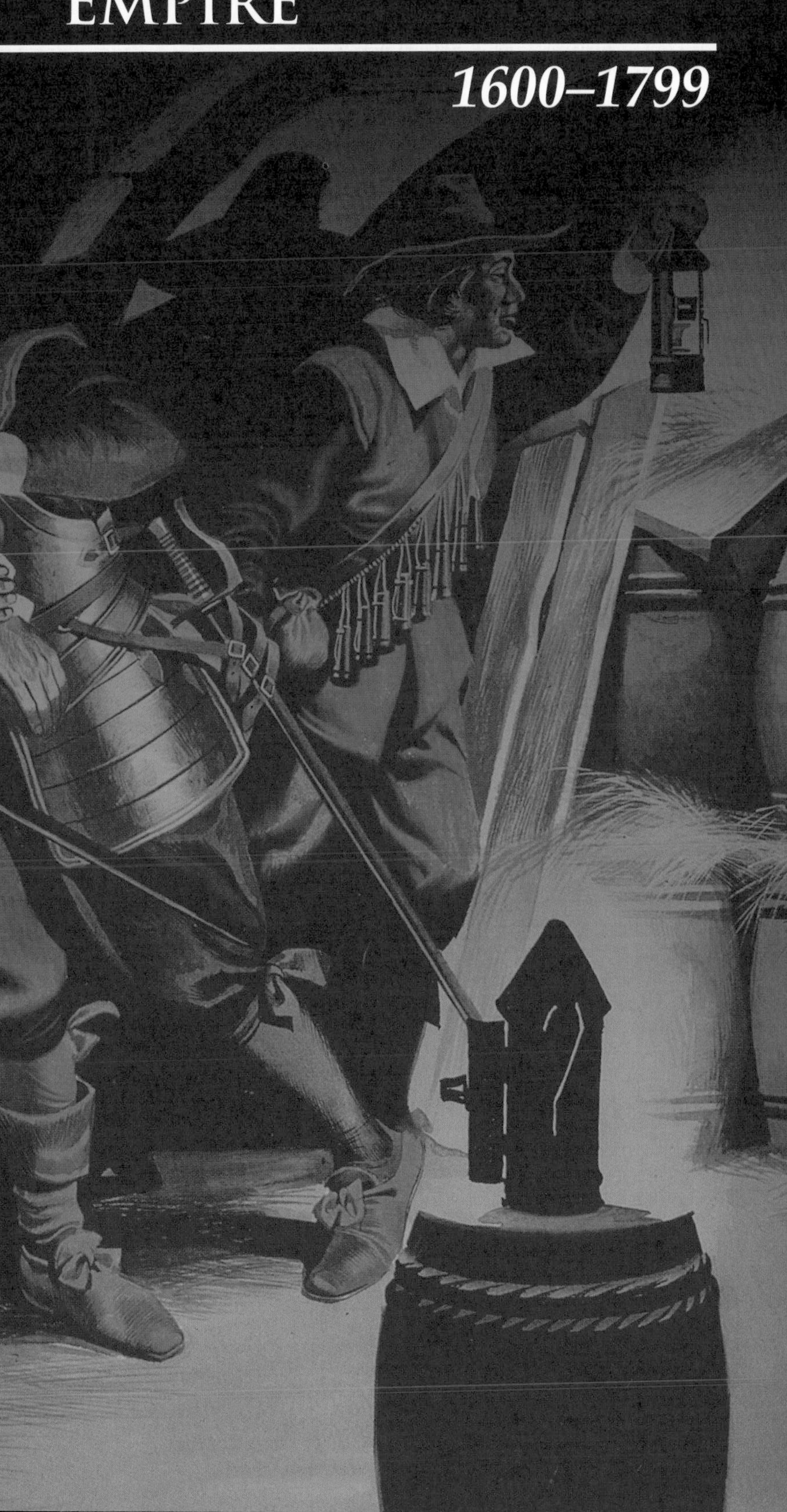

1600 **Wallachia** Simion Movilă, illegitimate son of Mihnea the Turned-Turk, becomes prince.

1601 **Wallachia** Radu Mihnea, son of Mihnea the Turned-Turk, becomes prince.

1602 **Wallachia** Simion Movilă becomes prince for the second time, and then loses power to Radu Şerban.

1603 **Great Britain** Elizabeth I, last of the Tudor monarchs, dies without issue; the Union of the Crowns takes place; James VI of Scotland, great-great-grandson of Henry VIII, also becomes James I of England, the first king of England from the House of Stuart.

1604 **Monaco** Hercule, lord of Monaco, is murdered; his 6-year-old son, Honoré II, becomes ruler under the regency of his father's brother-in-law, Frederico Landi; Honoré is the first ruler to be called prince of Monaco.

1605
England The Gunpowder Plot to blow up king and Parliament fails.

1605 **Rome** Cardinal Alessandro Ottaviano de' Medici is elected pope as Leo XI; he reigns for just 27 days; Cardinal Camillo Borghese is elected pope as Paul V. **Russia** Fyodor II becomes tsar, aged 16, on 10 June; the Time of Troubles begins when on 20 July he and his mother are strangled by a group of discontented *boyars* (high-ranking aristocrats); False Dimitri, an impostor claiming to be the son of Ivan the Terrible, becomes tsar.

1606 **Venice** Leonardo Donato is elected doge. **Russia** Tsar False Dimitri is shot dead, probably by supporters of Prince Vasili Shuisky, after a reign lasting 10 months; Vasili IV Shuisky becomes tsar, but is never generally recognized as such.

1608 **Germany** The Protestant Union, a coalition of Protestant German states with the objective of defending the rights, lands and person of its members, is formed in Germany by Frederick IV. **Liechtenstein** Karl I, prince of Liechtenstein, founds the Princely Family of Liechtenstein, after being created hereditary prince by the heir to the throne of the Holy Roman Empire, Archduke Mathias; the honour is given for his support for the archduke in a land dispute with his father, Emperor Rudolf II.

1609 **Netherlands** The Twelve Years' Truce virtually ensures independence for the Netherlands. **Germany and the Holy Roman Empire** Becoming increasingly unstable and ineffectual, Rudolf II is imprisoned and stripped of effective power by his brother Matthias in Prague.

1610 **France** Henri IV is stabbed to death by fanatical Catholic François Ravaillac, while riding in his coach; Louis XIII becomes king, aged 13; his mother, Marie de' Medici, rules as regent until 1614; with the help of his chief minister, Cardinal Richelieu, appointed 1624, he will become the epitome of the absolute monarch. **Sweden** Gustav Adolf II, widely known as Gustavus Adolphus, becomes king; he leads Sweden successfully in the Thirty Years' War, invading Germany and creating a small empire. **Wallachia** The Hungarian Gabriel Báthory, prince of Transylvania, seizes power. **Russia** Vasili IV Shuisky is deposed and becomes a monk; the country is governed by a council of Seven Boyars until 1612; they elect as king Władysław IV Vasa, son of the Swedish King Gustav I, but he never takes the throne, due to unrest and his father's opposition.

1611 **Germany and the Holy Roman Empire** Rudolf II is forced to cede his crowns to his brother Matthias. **Wallachia** Radu Mihnea returns to power for the second time, is ousted by Radu Şerban and then returns to power once again.

1612 **Venice** Marcantonio Memmo is elected doge. **Holy Roman Empire** Matthias, also king of Hungary and king of Bohemia, is crowned Holy Roman Emperor.

1613 **Russia** Aged 17, Mikhail I Fyodorovich Romanov is unanimously elected tsar of Russia by a national assembly; he is the first king of the Romanov dynasty, which will rule Russia until 1917.

1614 **Hungary** Transylvanian Prince Bethlen Gabor comes to power.

1615 **Venice** Giovanni Bembo is elected doge.

1616 **Wallachia** Gabriel Movilă, son of Simion, becomes prince, he is replaced soon after by Alexandru Iliaş.

1617 **Bohemia** Catholic Archduke Ferdinand, son of Charles II of Austria, becomes king.

1618 **Venice** Nicolò Donato is elected doge; Antonio Priuli is elected doge. **Hungary** Ferdinand II becomes king. **Wallachia** Gabriel Movilă returns to the throne.

1619 **Holy Roman Empire** Ferdinand II, nephew of Maximilian II and king of Bohemia and Hungary, becomes emperor; his suppression of Protestantism marks the early years of the Thirty Years' War.

1620 **Navarre** The Kingdom of Navarre is merged into France; French kings use the title 'King of Navarre' until the French Revolution in 1791; it is revived from 1814 to 1830 during the restoration of the French monarchy. **Wallachia** Radhu Mihnea returns to power for the fourth time.

1621 **Spain and Portugal** Philip IV becomes king of Spain and Philip III of Portugal; during his reign, Spain goes into decline. **Rome** Cardinal Alessandro Ludovisi is elected pope as Gregory XV.

1622 **England** James I dissolves Parliament.

1623 **Venice** Francesco Contarini is elected doge. **Rome** Cardinal Maffeo Barberini is elected pope as Urban VIII; he is the last pope to expand the papal territory by force of arms. **Wallachia** Alexandru Coconul, son of Radhu Mihneal, becomes prince.

1624 **Venice** Giovanni Corner is elected doge.

1625 **Great Britain** Charles I becomes king and dissolves the English Parliament. **Denmark** Christian IV enters the war against Holy

Roman Emperor Ferdinand II. **Hungary** Ferdinand III, son of Ferdinand II, becomes king.

1626 **Denmark** Christian IV loses the Battle of Lutter.

1627 **Liechtenstein** Karl Eusebius becomes the second prince of Liechtenstein, aged 16; he will restore his lands after the ravages of the Thirty Years' War, and becomes a patron of architecture. **Bohemia** The hereditary rule of the Habsburgs is confirmed. **Wallachia** Alexandru Iliaş returns to power.

1628 **England** The Petition of Right is created; Parliament curtails the King's powers.

1629 **England** Charles I dissolves Parliament again and rules personally until 1640. **Wallachia** Leon Tomşa becomes prince.

1630 **Sweden** Gustavus Adolphus enters the war against Ferdinand II. **Venice** Nicolò Contarini is elected doge.

1631 **Venice** Francesco Erizzo is elected doge.

1632 **Sweden** Gustavus Adolphus is victorious, but dies in the Battle of Lützen; aged just 6, Queen Christina takes the throne; Axel Oxenstierna, lord high chancellor of Sweden, becomes regent; Christina is brought up as a prince and becomes known as the 'Girl King'. **Polish-Lithuanian Commonwealth** Władysław IV Vasa, son of Sigismund IV Vasa, is elected king; during his reign, he prevents the Commonwealth from being embroiled in the Thirty Years' War and defends it successfully from invasion. **Wallachia** Matei Basarab becomes prince; he spends much of his reign fighting off Moldavian incursions.

1633 **Monaco** Philip IV of Spain recognizes Monaco as a principality, confirming its rulers' right to be called prince.

1636 **Germany** Ferdinand III is elected king. **Montenegro** On the death of Ruvim II Boljević-Njegos, the prince-bishopric remains vacant until 1639.

1637 **Holy Roman Empire** Ferdinand III, king of Germany, Hungary and Bohemia, becomes emperor.

1638 **Scotland** Scottish Presbyterians sign the Solemn League and Covenant, in effect a treaty between Scotland and the English Parliamentarians, agreeing to the preservation of the reformed religion in Scotland and its promotion in England and Ireland.

1639 **Scotland** The First Bishops' War breaks out between Charles I and the Scottish Church. **Montenegro** Mardarije I Kornečanin becomes prince-bishop.

1640
England The Long Parliament takes place (until 1660).

1640 **Scotland** The Second Bishops' War in Britain ends with the Treaty of Ripon. **Monaco** reverts from Spanish to French protection under the Treaty of Péronne. **Portugal** A revolution elevates João IV to the Portuguese throne, first king of the House of Braganza, launching the protracted Portuguese Restoration war in which Portugal fights against Castile, until 1668.

1642 **England** Civil war erupts in England between Cavaliers (Royalists) and Roundheads (Parliamentarians); it lasts until 1647.

1643 **England** The Solemn League and Covenant is signed by the English Parliament. **France** Louis XIV, 'the Sun King', becomes king, aged 5; Cardinal Mazarin is his chief minister.

1644 **England** Oliver Cromwell wins the Battle of Marston Moor. **Holy Roman Empire** Ferdinand III gives the rulers of the German states the right to conduct their own foreign policy, in an effort to gain allies in negotiations with the French and the Swedes; in reality, this decision helps to erode imperial authority in the Holy Roman Empire. **Rome** Cardinal Giovanni Battista Pamphilj is elected pope as Innocent X.

1645 **England** Cromwell forms his New Model Army; Parliamentarians win the Battle of Naseby. **Russia** Alexis I becomes tsar, aged 16.

THE NEW MODEL ARMY
FORMED IN 1645

At the very start of the English Civil War, Parliament relied on soldiers who were recruited by large landowners who supported their cause. However, in February 1645, Parliament decided they needed to form their own army of professional soldiers and made General Thomas Fairfax its commander-in-chief. Oliver Cromwell, who was in charge of the recruitment for the cavalry, believed that the New Model Army, as it became known, should only have men who truly believed in what they were fighting for. Where possible he recruited men who, like himself, held strong Puritan views.

The New Model Army was a military force that was based on a person's ability rather than their position in society. It was made up mainly of light cavalry and the riders wore thick leather jerkins for protection, rather than heavy armour which would have slowed down their horses. Discipline was strict and the training was tough and thorough. The first major battle for the New Model Army was the Battle of Naseby in June 1645, where over 1,000 Royalist soldiers were killed and another 4,500 taken prisoner. After such a major defeat the Royalists never really regained their strength.

1646 **Scotland** Charles I surrenders to the Scots. **Venice** Francesco Molin is elected the 100th doge of Venice. **Bohemia** Ferdinand, son of Holy Roman Emperor Ferdinand III, becomes king.

1647 **England** Charles I is handed over to the English Parliament; he escapes and makes a secret treaty with the Scots. **Hungary** Ferdinand, already king of Bohemia, becomes king.

1648 **Scotland** invades England and is defeated by Cromwell at the Battle of Preston. **France** The Frondes five years of revolts take place against Mazarin's rule in France. **Denmark and Norway** Frederick III becomes king. **Holy Roman Empire** In the Peace of Westphalia, Emperor Ferdinand III's titles are given as: Ferdinand the Third, elected Roman emperor, always August; king of Germany, Hungary, Bohemia, Dalmatia, Croatia and Slavonia; archduke of Austria; duke of Burgundy, Brabant, Styria, Carinthia and Carniola; Margrave of Moravia; duke of Luxembourg, of the Higher and Lower Silesia, of Wurtemburg and Teck; prince of Swabia; count of Habsburg, Tyrol, Kyburg and Goritia; marquess of the Sacred Roman Empire, Burgovia, the Higher and Lower Lusace and lord of the marquisate of Slavonia, of Port Naon and Salines. **Polish-Lithuanian Commonwealth** John II Casimir, brother of Władysław IV Vasa, is elected king of Poland and grand duke of Lithuania, the third and last monarch from the House of Vasa; his reign is dominated by the Russo-Polish war (1654–1667) and the invasion and occupation of Poland by Sweden (1655–1660).

1649 **England** Charles I of England, Wales and Scotland is executed; the Commonwealth is founded; England is a republic until 1660. **Montenegro** Visarion I becomes prince-bishop.

1650 **Scotland** Charles II lands in Scotland and is proclaimed king.

1651
England Charles II invades England but loses the Battle of Worcester and flees to France.

1653 **England** Cromwell dismisses the Rump Parliament; he becomes lord protector of England. **Germany** Ferdinand IV is elected co-king with his father Ferdinand III; he dies shortly after; his younger brother Leopold, becomes heir.

1654 **Sweden** Queen Christina abdicates and moves to Rome, unmarried and without issue, to openly practise her Catholicism; Charles X Gustav, grandson of Charles IX, becomes king. **Wallachia** Constantin Şerban becomes prince.

1655 **Venice** Carlo Contarini is elected doge. **Rome** Cardinal Fabio Chigi is elected pope as Alexander VII. **Hungary** Leopold, son of Emperor Ferdinand III, becomes king.

1656 **Portugal** The mentally unstable and physically disabled Afonso VI becomes king, aged 13; his mother, Luisa of Medina-Sidonia, acts as regent for six years. **Venice** Bertucci Valiero is elected doge. **Russia, Denmark and the Holy Roman Empire** declare war on Sweden.

1658 **England** Oliver Cromwell dies; he is succeeded by his son Richard. **Venice** Giovanni Pesaro is elected doge. **Holy Roman Empire** Leopold I, king of Hungary, Bohemia and Croatia, becomes emperor-elect; his reign sees wars against the French and the Turks.

Wallachia Mihnea III, also prince of Moldavia, comes to the throne; he moves the capital from Târgovişte to Bucharest.

1659 **England** The English army forces Richard Cromwell to resign, and the Rump Parliament is restored. **Venice** Domenico II Contarini is elected doge. **Montenegro** Mardarije II Kornečanin becomes prince-bishop. **Bohemia** Leopold I, Holy Roman Emperor-elect and king of Hungary, becomes king. **Wallachia** Gheorghe Ghica becomes prince.

1660 **Great Britain** Charles II is restored to the throne of England, Wales, Scotland and Ireland. **Sweden** Charles XI becomes king, aged 5. **Denmark** King Frederick III changes the Danish monarchy from elective to absolute.

> ***“You had better have one King than five hundred.”***
>
> Charles II

1661 **France** The death of Cardinal Mazarin; Louis XIV becomes absolute monarch in France. **Wallachia** Grigore I Ghica becomes prince.

1662 **Monaco** Louis I (not to be confused with the earlier Louis I, lord of Monaco) becomes sovereign prince.

1664 **Wallachia** Grigore I Ghica is deposed; Radu Leon becomes prince; his authority relies on the support of the Phanariots, prominent Greeks living in Phanar, and especially the noble Cantacuzino family.

1665 **Spain** Charles II becomes the last Habsburg king of Spain.

1667 **Portugal** Afonso VI is forced by his brother Pedro, duke of Beja, the future Pedro II, to exile himself, while he becomes prince-regent. **Rome** Cardinal Giulio Rospigliosi is elected pope as Clement IX.

1668 **Portugal** Spain recognizes Portugal's independence. **Polish-Lithuanian Commonwealth** John II Casimir abdicates to become a Jesuit.

1669 **Liechtenstein** Hans-Adam, nicknamed Hans-Adam the Rich, becomes the third prince of Liechtenstein; in 1699 he purchases the territory of Schellenberg, and in 1712 the County of Vaduz, the two areas that will later constitute the Principality of Liechtenstein. **Polish-Lithuanian Commonwealth** Michał Korybut Wiśniowiecki, son of controversial military commander Jeremi Michał Wiśniowiecki, is elected king; his reign is disastrous. **Wallachia** Anti-Greek sentiment brings down Radu Leon; Antonie din Popeşti, supported by the Cantacuzino family, replaces him as prince.

1670 **Rome** Cardinal Emilio Altieri is elected pope as Clement X. **Denmark and Norway** Christian V becomes king; he is loved by the people and hated by the nobles.

1672 **England** The Test Act deprives Catholics and Nonconformists of the right to hold public office. **Wallachia** Antonie din Popeşti is deposed on the orders of the Ottoman Grand Vizier; Grigore I Ghica is restored to power.

1673 **Polish-Lithuanian Commonwealth** John III Sobieski, a brilliant Polish military commander, is elected king of Poland and grand duke of Lithuania; he takes a country ravaged by half a century of war, stabilizes it and gains a famous victory over the Turks at the 1683 Battle of Vienna. **Montenegro** Ruvim III Boljević becomes prince-bishop. **Wallachia** The Greek George Ducas becomes prince.

1674 **Venice** Nicolò Sagredo is elected doge. **Polish-Lithuanian Commonwealth** Jan III becomes king after defeating the Turks and the Cossacks.

1676 **Venice** Luigi Contarini is elected doge. **Rome** Cardinal Benedetto Odescalchi is elected pope as Innocent XI. **Russia** Fyodor III becomes tsar; he has been an invalid since birth.

1678 **England** An imaginary Catholic plot to overthrow Charles II of England is invented by Titus Oates. **Wallachia** George Ducas loses support and is replaced as prince by Şerban Cantacuzino.

1682 **Russia** The death of Fyodor III leads to the Moscow Uprising, when relatives of each of Fyodor's two wives try to gain power; Peter the Great becomes tsar, sharing power with his sickly half-brother Ivan V; their sister, Sophia Alekseyevna, is regent during their minority.

PETER THE GREAT

REIGN: 1682–1725

Peter the Great (Peter I) has been credited with modernising Russia and turning it into an empire. He was born on 30 May 1672 in Moscow, the grandson of tsar Michael Romanov. Peter was proclaimed Tsar at the age of 10, but due to a power struggle had to rule together with his brother Ivan. As the brothers were both under age, they came under the patronage of their elder sister Sophia. Sophia appointed her lover Prince Golitsin as chief minister, but this caused such chaos in the government, Sophia was eventually overthrown and exiled to a convent. When Ivan died in 1696, Peter was left the sole leader.

Peter the Great was a giant of a man standing at nearly 7 ft, and he ruled his country with incredible power and fortitude. One of his main goals was to regain access to the Baltic Sea and Baltic trade. He started the Northern War with Sweden which lasted for 21 years, and founded St Petersburg in 1703. At the end of the war Russia was victorious and had conquered vast tracts of land. In 1712 Peter moved the Russian capital to St Petersburg and paid special attention to the construction of his new and vast city. By the end of the war in 1721, Russia was declared an empire and Peter the Great proclaimed himself its emperor.

1683 **Portugal** Pedro II becomes king, marrying Queen Marie-Françoise of Savoy, the wife of his brother, Afonso VI, the former king. **Venice** Leonardo Donato is elected doge; Marcantonio Giusinian is elected doge.

1685 **Great Britain** On the death of Charles II, his brother James II of England and VII of Scotland, takes the throne; the duke of Monmouth's rebellion against the king is quashed. **Montenegro** Vasilije II Velikrasić becomes prince-bishop; Visarion II Bajica becomes prince-bishop.

1686 **England** James II ignores the Test Act and Catholics are appointed to public office.

1687 **England** James II extends tolerance to all religions in the Declaration of Indulgence. **Hungary** The Habsburg succession to the Hungarian throne is confirmed; Joseph I is crowned king.

1688 **Great Britain** James II and VII of England and Scotland's unpopular espousal of Catholicism leads to the Glorious Revolution; he is deposed and William of Orange and his wife take the throne as joint monarchs, William III and Mary II. **Venice** Francesco Morosini is elected doge. **Wallachia** Constantin Brâncoveanu becomes prince.

1689 **Russia** Sophia Alekseyevna's regency, on behalf of Peter the Great and his brother Ivan V, comes to an end. **Rome** The 81-year-old Cardinal Pietro Vito Ottoboni is elected pope as Alexander VIII.

> ***"I have conquered an empire but I have not been able to conquer myself."***

Peter the Great

1690 **Ireland** William III invades Ireland to quash a rebellion by supporters of James II; he wins the decisive Battle of the Boyne. **Germany** Joseph I becomes co-king. **Montenegro** The prince-bishopric falls vacant until 1694.

1691 **Rome** Cardinal Antonio Pignatelli is elected pope as Innocent XII.

1694 **Great Britain** Queen Mary II dies, leaving William III as sole ruler. **Venice** Silvestro Valiero is elected doge. **Montenegro** Sava I Kaluđerović becomes prince-bishop.

1696 **Polish-Lithuanian Commonwealth** Frederick Augustus I, elector of Saxony, is elected king of Poland and grand duke of Lithuania as Augustus II the Strong; he embroils the Commonwealth in the Great Northern War and remains in power chiefly through Russian support. **Montenegro** Danilo I, known as Vladiko Danilo, becomes prince-bishop; the first from the House of Petrović-Njegoš, he establishes ties with Russia and recovers Zeta from the Ottomans. **Russia** Ivan V dies, leaving Peter the Great as sole ruler.

1697 **Sweden** Charles XII becomes king; he fights the Great Northern War against a coalition made up of Saxony, Denmark-Norway, Poland and Russia. **Russia** Peter the Great begins several years of travel through western Europe incognito.

1699 **Hungary** The Treaty of Karlowitz concludes the Austro-Ottoman war of 1683–1697, in which the Ottoman side has finally been defeated; the Austrian Habsburgs gain almost all of Hungary, Transylvania and Slavonia; Podolia is returned to Poland; the Peloponnese Peninsula and Dalmatia are returned to Venice; this treaty signals the decline of the Ottoman Empire and the rise of the Habsburg monarchy to be the dominant Central European power. **Denmark and Norway** Christian V dies in a hunting accident; Frederick IV succeeds him.

1700 **Spain** Charles II of Spain dies without issue, bringing the Spanish Habsburg line to a close and throwing Europe into the Spanish War of Succession until 1701. **Monaco** Antonio I becomes sovereign prince of Monaco. **Venice** Alvise II Mocenigo is elected doge. **Rome** Giovanni Francesco Albani is elected pope as Clement XI.

1701 **Great Britain** The Act of Settlement establishes Protestant Hanoverian succession in Britain; the exiled James II dies. **Prussia** The elector of Brandenberg, Frederick III, takes the Prussian throne as Frederick I, after Leopold I, archduke of Austria and Holy Roman Emperor, is persuaded by Frederick to allow Prussia to be ruled as a kingdom.

1702
Great Britain William III dies; Princess Anne, sister of Queen Mary, becomes queen of England and Scotland.

1703 **Hungary** Ferenc II Rákóczi leads a Hungarian uprising against the Habsburgs, lasting until 1711, as prince of the 'Estates Confederated for Liberty of the Kingdom of Hungary'. **Russia** Peter the Great founds St Petersburg.

1705 **Holy Roman Empire** Joseph I, archduke of Austria, king of Hungary and Bohemia, becomes emperor.

1706 **Portugal** João V becomes king, aged 17; he strengthens the monarchy with the wealth of the newly discovered diamond and gold mines in the Portuguese colony of Brazil. **Polish-Lithuanian Commonwealth** The Swedish king, Charles XII, defeats a Polish-Saxon army several times in battle, forcing Augustus II to yield his throne to a Swedish candidate, the Polish nobleman Stanisław Leszczyński.

1707 **Great Britain** The Act of Union unites the parliaments of England and Scotland; having shared the same monarch for just over 100 years, the countries merge to form the Kingdom of Great Britain.

1709 **Sweden** Charles XII loses to Russia in the Battle of Poltova, marking the end of the Swedish Empire and the beginning of the Russian Empire; Charles goes into exile in Moldovia in the Ottoman Empire. **Venice** Giovanni Corner is elected doge. **Polish-Lithuanian Commonwealth** Augustus II is restored to the throne under Russian auspices and remains subservient to Russia for the remainder of his reign.

1711 **Holy Roman Empire** Emperor Joseph I dies of smallpox; Charles VI succeeds him as king of Hungary, Bohemia and Holy Roman Emperor. **Wallachia** The Phanariote Epoch begins in Wallachia and Moldavia, lasting until 1821; princes are mainly Phanariotes – Greeks from Phanar, the main Greek quarter of Constantinople – and are given the position of prince chiefly as a promotion by the dragoman offices of the Ottoman Empire.

1712 **Liechtenstein** Josef Wenzel, eldest son of Prince Philip Erasmus of Liechtenstein, becomes prince of Liechtenstein; he is a great military commander, appointed generalissimo in Italy and general chief commander in Hungary; he reorganizes the Habsburg artillery, partly from his own pocket. **Russia** Peter the Great marries Catherine, a woman of humble origins, and gives her the title empress, the first woman to be so-called in Russia.

1713 **Spain** The Treaty of Utrecht ends the war of Spanish Succession, confirming Philip V, grandson of Louis XIV of France, as the first Bourbon king of Spain; Spain is forced to give away Spanish Netherlands, Sicily and Naples. **Austria** Charles VI has no male heirs and, consequently, introduces the Pragmatic Sanction; it ensures that his realm cannot be divided and permits daughters to inherit the throne in the event of there being no male heir. **Prussia** Frederick William I becomes king of Prussia; he establishes a standing army of 80,000 men. **Sicily** Victor Amadeus II, duke of Savoy, becomes king of Sicily.

1714 **Great Britain** Queen Anne dies having given birth to 18 children, none of whom live beyond 11 years. George I, the elector of Hanover, great-grandson of James I, becomes the first Hanoverian king of Great Britain and Ireland. **Wallachia** Ştefan Cantacuzino becomes prince.

1715 **Great Britain** The first Jacobite rising takes place in Britain in support of James the Old Pretender, son of James II. **France** Louis XIV dies after the longest reign by a European monarch, 72 years and three months; Louis XV becomes king.

1718 **Sicily** Philip V of Spain invades Sicily, trying to win it back; the Quadruple Alliance of Great Britain, France, Austria and the Dutch Republic is formed, and defeats Spain.

1719 **Liechtenstein** The Liechtenstein family's purchase of the lands of Schellenberg and Vaduz, between Switzerland and Lower Austria, qualifies it for a seat in the Reichstag, the parliament of the Holy Roman Empire; Emperor Charles VI declares that Schellenberg and Vaduz are united and names them Liechtenstein, which becomes a sovereign member state of the empire; the princes of Liechtenstein do not actually live in their principality until 1938; Josef Wenzel steps down and Anton Florian becomes the first prince of the Principality of Liechtenstein; Luxembourg and Liechtenstein are the only two states of the Holy Roman Empire that still exist.

1720 **Spain and Sicily** The Treaty of the Hague is signed between the Quadruple Alliance and Spain, concluding the war of the Quadruple Alliance; Philip V agrees to abandon his Italian claims; King Victor Amadeus is forced by the Alliance to change his title to the less important 'King of Sardinia'; he cedes Sicily to Austria; Charles IV, son of Leopold I, Holy Roman Emperor, becomes king; he is also king of Bohemia and Hungary and a claimant to the Spanish throne; Sicily comes under direct Austrian rule. **Sweden** Charles XII is killed while invading Norway; he is unmarried and his sister, Ulrika Eleonora, regent while he has been absent, is elected queen, and then abdicates in favour of her husband Frederick I, son of Landgrave Charles I of Hesse-Kassel in the Holy Roman Empire.

1721 **Rome** Cardinal Michelangelo Conti is elected pope as Innocent XIII. **Liechtenstein** Josef Johann Adam becomes prince of Liechtenstein. **Russia** Peter the Great is acclaimed 'Emperor of all Russia'.

1722 **Venice** Sebastiano Mocenigo is elected doge.

1724 **Spain** Philip V of Spain abdicates in favour of his 17-year-old son Louis, but Louis dies after nine months; Philip returns to the throne and reigns for a further 22 years. **Rome** Cardinal Pierfrancesco Orsini is elected pope as Benedict XIII.

1725 **Russia** Peter the Great dies, having westernized Russia, creating an empire and transforming it into a major European power; Empress Catherine I, his second wife, succeeds to the throne on her husband's death; she continues his modernisations.

1727 **Great Britain** George II becomes king. Spain is at war with Britain and France (until 1729). **Russia** Peter II, son of Tsarevich Alexei Petrovich, and grandson of Peter I, becomes emperor.

1730 **Rome** Cardinal Lorenzo Corsini is elected pope as Clement XII; he is blind and bedridden. **Denmark and Norway** Christian VI becomes king. **Russia** Peter II dies of smallpox on his wedding day; his new wife jumps into his deathbed in a futile effort to become pregnant; he is buried in the Kremlin, the only Russian monarch after Peter the Great to be given that honour; with him, the direct male line of the Romanov dynasty comes to an end; Anna Ioannovna, daughter of Ivan V, becomes empress.

1731 **Monaco** Antonio I dies without male issue; his daughter Louise Hyppolyte becomes sovereign princess; it has already been decided, with the permission of the French king Louis XIV, that her future husband will take the name Grimaldi and will rule Monaco jointly with her; in 1715 she marries Jacques Francois Goyon de Matignon; she dies of smallpox 10 months later and her husband becomes Jacques I, sovereign prince.

1732 **Liechtenstein** Josef Wenzel acts as regent for 8-year-old Johann Nepomuk Karl, prince of Liechtenstein, until 1745. **Venice** Carlo Ruzzini is elected doge.

1733 **Monaco** Honoré III becomes sovereign prince of Monaco; he chooses to live in Paris, and Antoine Grimaldi, known as 'le Chevalier de Grimaldi', is regent until 1784. **Polish-Lithuanian Commonwealth** August II the Strong dies, having fathered, according to some reports, more than 300 children during his life; opposed by Russia, Stanisław I Leszczyński is elected king of Poland and grand duke of Lithuania for a second time; the Russians decide to elect August III, son of August the Strong, as ruler; the war of the Polish Succession begins, in which the two Bourbon powers, France and Spain, try to limit Habsburg ambition in western Europe, going to war against Austria and Russia.

1735 **Venice** Alvise Pisani is elected doge. **Naples and Sicily** Retaken by Spain during the war of the Polish Succession, Sicily is merged with Naples, and Charles V, son of Philip IV of Spain, is named king. **Polish-Lithuanian Commonwealth** The war of the Polish Succession ends with victory for Spain and France; the Treaty of Vienna confirms Augustus as undisputed king; Stanisław I is compensated with the duchy of Lorraine, which passes, on his death, to France; Charles III of Spain gives up his right to the Grand Duchy of Tuscany, but is confirmed as king of Sicily and Naples. **Montenegro** Sava II Petrović Njegoš becomes prince-bishop.

1740 **Prussia** Frederick II the Great becomes king, greatly expanding Prussian territory and making it a major power in Europe; Prussia attacks Austria and drags much of Europe into the war of Austrian Succession, until 1748. **Holy Roman Empire** Cardinal Prospero Lorenzo Lambertini is elected pope as Benedict XIV. **Russia** Empress Anna Ioannovna dies, and her 8-month-old grand-nephew, Ivan VI, whom she has adopted, succeeds her.

1741 **Venice** Pietro Grimani is elected doge. **Hungary, Croatia and Bohemia** Emperor Charles VI's Pragmatic Sanction allows his daughter, Maria Theresa, to become queen of Hungary, Croatia and Bohemia. **Russia** Thirteen months after Ivan VI has come to the throne, a coup replaces him with the daughter of Peter the Great, Tsarevna Elizabeth; Ivan and his family are imprisoned; Ivan's guards are instructed to kill him if anyone tries to free him; he will be killed after 20 years of solitary confinement, when sub-lieutenant Vasily Mirovich attempts to free him and proclaim him emperor.

1742 **Germany and the Holy Roman Empire** Charles VII, son of the elector of Bavaria and husband of Maria Amalia, daughter of Joseph I, becomes king and emperor.

1745 **Great Britain** The 'Forty-Five' – a Jacobite rebellion in Great Britain led by Charles Edward Stuart, the 'Young Pretender'; government forces are defeated at the Battle of Prestonpans.

THE 'FORTY-FIVE'
1745

The major Jacobite Risings of 1715 and 1745 were known respectively as 'The Fifteen' and 'The Forty-five'. They formed part of a larger series of military campaigns by Jacobites who were attempting to restore the Stuart kings to the thrones of Scotland and England. The 'Forty-five' was led by Bonnie Prince Charlie and, despite having all the odds against against him and his 20,000 clansmen, they went on to defeat the government forces at Prestonpans. However, threatened by superior forces Charlie and his clan retreated to Scotland. The Jacobites' hopes were dashed when the Duke of Cumberland went in pursuit and Charlie lost over 1,200 men on Culloden Moor in April 1946. In the aftermath of the uprising, the wearing of tartan, the bearing of arms and the playing of bagpipes were all banned in Scotland.

1745 **Austria** In the war of Austrian Succession, French forces defeat an Anglo-Dutch-Hanoverian army in the Battle of Fontenoy. **Holy Roman Empire** The grand duke of Tuscany, Franz I, becomes emperor, founding the Habsburg-Lorraine dynasty; he is married to Maria Theresa, daughter of Emperor Charles VI, who is queen of Hungary, Croatia and Bohemia; she styles herself 'Holy Roman Empress'; the couple will soon be parents of Marie-Antoinette, queen of France.

1746 **Great Britain** The Jacobites are defeated at the Battle of Culloden; Charles Stuart flees, Highland clan culture is suppressed – including the banning of the kilt – and many Scots emigrate. **Spain** Ferdinand VI the Wise becomes king. **Denmark and Norway** Frederick V becomes king.

1748 **Liechtenstein** Johann Nepomuk Karl dies without male issue; Josef Wenzel returns to rule as prince of Liechtenstein for a third time.

1750 **Portugal** José I becomes king; he places power in the hands of Sebastião José de Carvalho e Melo, better known today as the marquis of Pombal, who becomes head of government; José declares his daughter Maria, princess of Beira, to be his heir; he creates her princess of Brazil, the official title of the heir to the Portuguese throne. **Montenegro** Vasilije III rules jointly with Sava II as prince-bishop, until 1766.

1751 **Sweden** Adolf Frederick is elected king; he is the son of Christian August of Holstein-Gottorp and is descended from Gustav I and

Charles X; he is ineffectual, the real power lying with his imperious wife Louisa Ulrika, sister of Prussian king Frederick the Great.

1757 **Venice** Francesco Loredan is elected doge. **Prussia** The Battle of Rossbach; Prussian King Frederick the Great defeats the French and the Austrians.

1758 **Rome** Cardinal Carlo della Torre Rezzonico is elected pope as Clement XIII.

1759 **Spain** Ferdinand VI dies insane; Charles III, his brother and fifth son of Philip V, becomes king; he begins Bourbon reforms, expelling the Jesuits from Spain. **Naples and Sicily** Charles IV abdicates in favour of his son, Ferdinand III, in order to take the Spanish throne as Charles III.

1760 **Great Britain** George III, grandson of George II, becomes king; he will have 15 children. **Portugal** Maria, princess of Brazil, marries her uncle, Pedro; he becomes prince of Brazil in his wife's right.

1762 **Venice** Marco Foscarini is elected doge. **Polish-Lithuanian Commonwealth** August III dies; his reign has seen the Seven Years' War, involving all the major European powers and the refining of the plans of Prussia, Austria and Russia to partition the Commonwealth. **Russia** Empress Elizabeth dies; she is the last of the Russian Romanovs; future rulers will call themselves by the name of Romanov but, apart from Peter II, they are descended from the German Catherine II; the mentally immature Peter III becomes emperor in January; he is the son of Karl Friedrich, duke of Holstein-Gottorp, and Anna Petrovna, daughter of Peter the Great; he immediately makes himself unpopular and is forced to abdicate in June; he is succeeded by his wife, Catherine II the Great, daughter of Christian August, prince of Anhalt-Zerbst, a Prussian general.

1763 **Venice** Alvise Giovanni Mocenigo is elected doge.

1764 **Polish-Lithuanian Commonwealth** Stanisław II August Poniatowski is elected king; the last king of Poland and last grand duke of Lithuania, he is controlled by Russia and Prussia.

1765 **Germany and Holy Roman Empire** Joseph II becomes king and emperor; his mother, Maria Theresa, wields the real power.

1766 **Denmark and Norway** Christian VII becomes king; he may be schizophrenic and his reign is debauched and scandalous.

1767
Russia Catherine the Great commissions a new code of laws.

1767 **Montenegro** Šćepan Mali claims to be Russian tsar Peter III, recently murdered by Catherine II of Russia; Sava II hands him power and he rules as an absolute ruler; he is actually a farmer from Dalmatia.

1769 **Rome** Cardinal Giovanni Vincenzo Antonio Ganganelli is elected pope as Clement XIV.

1770 **Polish-Lithuanian Commonwealth** Stanisław II August Poniatowski is briefly dethroned and imprisoned by the Council of the Bar Confederation, an association of Polish nobles.

1771 **Sweden** Gustav III becomes king.

1772 **Liechtenstein** Josef Wenzel dies without surviving male issue; his nephew, Franz Josef I, becomes prince of Liechtenstein. **Polish-Lithuanian Commonwealth** In the First Partition, the Commonwealth loses about a third of its territory.

1773 **Montenegro** Šćepan Mali, who claims to be former Russian emperor Peter III, is killed by one of his own people.

1774 **France** Louis XV dies, having lost Canada and sold Louisiana during his reign; Louis XVI, grandson of Louis XV, becomes king.

> ***"It is not a revolt, it is a revolution."***

King Louis XVI

1775 **Rome** Cardinal Count Giovanni Angelo Braschi is elected pope as Pius VI.

1777 **Portugal** Maria I, oldest of the four daughters of José I, becomes Portugal's first queen regnant; her husband becomes king consort and is known as Pedro III; her first act is to dismiss the powerful head of government, the marquis de Pombal.

1779 **Venice** Paolo Renier is elected doge.

1780 **Holy Roman Empire** Joseph II, Holy Roman Emperor and co-ruler of Austria with his mother, Maria Theresa, becomes sole ruler on her death, beginning a 10-year period of important reforms; he also becomes king of Hungary, Croatia and Bohemia.

1781 **Liechtenstein** Alois I, third son of Franz Josef I, becomes prince of Liechtenstein.

1782 **Montenegro** Petar I becomes prince-bishop; he becomes the most popular spiritual as well as military leader from the House of Petrović-Njegoš.

1785 **Germany** The League of German Princes is formed by Frederick the Great, against Austria.

1788 **Spain** Charles IV, second son of Charles III, becomes king; patron of Goya, he is closer to painters than to military and naval matters; the English will defeat him at Trafalgar in 1805.

1789 **France** The Estates-General meet at Versailles; the French Revolution begins; the Third Estate forms the National Assembly; the Bastille is stormed; the *Declaration of the Rights of Man and the Citizen* is issued. **Venice** Ludovico Manin is elected last doge of Venice.

1790 **Holy Roman Empire** Leopold II, younger brother of Joseph II, becomes emperor and ruler of the Habsburg lands of Hungary, Croatia and Bohemia; his sister is Marie Antoinette, queen consort of France.

1791 **France** Amid the turmoil, Louis XVI and his family flee, but are captured; Louis accepts the new constitution.

1792 **France** is declared a republic; Louis XVI and his queen, the Austrian Marie Antoinette, are beheaded. **Sweden** Gustav III is assassinated at an Opera House Ball by an army captain named Anckarström; Gustav IV Adolf becomes king. **Holy Roman Empire** Franz II becomes the last Holy Roman Emperor, archduke of Austria and king of Hungary, Croatia and Bohemia. **Polish-Lithuanian Commonwealth** Following the Second Partition, the Commonwealth is left with only about a third of its 1772 population.

1793 **France** Exiled French Royalists declare Louis XVII king. **Monaco** comes under French control until 1814.

1794 **France** The execution of Danton and Robespierre; the Reign of Terror draws to a close.

1795 **France** Louis XVII dies uncrowned, a prisoner in the Temple prison; the Directoire rules France. **Russia** Catherine 'the Great' dies, having taken countless lovers and expanded and modernized the Russian Empire; she may have died of a stroke, but one unsubstantiated rumour suggests that a horse fell on her during an act of bestiality; Paul I, son of Peter III and Catherine 'the Great', and a man of violent temper and capricious nature, becomes emperor. **Polish-Lithuanian Commonwealth** The Commonwealth ceases to exist, following the Third Partition of the territory which shares its remaining lands between Russia, Prussia and Austria; Poland and Lithuania become separate independent countries again; Stanisław August Poniatowski abdicates and, from this date on, Russian emperors assume the title of grand duke of Lithuania.

1796 **France** Napoleon Bonaparte, leading the French army, conquers most of Italy.

NAPOLEON BONAPARTE
1769–1821

Napoleon Bonaparte was the emperor of France and is considered to be one of the greatest military leaders in history. He was educated in a military school and by 1796 had gained the position of commander of the French army in Italy.

Napoleon summed up his own career with the words:

'I closed the gulf of anarchy and brought order out of chaos. I rewarded merit regardless of birth or wealth, wherever I found it. I abolished feudalism and restored equality to all regardless of religion and before the law. I fought the decrepit monarchies of the Old Regime because the alternative was the destruction of all this. I purified the Revolution.'

Napoleon's brief reign ended after the Battle of Waterloo in 1815. He was captured and imprisoned by the British on the remote island of St Helena. Napoleon died on the island on 5 May 1821.

1797 **Venice** Napoleon invades Venice; the doge is forced to abdicate; the city is incorporated into the Kingdom of Italy, under French rule, ending more than 1,000 years of independence.

1798 **Rome** The French occupy Rome, creating a Roman Republic; the pope is ordered to renounce his temporal authority and, refusing, is taken prisoner.

1799 **France** A coalition is formed of Britain, Austria, Russia, Portugal and the Ottoman Empire against the French; Bonaparte returns to France and becomes 'First Consul'; the French are driven out of Italy. **Portugal** Queen Maria I's mental instability – possibly caused by porphyria, the disease with which George III of Britain had been afflicted – renders her incapable of handling affairs of state; her son, Prince João, acts as prince regent.

1799
Rome Pope Pius VI dies in captivity in Valence, in France; his pontificate is the longest in historical times at 24 years, 6 months and 15 days.

1799 **Naples and Sicily** The Kingdom of Naples is abolished and replaced, for six months, by the Parthenopaean Republic; Ferdinand is restored to the throne.

REBELLION AND REVOLUTION

1800-1918

1800 **United Kingdom** The Act of Union formally unites Great Britain and Ireland as the United Kingdom. **Etruria** Napoleon dispossesses Ferdinand, grand duke of Tuscany, and creates the Kingdom of Etruria; the crown prince of Parma is crowned Louis I. **Rome** Cardinal Count Barnaba Niccolò Maria Luigi Chiaramonti Pius VII is elected pope. **Holy Roman Empire** The Treaty of Lunéville between France and Austria, marking the end of the Second Coalition, leads to the break-up of the Holy Roman Empire; the Austrian emperor has to renounce all claims to the empire. Bonaparte, meanwhile, has time to prepare his troops for greater triumphs.

1801 **France** Napoleon signs a concordat with the Catholic Church, seeking to reconcile the Catholics under his control. **Spain** Supported by Napoleon, Spanish dictator Manuel de Godoy, prime minister of Portugal from 1792 to 1797 and known as the Prince of the Peace, unsuccessfully invades Portugal. **Russia** Emperor Paul I is assassinated by being strangled and stamped to death by a group of disgruntled army officers, annoyed by reforms disadvantaging the nobility; Alexander I becomes emperor.

1802 **France** Napoleon Bonaparte is created 'First Consul for Life'.

1803 **Etruria** Louis II becomes king of Etruria.

1804 **France** Napoleon is crowned emperor of France; his civil code is created and adopted by many other countries. **Austrian Empire** Archduke Franz founds the Austrian Empire, consisting of all the Habsburg lands, including Austria, Lombardy and Venetia, Hungary, Croatia and Dalmatia, becoming Emperor Franz I.

1805 **Bavaria** Maximilian I Joseph, the elector of Bavaria, is rewarded by Napoleon for his support; the treaty of Pressburg makes Bavaria a kingdom, and Swabia and Franconia are added to its territory; Maximilian I becomes king. **Liechtenstein** Prince Alois I dies childless; his brother, Johann I Josef, becomes the last prince of Liechtenstein to rule under the Holy Roman Empire. **Italy** Napoleon takes control of much of the north of the country and becomes king of Italy.

1806 **Netherlands** Louis Bonaparte, brother of Napoleon, is named king of Holland, a puppet kingdom created by Napoleon. **Liechtenstein** Napoleon incorporates Liechtenstein into the Confederation of the Rhine and makes it a sovereign state. **Württemberg** becomes a kingdom, having been ruled by the same family for 700 years; Duke Frederick II assumes the title of King Frederick I, abrogates the constitution and unites old and new Württemberg; he marries Princess Charlotte, daughter of George III of Great Britain, and allies with Napoleon, deserting him for the Allied cause in 1813. **Austrian Empire and Holy Roman Empire** Emperor Franz II dissolves the Holy Roman Empire after the disastrous defeat of the Third Coalition by Napoleon at the Battle of Austerlitz; he is left only with the titles emperor of Austria; king of Jerusalem, Hungary, Bohemia, Dalmatia, Croatia, Slavonia, Galicia and Lodomeria; archduke of Austria; duke of Lorraine, Salzburg, Würzburg, Franconia, Styria, Carinthia and Carniola; grand duke of Cracow; grand prince of Transylvania; margrave of Moravia; duke of Sandomir, Masovia, Lublin, Upper and Lower Silesia, Auschwitz and Zator, Teschen and Friule; prince of Berchtesgaden and Mergentheim; princely count of Habsburg, Gorizia and Gradisca and of the Tyrol and margrave of Upper and Lower Lusatia and Istria. **Naples and Sicily** Napoleon I deposes Ferdinand, replacing him with his brother, Joseph Bonaparte.

BATTLE OF JENA
14 OCTOBER 1806

The Battle of Jena was a military engagement during the Napoleonic Wars and took place at Jena and Auerstädt in Saxony (modern Germany). On 14 October 1806, Napoleon attacked Prince Friedrich of Hohenlohe-Ingelfingen and his force with his main army of over 56,000 men. It was a bitter conflict and throughout the night new units moved up to reinforce the French army. They used a parade ground formation, firing volleys into the enemy when ordered. The Prussian force under Marshal Lannes soon started to weaken and he sent for immediate reinforcements hoping to hold out until they arrived.

Unfortunately for Lannes, an impatient Marshal Ney launched an assault in the centre and neither side could believe his stupidity. It left the Prussian army completey exposed. At 1.00 p.m. Bonaparte ordered a general advance and within two hours the exhausted Prussians surrendered. Jena cost Bonaparte some 5,000 men; nothing compared to the staggering 25,000 Prussian casualties.

1807 **Portugal** refuses to join in the Continental Blockade of Britain; France and Spain invade; the entire Braganza dynasty flees to Brazil, where it sets up a court in exile in Rio de Janeiro; Rio will be capital of Portugal until 1821; Napoleon appoints as governor, French General Jean-Andoche Junot, 1st Duc d'Abrantès. **Westphalia** Napoleon creates the Kingdom of Westphalia from Hesse-Kassel, Brunswick and large areas of Russia, Hanover and Saxony; he names his brother, Jérôme Bonaparte, as king of what is effectively a French vassal state.

1808 **Spain and Portugal** Charles IV abdicates in favour of his son, who takes the throne as Ferdinand VII; France occupies Spain; Napoleon persuades Charles IV to rescind his abdication in favour of his son and change it to favour his brother Joseph, who is already king of Naples and Sicily, and becomes king of Spain; British General Arthur Wellesley, later the duke of Wellington, lands in Lisbon with a force, initiating the Peninsular War, which lasts until 1814. **Rome** The French take the Papal States and Pope Pius VII is taken prisoner; he is held for more than six years. **Denmark and Norway** Christian VII dies following a scandalous and unpopular reign; during the reign of his successor, Frederick VI, Denmark loses Norway. **Etruria** The Kingdom of Etruria is revoked by Napoleon; he restores the Grand Duchy of Tuscany and gives it to his sister Elizabeth, princess of Lucca. **Naples and Sicily** Napoleon names his brother-in-law, Joachim Murat, king as Joachim I.

1809 **Sweden** A military coup ousts Gustav IV Adolf; Charles XIII, second son of King Adolf Frederick and uncle of Gustav IV, becomes king.

1810 **United Kingdom** George III is declared insane; George, prince of Wales, becomes regent. **Netherlands** King Louis Napoleon has attempted to serve Dutch interests as well as his brother's; he is forced to abdicate; his 5-year-old son, Napoleon Louis, succeeds him as Louis II; he reigns for just 10 days; Napoleon invades and dissolves the kingdom; the country is annexed and becomes part of the French Empire. **Sweden** Jean-Baptiste Bernadotte, created marshal of France by Napoleon Bonaparte, is offered the throne partly because he will be acceptable to Napoleon; he becomes Charles XIV John of Sweden, first king of the House of Bernadotte; he never learns Swedish; the House of Bernadotte still reigns.

1811 **Portugal** The French are driven out of Portugal.

1813 **France** Napoleon is defeated in the Battle of the Nations at Leipzig; Allied forces invade France and enter Paris. **Spain** The French are driven out by Wellington; the House of Bourbon is restored and Ferdinand VII, son of Charles IV, becomes king, having been a prisoner of the French; he rules despotically and loses Spain's South American colonies in 1820. **Westphalia** Following the Battle of Leipzig, the Kingdom of Westphalia ceases to exist; Jerome Bonaparte flees.

1814
France Napoleon abdicates and is exiled to Elba; Louis XVIII (left), brother of beheaded Louis XVI, becomes king of France.

1814 **Lombardy** The Congress of Vienna combines Lombardy, ruled by the Habsburgs since the 16th century, with Venetia into the Kingdom of Lombardy, under the rule of the Habsburgs; the former Holy Roman Emperor, Franz I, becomes king. **Tuscany** Grand Duke Ferdinand is restored; Lucca unites with Tuscany. **Rome** Pope Pius VI is freed by allied forces and returns to the Vatican; the Congress of Vienna restores the Papal States to Rome. **Norway** Christian VIII of Denmark is elected regent of Norway; after trying to unite Norway with Sweden – Norwegian forces are defeated by Swedish Crown Prince Karl-Hans – he abdicates; Norway forms a union with Sweden and Charles XIII of Sweden is elected Karl II of Norway. **Hanover** The Treaty of Vienna raises Hanover to the status of a kingdom; George-William-Frederick, George III of Great Britain and Ireland, becomes the country's first king. **Liechtenstein**

The Vienna Congress confirms Liechtenstein's status as a sovereign state; Johann I Josef is restored as prince.

1815 **France** The hundred days war; Napoleon escapes from Elba and marches on Paris; at the Battle of Waterloo, Napoleon is defeated by Wellington and exiled to St Helena; Napoleon II, aged 4, becomes emperor of the French from 22 June until 7 July; Louis XVIII is restored to the French throne.

> ***"My business is to succeed, and I'm good at it. I create my Iliad by my actions, create it day by day."***

Napoleon Bonaparte

1815 **The United Kingdom of the Netherlands** formally unites Belgium and Holland. **Monaco** becomes a protectorate of the Kingdom of Sardinia under the Congress of Vienna; Honoré V becomes sovereign prince. **Portugal** Exiled in Brazil, Queen Maria I elevates Brazil to the status of a kingdom, and is proclaimed queen of the United Kingdom of Portugal, Brazil and the Algarves; on the eventual defeat of Napoleon, she and her family remain in Brazil. **Prussia** King Frederick William III is restored and, following the Napoleonic wars, Prussia becomes the dominant state in Germany. **Württemberg** joins the German Confederation. **Netherlands** Prince William of Orange becomes William I. **Luxembourg** is promoted to a Grand Duchy, ; William I, king of the Netherlands, from the House of Orange-Nassau, becomes grand duke. **Austria** The Austrian monarchy is restored, with Franz I as emperor. **Naples and Sicily** Ferdinand III is restored to the throne, for a third time, with the Austrian victory at the Battle of Tolentino. **Serbia** The Serbs revolt against Turkish rule; Milosh Obrenovich becomes prince of Serbia; he is the first king of the House of Obrenovich that will reign until 1903 (apart from 1842 until 1858). **Grand Duchy of Posen** The territory formerly known as Greater Poland becomes an autonomous province of the Kingdom of Prussia, under Hohenzollern rule; the kings of Prussia assume the title grand duke of Posen, the first being Frederick William III.

1816 **Portugal** João VI becomes king; he remains in Brazil. **Württemberg** William I becomes king; he abolishes serfdom. **Naples and Sicily (The Kingdom of the Two Sicilies)** are merged into the new Kingdom of the Two Sicilies; Ferdinand I, third son of King Charles III of Spain, becomes king.

1818 **Sweden and Norway** Charles XIII (Karl II of Norway) dies without issue; Jean-Baptiste Bernadotte, king of Sweden, also becomes king of Norway, as Karl III Johan.

1820 **Portugal** A peaceful revolution results in the proclamation of a constitutional government. **Bavaria** George IV becomes King George-Augustus-Frederick of Hanover, as well as king of Great Britain and Ireland.

1821 **France** Napoleon Bonaparte dies on St Helena. **Portugal** João VI returns to the country after spending 14 years in Brazil; he swears to support the constitutional government. **Greece** The Greek war of Independence against Turkish rule begins.

1823 **Spain** A Spanish revolution fails. **Portugal** João VI's younger son, Prince Miguel, leads an unsuccessful revolt against his father. **Rome** Cardinal Count Annibale Sermattei della Genga, a ferocious fundamentalist fanatic, is elected pope as Leo XII.

1824 **France** Charles X, Louis XVIII's brother, becomes the last Bourbon king of France in the only normal succession of French heads of state in the 19th century. **Portugal** Prince Miguel is banished by his father.

1825 **Bavaria** Ludwig I becomes king. **Russia** Emperor Alexander I dies of typhus on a journey to southern Russia for his wife's health; rumours persist that he has not actually died but has become a monk or a hermit; when his tomb is opened, in 1925, it is found to be empty; confusion reigns following Alexander's death; his son and heir, Constantine Pavlovich, has already secretly renounced his right to the throne, in 1822; the Decembrist uprising is brutally suppressed by Constantine Pavlovich's younger brother, who becomes the antireformist Emperor Nicholas I. **The Kingdom of the Two Sicilies** Francis I The Bourbon becomes king.

1826 **Portugal** João VI dies; his son, Pedro IV, who has declared Brazil independent from Portugal and himself emperor, becomes king; he is forced to abdicate and names his daughter Maria II, aged 7, as queen; Pedro's brother, Miguel, is named as regent, on the condition that he marries Maria.

1828 **Portugal** Miguel reneges on his promise to marry his niece, Maria II; he deposes her and proclaims himself king, abrogating the constitution; he begins a reign of terror.

1829 **Spain** Ferdinand VII, having had only two daughters, sets aside the Salic Law, the law of succession which gives preference to all males in a family, to allow his daughter Isabella to become queen; this leads, eventually, to civil war. **Rome** Cardinal Francesco Saverio Castiglioni is elected pope, as Pius VIII.

1830
United Kingdom William IV becomes king of Britain and Ireland as well as King William-Henry of Hanover.

1830 **France** The efforts of the French king, Charles X, to compensate nobles for losses in the French Revolution, lead to the July Revolution; Charles abdicates in favour of his grandson, Henri V, who is, disputedly, king of France for 7 days; Charles's son, the Dauphin

Louis-Antoine, is sometimes considered to have legally been the king of France, as Louis XIX, in the 20 minutes that passed between Charles X's formal signature of abdication and the dauphin's own signature, the shortest-reigning monarch on record; Louis-Philippe, Duc d'Orléans, great-great-great-great-grandson of Louis XIII, is elected to the vacant French throne as king of the French, as opposed to king of France; he is known as *le Roi-Citoyen* – the Citizen-King. **Belgium, Poland, Italy and Germany** all experience revolutions. **The Kingdom of the Two Sicilies** Ferdinand II becomes king. **Greece** gains independence from the Ottomans. **Montenegro** Petar II becomes prince-bishop; he transforms the country from a theocracy into a secular state.

1831 **Belgium** Leopold I, of the House of Saxe-Coburg-Gotha, the youngest son of Franz Frederick Anton, duke of Saxe-Coburg-Saalfeld, and Countess Augusta Reuss-Ebersdorf, becomes the first king of the Belgians, having refused the Greek throne; he was married to Princess Charlotte Augusta of Wales, the only legitimate child of the British prince-regent – later King George IV of the United Kingdom – who was heiress to the British throne until her early death in 1817. **Portugal** Pedro forces Miguel to abdicate, and Maria is restored to the throne. **Rome** Conservative Cardinal Bartolomeo Alberto Cappellari is elected pope as Gregory XVI.

THE HOUSE OF SAXE-COBURG-GOTHA

REIGN: 1762–1796

The House of Saxe-Coburg-Gotha was formed from two Saxon duchies – Saxe-Coburg and Saxe-Gotha – both held by the Wettin dynasty. Leopold I (1790–1865) was the first king of Belgium and also the founder of the Belgian line of the House of Saxe-Coburg-Gotha.

The name Saxe-Coburg-Gotha came to the British royal family in 1840 when Queen Victoria married Prince Albert, son of Ernst, duke of Saxe-Coburg and Gotha. Victoria, however, remained a member of the House of Hanover.

The only British monarch of the House of Saxe-Coburg-Gotha was King Edward VII, who reigned for nine years (1901–1910).

The German-sounding title was replaced by King George V during the First World War, changing the name to the House of Windsor. The name Saxe-Coburg-Gotha survived in other European monarchies, including the current Belgian royal family.

1832 **Greece** Otto I of the House of Wittelsbach, second son of Ludwig of Bavaria, is chosen as king of the Hellenes.

1833 **Spain** The 3-year-old Isabella II becomes queen.

1834 **Spain** The Pretender Don Carlos tries to take the Spanish throne, leading to the civil war known as the Carlist wars, until 1839.

1835 **Austrian Empire** The epileptic and mentally unstable Ferdinand becomes emperor. **Lombardy** Emperor Ferdinand I becomes king. **Greece** Aged only 20, Otto I takes personal control of the government.

1836 **Portugal** Maria II marries Prince Ferdinand of Saxe-Coburg and Gotha; he rules with her as co-monarch, as Ferdinand II; he is the first ruler from the House of Braganza-Wettin (Saxe-Coburg and Gotha). **Liechtenstein** Alois II becomes prince of Liechtenstein.

1837 **United Kingdom** Aged 18, Victoria, daughter of Edward, duke of Kent, fourth son of George III, becomes the last Hanover queen of Great Britain and Ireland. **Hanover** Due to the fact that women are not allowed to become queen in Hanover, Queen Victoria cannot also become queen of Hanover on the death of King William-Henry (William IV of Great Britain and Ireland); Hanover is separated from Great Britain and Ernest-Augustus, fifth son of George III, becomes king. **The Kingdom of the Two Sicilies** Ferdinand II violently suppresses rebels demanding a constitution.

1839 **Denmark** Christian VII's half-brother, Christian VIII, becomes king.

1840
United Kingdom Queen Victoria marries Prince Albert of Saxe-Coburg and Gotha.

1840 **Luxembourg** Grand Duke William abdicates; William II of the Netherlands becomes grand duke. **Grand Duchy of Posen** Frederick William IV, king of Prussia, becomes grand duke.

1841 **Monaco** Florestan I, second son of Prince Honoré IV, becomes sovereign prince; an actress in Paris's Théâtre de l'Ambigu-Comique, his wife, Maria Caroline Gibert de Lametz, holds the real power.

1844 **Sweden and Norway** Oscar I becomes king.

1846 **Rome** Liberal Cardinal Count Giovanni Maria Mastai-Ferretti is elected pope as Pius IX.

1848 **Europe** A year of revolution in Europe – revolutions in Milan, Naples, Venice and Rome, Berlin, Vienna, Prague and Budapest. **France** The unpopular and repressive Louis Philippe abdicates, and Napoleon Bonaparte's nephew, Louis Napoleon, becomes president. **Germany** The Frankfurt National Assembly meets to discuss the unification of Germany. **Bavaria** Ludwig I of Bavaria abdicates following a scandal caused by his relationship with the dancer Lola Montez; Maximilian II becomes king. **Austrian Empire** Emperor Ferdinand abdicates due to ill health; his nephew, Franz-Joseph, becomes emperor. **Lombardy** Holy Roman Emperor Franz-Joseph becomes king. **Rome** Pope Pius IX is forced to flee Rome in the face of rebellion and rioting. **Denmark** Frederick VII becomes an undistinguished king. **The Kingdom of the Two Sicilies** Following a series of rebellions, Ferdinand II is forced to grant a constitution. **Hungary** Austrian Emperor Franz-Joseph becomes apostolic king, a hereditary title borne by the king of Hungary.

1849 **Italy and Hungary** The revolutions in Italy and Hungary are crushed. **Grand Duchy of Posen** The Grand Duchy's autonomy is abolished; the territory is reduced to a province, although the Prussian kings up to Kaiser Wilhelm II in 1918 continue to hold the title of grand duke of Posen. **Russia** William III becomes grand duke.

1851 **Hanover** George V becomes the last king. **Montenegro** Prince Danilo II becomes ruler; he travels to Russia where Nicholas I endorses him as prince of Montenegro instead of prince-bishop; he is the first ruler of the country since 1516 not to be a vladika (prince-bishop); Montenegro becomes a lay-principality instead of a bishopric-principality.

1852 **France** Napoleon III stages a coup and declares the Second Empire, with himself as emperor.

1853 **Portugal** On the death of Maria II, the popular, modernising Pedro V becomes king, aged 15; his father, King Consort Ferdinand II, rules as regent until his majority.

1854 **Spain** Liberal revolution overthrows the government.

1855
Russia Emperor Nicholas I dies; many claim that he has poisoned himself following the crushing defeat of his army at the Battle of Eupatoria, during the Crimean War; Alexander II becomes emperor.

1856 **Monaco** Florestan I dies, leaving a principality divided and poor; Charles III becomes sovereign prince; he founds the casino in Monte Carlo.

1858 **Liechtenstein** Johann II the Good becomes prince of Liechtenstein; he will make the principality a constitutional monarchy, cool its relationship with its traditional ally, Austria-Hungary, and forge closer relations with Switzerland, particularly after the First World War.

1859 **Lombardy** The Lombardy part of the kingdom is annexed to the new Italian state by the Treaty of Zurich, signed after the Second Italian War of Independence. **Sweden and Norway** Oscar I's son becomes Charles XV of Sweden and Karl IV of Norway; although none of Charles's direct descendants have become king of Sweden, his descendants are, or have been, on the thrones of Denmark, Luxembourg, Greece, Belgium and Norway. **The Kingdom of the Two Sicilies** Ferdinand II dies from a wound he received in an assassination attempt three years previously; Francis II becomes king. **Romania** The Ottoman vassal states of Wallachia and Moldavia are united under Moldavian-born politician Alexandru Ioan Cuza, as prince of Romania or domnitor.

1860 **Italy** Parma, Modena, Tuscany and Romagna unite with Piedmont; the Italian parliament meets in Turin; Garibaldi takes southern Italy; most of Italy is unified. **Montenegro** As he boards a ship at the port of Kotor, Prince Danilo II is assassinated by an Austrian agent in protest at brutal mistreatment of the Montenegrin Bjelopavlići tribe by Danilo's troops; he dies without achieving his ambition of turning Montenegro into a kingdom; Nikola I Mirkov Petrović-Njegoš, elder brother of Danilo II, becomes prince.

1861 **United Kingdom** Prince Albert, husband of Queen Victoria, dies. **Monaco** In the Franco-Monegasque Treaty, France recognizes Monaco's status as an independent principality. **Portugal** Pedro V, his brother Ferdinand, and many other members of the royal family die in a cholera epidemic; Pedro dies without issue; his younger brother, Luis I, becomes king. **The Kingdom of the Two Sicilies** Garibaldi deposes Francis I, and the Kingdom of the Two Sicilies is merged into the fledgling Kingdom of Italy. **Italy** Vittorio-Emanuele II, of the House of Savoy, king of Piedmont, Savoy and Sardinia, becomes the first king of a united Italy (all except Rome and Venice); his titles are: Vittorio-Emanuele II, by the Grace of God; king of Italy, Sardinia, Cyprus, Jerusalem and Armenia; duke of Savoy; count of Maurienne; marquis (of the Holy Roman Empire) in Italy; prince of Piedmont, Carignano, Oneglia, Poirino and Trino; prince and perpetual vicar of the Holy Roman Empire; prince of Carmagnola, Montmellian with Arbin and Francin; prince bailiff of the duchy of Aosta, prince of Chieri, Dronero, Crescentino, Riva di Chieri e Banna, Busca, Bene and Brà; duke of Genoa, Montferrat and Aosta; duke of Chablais and Genevois; duke of Piacenza; marquis of Saluzzo (Saluces), Ivrea, Susa, del Maro, Oristano, Cesana, Savona, Tarantasia, Borgomanero e Cureggio, Caselle, Rivoli, Pianezza, Govone, Salussola, Racconigi con Tegerone, Migliabruna e Motturone, Cavallermaggiore, Marene, Modane e Lanslebourg, Livorno Ferraris, Santhià Agliè, Centallo e Demonte, Desana, Ghemme and Vigone; count of Barge, Villafranca, Ginevra, Nizza, Tenda, Romont, Asti, Alessandria, del Goceano, Novara, Tortona, Bobbio, Soissons, Sant'Antioco, Pollenzo, Roccabruna, Tricerro, Bairo, Ozegna and delle Apertole; baron of Vaud e del Faucigni; lord of Vercelli, Pinerolo, della Lomellina, della Valle Sesia and del marchesato di Ceva; overlord of Monaco and Roccabruna and 11/12th of Menton; noble patrician of Venice and patrician of Ferrara. **Russia** Tsar Alexander II abolishes serfdom and becomes known as 'the Liberator'.

1862 **Württemberg** William I dies, the oldest living sovereign of his day, at 83; Charles becomes king. **Greece** Faced with a revolution, King Otto flees, going into exile in his native Bavaria; the Greek National Assembly elects 17-year-old Danish Prince George, son of Christian IX of Denmark, as King George I; he is brother-in-law to Edward Albert, prince of Wales.

1863 **Denmark** Christian IX becomes king; he has married the king of Sweden's daughter; his son, George, is king of Greece, his daughter Alexandra marries King Edward VII, his daughter Dagmar marries the tsar of Russia, his daughter Tyra marries the duke of Cumberland, his grandson becomes Haakon VII of Norway. **Poland** The Poles rebel, unsuccessfully, against Russian rule.

1864 **Bavaria** The eccentric Ludwig II becomes king of Bavaria; he forges closer links with Prussia.

1865 **Belgium** Leopold II becomes king of the Belgians; the foundation of the Congo Free State in Africa brings him an immense fortune gained through cruelty and exploitation.

1866 **Germany** During the Austro-Prussian War, Hanover is annexed by Prussia and King George V goes into exile in Paris. **Romania** Following economic difficulties and a scandal involving his mistress, domnitor or prince of Romania, Alexander Ioan Cuza, is forced to abdicate and go into exile; Prince Karl of Hohenzollern-Sigmaringen is elected domnitor as Carol I; he is the first ruler from the House of Hohenzollern-Sigmaringen that will rule the country until 1947.

1867 **Austria-Hungary** To satisfy Hungarian dissatisfaction with Austrian rule, the Austro-Hungarian Compromise is introduced, whereby the dual monarchy of the Austro-Hungarian Empire is formed, replacing the Austrian Empire; the compromise has to be renegotiated every 10 years; Emperor Franz Josef also becomes king of Hungary.

1868 **Spain** Queen Isabella is deposed by a revolution; a two-year interregnum follows.

1869 **Württemberg** is absorbed by the German Empire.

1870 **France** The Franco-Prussian War; the Prussians besiege Paris; Napoleon III is deposed and the Third Republic is established in France (lasting until 1940); Napoleon III has the distinction of having been both the first titular president and the last monarch of France.

BATTLE AT SAINT-PRIVAT
18 AUGUST 1870

A short, bloody battle took place at the cemetery of Saint-Privat near Metz, on 18 August 1870. The conflict was part of the ongoing Franco-Prussian War, between Marshal Bazaine's French army and the first and second corps of the Prussian army. Despite both armies using advanced weapons, their tactics were outdated and losses were high. Neither side could claim a total victory and yet it was a precursor of the world war to come. It led to the downfall of an empire and the reconfiguration of a continent.

1870 **Spain** Amadeo, second son of Vittorio Emanuele II of Italy, is elected king of Spain; given the hereditary title of duke of Aosta, following his birth, he is the founder of the Aosta branch of Italy's royal

House of Savoy, which is junior in agnatic descent to the branch descended from King Umberto I that reigned until 1946, but senior to the branch of the dukes of Genoa. **Rome** The Papal States are annexed by the new Kingdom of Italy; Pope Pius IX rejects an offer of the use of the Vatican without sovereign power and calls himself a 'prisoner in the Vatican'; he is the last pope to hold temporal power; the infallibility of the pope is proclaimed by the Roman Catholic Church.

1871 **France** Paris surrenders and the Paris Commune is set up in opposition to the government and to the peace terms; Alsace-Lorraine is ceded to Germany. **Germany** The unification of Germany as the semi-constitutional monarchy of the German Empire; Prussian King William I becomes emperor.

1872 **Sweden and Norway** Oscar II becomes king.

1873 **Spain** Unable to rule without popular support, King Amadeo abdicates; a republic is declared.

1874 **Spain** After five presidents, the House of Bourbon is restored for the second time; Alfonso XII, Queen Isabella's son, becomes king; it is thought his father is not the king consort, but either of two of Isabella's lovers, Enrique Puigmoltó y Mayans, captain of the Royal Guard, or General Francisco Serrano.

1876 **United Kingdom** Queen Victoria is proclaimed empress of India. **Romania** Carol I, prince of Romania, personally leads his troops in the Russo-Turkish War.

1878 **Rome** Pope Pius IX dies following the longest pontificate in papal history, 32 years; Cardinal Gioacchino Vincenzo Raffaele Luigi Pecci is elected pope as Leo XIII, the 256th pope of the Catholic Church; he is known as the 'Pope of the Working Man' due to his championing of Catholic Social Teaching. **Italy** The deeply conservative Umberto I becomes king of Italy. **Bulgaria** The Treaty of Berlin creates the Principality of Bulgaria as a vassal state of the Ottoman Empire; it is comprised of the regions of Moesia, Thrace and Macedonia; the Prussian Alexander Joseph, second son of Alexander of Hesse of the House of Battenberg, is unanimously elected knyaz, or prince, as Alexander I, by the General National Assembly. **Romania** gains independence from the Ottoman Empire.

1880 **Romania** Heir to the Romanian throne, Crown Prince Leopold, elder brother of Carol I, renounces his right of succession in favour of his son William.

1881 **Romania** Following its independence, the Principality of Romania becomes a sovereign kingdom; Carol I is crowned its first king. **Bulgaria** Prince Alexander assumes absolute power. **Russia** Tsar Alexander II is assassinated when a bomb is thrown at him by Russian-Polish revolutionary Ignacy Hryniewiecki, in St Petersberg: his second son Alexander III, who has been openly critical of his father's reforms, takes the throne.

1883 **Bulgaria** Prince Alexander's absolute monarchy experiment fails and he restores the constitution.

1885 **Spain** Alfonso XII dies without an heir; his pregnant wife, Maria Christina, becomes a 'child-bearing regent' for six months.

1886 **Spain** Maria Christina gives birth to Alfonso XIII; he is the first child to be born already a king since the short-lived John I of France, in 1316. **Bavaria** Ludwig II drowns himself five days after abdicating, due to insanity; his mentally unbalanced brother, Otto, becomes king; his uncle, Prince Luitpold, acts as regent. **Austria-Hungary** Crown Prince Rudolf of Austria and his mistress, Baroness Mary

Vetsara, die in an apparent suicide pact at Mayerling. **Bulgaria** Discontented army officers seize Prince Alexander and force him to abdicate; he is restored by a counter-coup, but his position is untenable and he resigns the throne.

1887 **Bulgaria** Ferdinand of Saxe-Coburg, son of Prince August of Saxe-Coburg-Kohary and his wife Clémentine of Orléans, daughter of King Louis Philippe I of the French, is elected prince of Bulgaria; it becomes the leading Balkan state; he is also grand-nephew of Leopold I, first king of the Belgians, nephew of Ferdinand II of Portugal and a first cousin of Queen Victoria of Britain; he is also related to the medieval tsars of Bulgaria.

1888 **Germany** William II becomes kaiser (emperor). **Romania** The heir to the throne, Crown Prince William, surrenders his claim in favour of his son, Prince Ferdinand.

1889 **Monaco** Albert I becomes sovereign prince. **Portugal** Carlos I becomes king.

1890 **Luxembourg** Grand Duke William III dies, but his sons have also all died and, under the 1783 Nassau Family Pact, territories of the Nassau family in the Holy Roman Empire at the time of the Pact (Luxembourg and Nassau) are bound to use Salic Law, which forbids inheritance by the female line; his daughter Wilhelmina cannot inherit and 73-year-old Adolphe, the dispossessed duke of Nassau and head of the House of Nassau-Weilburg, becomes grand duke.

1891 **Portugal** The Portuguese Republican Revolution breaks out. **Württemberg** William II becomes king.

1894 **Russia** In spite of several assassination attempts, Alexander III dies of natural causes; Nicholas II, the last tsar of Russia, takes the throne.

1897 **United Kingdom** Queen Victoria celebrates her Diamond Jubilee.

1898 **Austria-Hungary** Empress Elisabeth, consort of Franz Joseph I, is assassinated by Italian anarchist Luigi Lucheni; 'I wanted to kill a royal,' he said. 'It did not matter which one.'

1900 **Italy** Umberto I is assassinated by the anarchist Gaetano Bresci, in revenge for the Bava-Beccaris massacre when hundreds of striking workers were killed by the army; Vittorio Emanuele III becomes king. **Montenegro** Nikola I begins to style himself 'Royal Highness'.

1901
United Kingdom Queen Victoria dies, after reigning for 64 years; she is succeeded by Edward VII who is almost 60, first king of the House of Saxe-Coburg and Gotha.

“Great events make me quiet and calm; it is only trifles that irritate my nerves.”

Queen Victoria

1901 **France** Church and state begin to separate. **Russia** The Russian Social Revolutionary Party (Bolsheviks) is founded.

1903 **Serbia** King Alexander is assassinated; the House of Karađorđević (the descendants of the revolutionary leader Đorđe Petrović) assumes power under Peter I. **Rome** Cardinal Giuseppe Melchiorre Sarto Pius X is elected pope.

1905 **Luxembourg** William IV becomes grand duke. **Germany** Kaiser William II visits Tangier and provokes a crisis with France. **Sweden and Norway** After some months of tension, the union between Sweden and Norway is dissolved and Sweden recognizes Norway as an independent constitutional monarchy; Oscar II renounces his and his family's claim to the Norwegian throne, and prince Karl of Denmark, son of future King Frederick VIII of Denmark, is elected king of Norway as Haakon VII; a referendum, called for by Karl, confirms the monarchy. **Montenegro** Nikola I gives his country its first constitution.

1906 **Denmark** Frederick VIII becomes king; Iceland gains independence from Denmark during his reign.

1907 **Luxembourg** Following the death of his uncle, the only other legitimate male in the House of Nassau Weilburg, the grand duke declares his eldest daughter Marie-Adélaïde as 'Heir Apparent to the Grand Duchy', overturning the Salic Law that has previously applied. **Sweden** Gustav V becomes king; he maintains Sweden's neutrality during the two world wars.

1908 **Portugal** Carlos I is assassinated by two Republicans in Lisbon, while travelling in an open carriage with the royal family, the first Portuguese king to die violently since Sebastião I in 1578; the heir to the throne, Luís Filipe, is also wounded, dying 20 minutes later; Prince Manuel, wounded in the arm in the incident, is declared king as Manuel II; he will be the last king of Portugal. **Austria-Hungary** Austria annexes Bosnia and Herzegovina. **Bulgaria** declares independence from Turkey; Prince Ferdinand I becomes tsar. **Greece** Crete unifies with Greece.

1909 **Belgium** Albert I becomes king of the Belgians.

1910 **United Kingdom** George V, second son of Edward VII, becomes king. **Portugal** Revolution breaks out; following three days of street fighting, Manuel II flees on the royal yacht to British-ruled Gibraltar; he lives in exile in Britain; Portugal becomes a republic. **Montenegro** In celebration of his jubilee, Prince Nikola I assumes the title of king of Montenegro.

1911 **Portugal** The monarchy is abolished and a republic is declared.

1912 **Luxembourg** Marie-Adélaïde becomes the first grand duchess; she is also the first sovereign of Luxembourg, since 1296, to have been born within the country. **Denmark** Christian X becomes a much-loved king; in 1943 he will be imprisoned by the Nazis.

1913 **Bavaria** Ludwig III becomes the last king of Bavaria when he deposes his cousin Otto. **Greece** King George I is assassinated by Alexandros Schinas, variously described as a socialist and an alcoholic vagrant; Constantine I becomes king and leads Greece to victory in the Balkan wars. **Albania** After British traveller, diplomat and MP, Aubrey Herbert, turns down the crown, William of Wied, from Rhineland-Palatinate in Germany, becomes sovereign of the principality of Albania.

1914 The First World War; **Austria-Hungary** Archduke Franz Ferdinand, heir to the Austrian throne, is assassinated by Bosnian student Gavrilo Princip, triggering the outbreak of the First World War. **Rome** Cardinal Giacomo Della Chiesa is elected pope as Benedict XV. **Albania** Prince William, sovereign only from March to September, goes into exile due to lack of support.

1916 **Romania** Romania's first king, Carol I, dies childless, after 48 years on the throne; his great-nephew, King Ferdinand I, married to British Princess Marie of Edinburgh, takes the throne; the Romanian Constitution specifically bars the heir to the throne from being married to a woman of Romanian birth; when Ferdinand enters the First World War on the side of the Triple Entente, German Kaiser Wilhelm has his name erased from the Hohenzollern House register.

1917 **United Kingdom** Due to the First World War, George V changes the royal family name from the German Saxe-Coburg and Gotha to the more British-sounding 'Windsor'. **Montenegro** The royal family flees to Italy. **Greece** Constantine I is forced to abdicate in favour of his second son, Alexander I, due to his lack of sympathy for the Allies in the First World War. **Russia** Tsar Nicholas II's reign ends in the October Revolution, when the Bolsheviks, led by Vladimir Lenin, seize power and declare a republic; the tsar and his family are imprisoned; he is forced to abdicate, initially in favour of his 12-year-old son, Alexei, but because of Alexei's haemophilia, he changes it to his brother Mikhail; Mikhail defers his acceptance and never actually rules.

1918 **Germany** Revolution breaks out; William II abdicates and goes into exile in Holland, where he will live as a private citizen until his death in 1941; a republic is declared. **Bavaria** Ludwig III is the first of the monarchs in the German Empire to be deposed; it marks the end of 738 years of Wittelsbacher rule in Bavaria. **Württemberg** William II is deposed by a revolution that leads to a republic being declared. **Austria-Hungary** Archduke Karl I steps down but never abdicates. **Serbia, Croatia and Slovenia** Peter I, son of Alexander, prince of Serbia, emerges from a 60-year exile, to be elected the first king of the Serbs, Croats and Slovenes; due to Peter's ill health, Crown Prince Alexander acts as regent. **Montenegro** His kingdom having been united with the other south Slav lands, King Nikola I goes into exile in France. **Romania** Following his support for the Triple Entente in the First World War, Ferdinand I's country is greatly enlarged with the union of Bessarabia, Bukovina and Transylvania. **Bulgaria** Following a heavy defeat by the Allies in Greece, Tsar Ferdinand I abdicates in order to save the Bulgarian throne; his son, Boris III, becomes tsar and is a target of several assassination attempts. **Russia** On the night of 17 July, Tsar Nicholas and his family are executed by the Bolsheviks.

THE STRUGGLE TO SURVIVE

1919–present day

1919 **Luxembourg** Grand Duchess Marie-Adélaïde abdicates without marrying and enters a convent following criticism of her cordial relationship with German occupiers during the First World War; her younger sister, Charlotte, becomes Grand Duchess; a referendum votes 77.8% in favour of retaining a grand ducal monarchy with Charlotte as head of state; she marries Felix of Bourbon, prince of Parma, creating the House of Nassau-Weilburg and Bourbon-Parma. **Germany** adopts the Weimar Constitution. **Austria-Hungary** The Treaty of St Germain ends the Habsburg monarchy, and Czechoslovakia, Poland, Yugoslavia and Hungary gain independence.

1920 **Greece** Alexander I dies after being bitten by his two pet monkeys; following a plebiscite in which he won 99% of the vote, Constantine I is reinstated as king.

ALEXANDER I
REIGN: 1917–1920

Alexander I was born on 1 August 1893 at Tatoi near Athens. He was the second son of Constantine I and Sophie of Prussia.

During the First World War Constantine was insistent that Greece remained neutral, while the prime minister, Eleftherios Venizelos, was determined to go to war. When troops entered Greece, Constantine and his first born son George were forced into exile. The young Alexander took the throne, although he had very little say in the matters of his country as he was overpowered by the prime minister.

Alexander made relations with Venizelos worse by eloping with Aspasia Manos, who the prime minister considered to be a commoner. The wedding was finally legalised but they were not allowed to travel together or attend official functions together.

Following the Treaty of Sèvres in 1920, Greece increased its territories making Alexander the ruler of a much larger kingdom. Alexander died prematurely at the age of 27. He was taking a walk through the royal gardens when his pet dog was attacked by two monkeys. He tried to fight the monkeys off with a stick but received a couple of bites which became infected. He died from a severe reaction to the infection on 25 October 1920. Alexander had one daughter, Princess Alexandra, who was born after his death, in 1921.

1921 **Bavaria** Former King Ludwig II dies in exile; Crown Prince Rupprecht becomes titular heir to the throne and head of the Wittelsbach family; he is also the Jacobite heir to the thrones of England, Scotland, Ireland and France, through his mother, Archduchess Maria Theresia of Austria-Este, although he never lays claim to these titles. **Liechtenstein** Prince Aloys, heir to the principality, renounces his right of succession in favour of his son, Franz Josef II, who becomes heir. **Serbia, Croatia and Slovenia**

Alexander I becomes king; his dictatorial style makes him unpopular. **Montenegro** Former King Nikola I dies; he has continued to claim the throne of his country since he began his exile; Crown Prince Danilo Aleksandar Petrović-Njegoš becomes claimant to the Montenegrin throne, leading an unrecognized government in exile; for unknown reasons, he abdicates after only six days, in favour of his nephew Prince Michael Petrović-Njegoš.

1922 **Monaco** Louis II becomes sovereign prince; during his reign, Monaco football club is founded and the first Monaco Grand Prix takes place. **Rome** Cardinal Achille Ambrogio Damiano Ratti is elected pope as Pius XI. **Romania** Ferdinand I is crowned king of his greatly enlarged nation in a lavish ceremony.

1922
Greece Constantine I abdicates again, after disastrous losses in the Greco-Turkish War; his eldest son, a great-grandson of Britain's Queen Victoria, becomes George II.

1923 **Spain** General Primo de Rivera becomes dictator, until 1930. **Greece** George II goes into exile in his wife's native Romania, following a coup.

1924 **Greece** George II is officially deposed and stripped of his Greek nationality. **Russia** After a gap of six years, Grand Duke Cyril Vladimirovich, grandson of Tsar Alexander III and heir to the Russian throne, becomes head of the imperial family, 'Titular Emperor and Autocrat of all the Russias'; he spends his exile in France.

1925 **Romania** Following a scandal, Crown Prince Carol renounces his right of succession to the Romanian throne in favour of his son Michael.

1927 **Romania** Ferdinand I's grandson, a great-great-grandson of Britain's Queen Victoria, becomes king as Michael I, aged 6; a regency acts on his behalf.

1928 **Albania** Zog (Ahmed Bey Zogu), former president, becomes king.

1929 **Rome** The State of the Vatican City, a landlocked sovereign city-state ruled by the pope, is created. **Liechtenstein** Johann II the Good dies; his reign of 70 years and 3 months is the longest in European royal history; he has never married and dies without issue; his brother, Franz I, becomes prince of Liechtenstein. **Serbia, Croatia and Slovenia** King Alexander abolishes the constitution, prorogues parliament and introduces a personal dictatorship; he changes the name of the country to the Kingdom of Yugoslavia. **Montenegro** The claimant to the Montenegrin throne, Michael, renounces his dynasty's claim and swears allegiance to the Kingdom of Serbs, Croats and Slovenes; he is rewarded by the king with a pension from the Civil List.

VATICAN CITY
BUILT: 1929

The Vatican City is the smallest independent state in the world. It occupies an area of 44 hectares (109 acres), the borders of which are represented by its walls and its travertine (or rock) curved pavements that join the two wings of the colonnades in St Peter's Square.

Even before the arrival of Christianity, this previously uninhabited tract of land on the opposite side of the Tiber from the city of Rome (*ager vaticanus*), had always been considered sacred. The first person to make use of the land was Agrippina the Elder (14 BC–AD 33). She had the land drained and built her gardens there in the early 1st century AD.

The Vatican City State was founded after the signing of the Lateran Pacts between the Holy See and Italy on 11 February 1929, which granted Roman Catholicism special status in Italy. The Vatican City is unique in that the head of the Catholic Church, or pope, takes complete power in place of a monarchy. He exercises judicial power of the Vatican City, an entity which is completely separate from the Holy See. The government of the city also has a unique structure. Although the pope is the sovereign of the state, legislative authority is vested in the Pontifical Commission – a body of cardinals appointed by the pope for a period of five years. Executive power is given to the president of that commission, who in turn is assisted by the general secretary and deputy general secretary. The pope is currently the only absolute monarch in the whole of Europe.

1930 **Romania** King Michael I's father, Carol II, returns suddenly; dissatisfaction with the regency results in Carol being proclaimed king as Carol II.

1931 **United Kingdom** The Statute of Westminster makes dominions of the British Empire self-governing. **Spain** The Second Spanish

Republic is declared; King Alfonso XIII leaves the country but refuses to abdicate. **Albania** During an assassination attempt, King Zog opens fire on his assailants; it is the only occasion in modern history when a head of state has returned fire on potential assassins.

1932 **Portugal** Former King Manuel II dies suddenly in exile in Twickenham, in England; some suspicion lingers due to the arrest the previous night of a prominent member of the Portuguese republican terrorist group, the Carbonária, in the grounds of his residence; Manuel dies without issue; he has declared his cousin from a previously rival branch of the family, Duarte Nuno, duke of Braganza, as the heir to his throne.

> ***"I rule a nation, not a road."***

Albert I of Belgium

1934 **Belgium** King Albert I of the Belgians dies in a mountaineering accident; Leopold III becomes king.

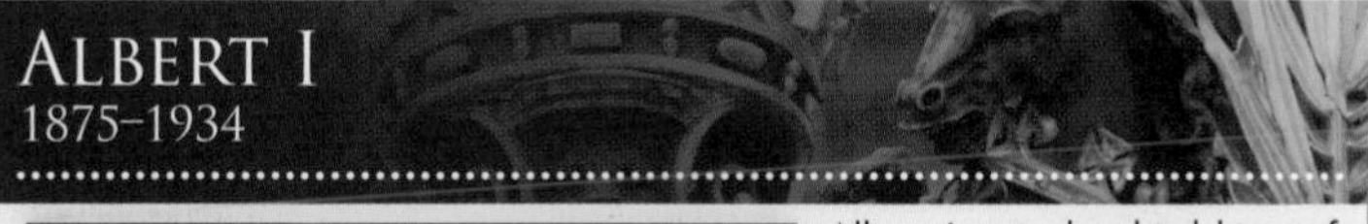

ALBERT I
1875–1934

Albert I was the third king of Belgium. He was the younger son of Prince Philippe, the count of Flanders, and came to the throne on 17 December 1909. At the onset of First World War, Albert resisted the German advance and managed to hold them off long enough for Britain and France to prepare themselves for the Battle of Marne (6–9 September 1914).

He fought on the front line and led his army through the Siege of Antwerp and the Battle of the Ysar. He returned to his home country a war hero.

Albert I tragically died in a climbing accident at the Marche-les-Dames in the Ardennes region of Belgium. He is buried in the royal vault at the Church of Our Lady in Laeken Cemetery, Brussels. Albert's death was mourned universally and he was succeeded by his son Leopold III.

1934 **Yugoslavia** The deeply unpopular Alexander I is assassinated on a state visit to France by a gunman, Vlado Chernozemski, on behalf of the Internal Macedonian Revolutionary Organization; it is the first assassination to be caught on film; Peter II becomes king, aged 11. **Bulgaria** A coup by the Zveno military and political organization and the Military Union, with the help of the Bulgarian army, establishes a dictatorship, abolishing political parties; Boris II is reduced to the status of puppet king.

1935 **Greece** A plebiscite shows 95% in favour of the restoration of the monarchy; George II is restored to the throne. **Bulgaria** Boris II stages a counter-coup and regains control of the country, introducing a form of parliamentary rule.

1936
United Kingdom Edward VIII becomes king, although never crowned; he abdicates to marry American double divorcee Wallis Simpson; his brother, George VI, becomes king.

1936 **Spain** The Spanish Civil War begins (until 1939).

1938 **Liechtenstein** Franz I abdicates, citing old age – he is 85 – as the reason he names the son of a cousin, Franz Josef, as regent; many believe that he has abdicated to avoid being on the throne when Germany invades; Franz Josef II becomes prince of Liechtenstein; he is the first prince of Liechtenstein to actually live in the principality. **Russia** On the death of his father, Grand Duke Cyril Vladimirovich claims the role of head of the imperial family, Titular Emperor and Autocrat of all the Russias, living in Madrid and France.

1939 **Rome** Cardinal Eugenio Maria Giuseppe Giovanni Pacelli is elected pope as Pius XIII. **Albania** Vittorio Emanuele III becomes king of Albania when Italy invades; King Zog spends the remainder of his life in exile. **Germany** The Second World War is declared after Germany invades Poland.

1940 **Romania** King Carol II is forced to abdicate by a pro-German government, after surrendering parts of his kingdom to foreign rule due to pressure from Hungary, Bulgaria, Italy and Germany; he goes into exile in Portugal in a train laden with royal treasure – paintings, jewels and other valuables; he goes on to live a life of extravagant luxury; his son, 18-year-old former king, Michael, is restored to the throne and crowned king again.

1941 **Spain** The former king, Alfonso, dies in Rome. **Montenegro** Prince Michael, former claimant to the throne, and his wife are arrested by the Germans and offered the throne of a new, independent Kingdom of Montenegro, but under the control and protection of the Axis forces; he rejects the offer and remains imprisoned until his release is secured in 1943 by his aunt, the queen of Italy; in France, he is rearrested by the Germans and sent to a concentration camp in eastern Germany, where his son, Prince Nicholas, is born a year later. **Greece** The Germans invade and George II flees to Egypt and then Britain.

1942 **Portugal** Duarte Nuno, duke of Braganza, claimant to the Portuguese throne, marries Princess Maria Francisca of Orleans-Braganza, princess of Brazil, uniting the two rival lines of the Portuguese royal family.

1943 **Bulgaria** Tsar Boris III dies, possibly poisoned by German agents or communists; he is replaced by his 6-year-old son, Simeon, under a council of regents.

1944 **Monaco** Hereditary Princess Charlotte cedes her succession rights to her son, Rainier, who becomes heir to the throne as hereditary prince. **Bavaria** While he is in Italy, the family of Crown Prince Rupprecht are captured by the Nazis and imprisoned in the Sachsenhausen and Dachau concentration camps, before being liberated by the Allies.

1945 **Yugoslavia** Peter II is exiled when Marshal Tito comes to power and abolishes the monarchy; he moves to the United States.

MARSHAL TITO
1892–1980

The Yugoslav statesman Marshal Tito became president of Yugoslavia in 1953. He directed the rebuilding of his country which was devastated in the Second World War and helped to unite his people until his death in 1980.

Tito was born Josip Broz on 25 May 1892, the son of an impoverished farmer. Tito himself had to work on the farm from the tender age of seven, but through determination built himself up to be a leader. Yugoslavia was left badly scarred at the end of the Second World War and it was during this devastation that Marshal Tito emerged as a leader. With wisdom he led Yugoslavia to peace and prosperity, lifting himself from his meagre background to a pinnacle of political power. He remained president of Yugoslavia for 35 years in succession and, despite often having barrels pointed at him from all directions, he still managed to transform his country into a Socialist nation.

1946 **Belgium** King Leopold III of the Belgians is exonerated of treason during the Second World War. **Italy** Having supported the fascist dictator Mussolini, until his fall, Vittorio Emanuele III retires from public life; Umberto II replaces him for a month before a referendum shows the Italian people favour a republic; Umberto and his descendants are barred from Italy forever, bringing an end to the 980-year reign of the House of Savoy in various Italian duchies and kingdoms. **Hungary** The Republic of Hungary is founded. **Bulgaria**

The communists seize control of Bulgaria and send King Simeon into exile in Egypt. **Montenegro** Prince Michael and his family are released from their incarceration in concentration camps and live in France. **Greece** A referendum in Greece votes, once again, in favour of restoring the monarchy; George II returns to the throne for a third time.

> ***"Any movement in history which attempts to perpetuate itself, becomes reactionary."***
>
> Marshal Tito

1947 **Sweden** Heir to the throne Prince Gustav Adolf dies in a plane crash near Copenhagen; his son, Prince Carl Gustav, becomes heir. **Denmark** Frederick IX becomes king; he changes the law to allow female succession. **Romania** King Michael I is forced to abdicate by his communist government, the last monarch behind the Iron Curtain to lose his throne; the government announces the abolition of the monarchy and its replacement by a People's Republic; Michael I leaves Romania, as did his father, with a number of valuable paintings; settling in Switzerland, he later becomes a commercial pilot and works for an aircraft equipment company. **Greece** George II dies; his younger brother, Paul, becomes king.

1948 **United Kingdom** Prince Charles, heir apparent to the British throne, is born.

1949

Monaco Prince Rainier, a descendant, through his mother Lady Mary Victoria Hamilton, of King James IV of Scotland, becomes sovereign prince; he reforms the country's constitution and expands its economy beyond its traditional gambling base.

1950 **United Kingdom** Princess Anne, only daughter of Queen Elizabeth, is born. **Belgium** Leopold III, having been 'held prisoner' by the Germans during the Second World War, wins a narrow majority in a referendum and remains on the throne. **Sweden** Gustav VI Adolf becomes king at the age of 67; he is the last Swedish monarch to possess any real constitutional power.

1951 **Belgium** Riots follow Leopold III's return to Brussels; he abdicates in favour of his son, Baudouin.

1952 **United Kingdom** Elizabeth II becomes queen; her husband, the ex-Prince Philip of Greece, becomes consort and is titled duke of Edinburgh. **Spain** Xavier, duke of Parma and Piacenza, head of the ducal House of Bourbon-Parma, publicly lays claim to the Spanish throne as Javier I, but is ignored by dictator Francisco Franco.

1953 **Romania** Former King Carol II dies in Portugal.

1955 **Bavaria** Crown Prince Rupprecht dies and is given a state funeral in Munich; Duke Albrecht becomes titular king of Bavaria.

1956 **Monaco** Prince Rainier III marries American Oscar-winning actress Grace Kelly; they have three children – Princess Caroline, Prince Albert and Princess Stephanie.

1957 **Norway** The much-loved Haakon VII dies, having reigned for 52 years; Olav V becomes king, reigning as the 'People's King'.

1958 **United Kingdom** Prince Charles is given the traditional heir to the throne's title of prince of Wales. **Rome** Cardinal Angelo Giuseppe Roncalli is elected pope as John XXIII; he becomes the first pope to leave Vatican territory since 1870.

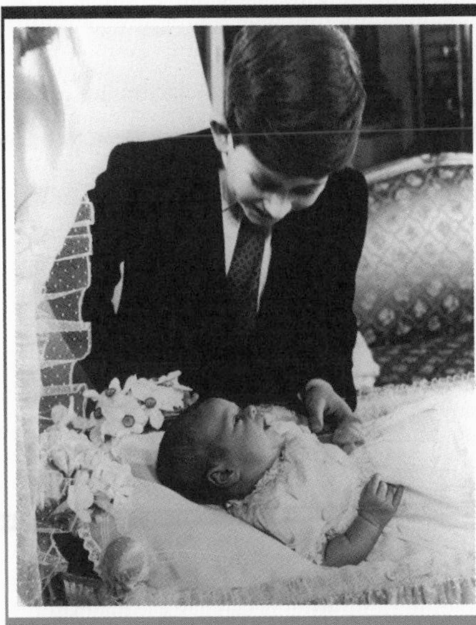

1960
United Kingdom Prince Andrew, duke of York, is born; he is fourth in line of succession to the throne. Here, Prince Charles can be seen admiring his new brother.

1961 **Albania** King Zog dies in exile in France; his son is declared King Leka I of the Albanians by Albanian exiles.

1963 **Rome** Cardinal Giovanni Battista Enrico Antonio Maria Montini is elected pope as Paul VI.

1964 **United Kingdom** Prince Edward, earl of Wessex, Queen Elizabeth's youngest child, is born. He is seventh in line of succession to the throne. **Luxembourg** Grand Duchess Charlotte abdicates in favour of her son, Prince Jean, who has been regent for three years; Prince Henri becomes heir apparent. **Greece** Constantine II becomes king.

1967 **Greece** A military junta abolishes the monarchy; Constantine II goes into exile.

1968 **Spain** Philip, heir to the throne, is born. **Denmark** Crown Prince Frederick is born.

1970 **Yugoslavia** Titular King Peter II dies in Denver; his son, Aleksandar Karađorđević, becomes crown prince of Yugoslavia, later becoming claimant only to the throne of Serbia on the break-up of his former country.

1972 **Denmark** Margarethe II becomes the first queen of Denmark; she is an accomplished painter under the pseudonym Ingahild Grathmer.

1973 **Sweden** On the death of his grandfather, Gustav VI Adolf, Carl XVI Gustav becomes king. **Norway** Haakon, crown prince of Norway, is born. **Greece** is declared a republic.

1974 **Greece** In a plebiscite, over two-thirds vote in favour of the abolition of the monarchy.

1975 **Spain** Dictator General Francisco Franco dies; King Juan Carlos I, grandson of Alfonso XIII, becomes king; the monarchy is restored after 44 years of dictatorship.

1976 **Portugal** Pretender to the throne Duarte Nuno, duke of Braganza, dies; his son, Duarte Pio, becomes claimant to the throne and duke of Braganza.

1977 **United Kingdom** Prince Charles first meets Lady Diana Spencer, while visiting her family's home, Althorp, as the companion of her elder sister, Lady Sarah. **Sweden** Crown Princess Victoria, heir to the throne, is born; if she ascends to the throne, she will be Sweden's third queen regnant, after Queen Christina and Queen Ulrika Eleonora.

LADY DIANA SPENCER
1961–1997

Diana, Princess of Wales, was formerly Lady Diana Frances Spencer, born on 1 July 1961. She was the youngest daughter of Earl Spencer and Mrs Shand-Kydd. Earl Spencer was Equerry to George VI from 1950 to 1952, and to the Queen from 1952 to 1954.

When Prince Charles first started to date Lady Diana she was working as a kindergarten teacher in London. On 24 February 1981, it was officially announced that the couple were engaged to be married. The ceremony took place at St Paul's Cathedral on 29 July 1981 and the route was lined by hundreds of thousands of well-wishers. The prince and princess made their principal home at Highgrove House near Tetbury in Gloucestershire and had two sons — William born in 1982 and Henry (Harry) in 1984. However, the marriage had its problems and the couple agreed to separate in December 1992.

Princess Diana was the people's favourite and had loyal fans throughout the world and the news of her death on 31 August 1997 was met with both shock and disbelief. She died in a car accident in Paris after the princess left the Ritz Hotel with her companion Dodi Al Fayed, who was the son of Harrod's owner, Mohammed Al Fayed.

The death of the Princess of Wales was so momentous that for a long time it shed a veil of doubt over the sincerity of the English monarchy.

1978 **Rome** A year of three popes; Cardinal Albino Luciani succeeds Paul VI as John Paul I, but dies after 33 days amid numerous conspiracy theories; he is replaced by Polish Cardinal Karol Józef Wojtyła as Pope John Paul II; he is the first non-Italian pope for over 450 years; he will travel extensively, visiting over 100 countries.

1979 **United Kingdom** Lord Mountbatten, uncle of Prince Philip, is killed by an IRA bomb.

1981 **United Kingdom** Charles, prince of Wales, marries Lady Diana Spencer. **Rome** Pope John Paul II is shot by a Turk, Mehmet Ali Ağca, but survives. **Russia** Grand Duke George Mikhailovich is born to Grand Duchess Maria Vladimirovich; he is accepted by some as heir apparent to the disputed headship of the Russian imperial family, while others take Prince Dimitri Romanov (born 1926), designated by Nicholas Romanov, prince of Russia, as heir.

1982 **United Kingdom** Prince William of Wales is born; he is second in line of succession to the throne behind his father, Prince Charles. **Monaco** Princess Grace is killed in a car crash.

1984 **United Kingdom** Prince Henry, known as Harry, is born; he is third in line of succession to the throne. **Liechtenstein** Franz Josef II hands over the majority of his powers to heir apparent Hans-Adam II, who becomes prince of Liechtenstein.

1985 **Luxembourg** Former Grand Duchess Charlotte dies of cancer.

1986 **Luxembourg** Grand Duke Jean renounces the titles of the House of Bourbon-Parma for himself and his family following the marriage of his eldest son, Prince Henri, to Maria-Theresa Mestre; the duke of Parma, Carlos Hugo, had ruled the marriage unequal in 1981. **Montenegro** Prince Michael dies in Paris; Prince Nicholas becomes pretender to the throne of Montenegro.

1987
United Kingdom
Princess Anne is made 'Princess Royal'.

1988 **United Kingdom** Princess Beatrice, daughter of Prince Andrew, is born; she is fifth in line of succession to the throne.

1989 **Liechtenstein** Franz Josef II dies; his 51-year reign is the longest of any European monarch at the time; Hans-Adam succeeds him.

Montenegro The remains of King Nikola I, his queen Milena and two of their 12 children are reburied in Montenegro; he had gone into exile in 1918, dying in 1921.

1990 **United Kingdom** Prince Andrew's daughter, Princess Eugenie, is born; she is sixth in line of succession to the throne.

1991 **Norway** There is a huge outpouring of emotion in Norway when Olav V dies; his son, Harald V, succeeds him as king; he is the first Norwegian-born king since the birth of Olav IV in 1370.

1992 **United Kingdom** Prince Charles and Princess Diana separate. **Romania** Following the revolution that has overthrown the communist dictatorship, former King Michael draws such large crowds on his return to Romania for the first time since 1947 that he is banned from visiting again for five years. **Russia** On his death in Miami, Titular Emperor Cyril Vladimirovich is buried in the Peter and Paul Fortress in St Petersburg, the first Romanov to receive this honour since the revolution; his daughter, Grand Duchess Maria Vladimirovna, assumes the role of head of the imperial family, 'Titular Emperor and Autocrat of all the Russias', but this is disputed with Nicholas Romanov, prince of Russia.

1993 **Belgium** King Baudouin I of the Belgians dies without children; his brother, Albert II, becomes king.

1996 **United Kingdom** Prince Charles and Princess Diana divorce. **Portugal** Afonso, prince of Beira, is born to Duarte Pio, claimant to the Portuguese throne; he becomes his heir. **Bavaria** Franz, duke of Bavaria, becomes titular king; he is regarded by Jacobite sympathizers as the rightful king of England, Scotland, France and Ireland.

> ***“ Do you seriously expect me to be the first Prince of Wales in history not to have a mistress? ”***

Prince Charles (atrib.)

1997 **United Kingdom** Diana, princess of Wales, dies in a car crash in Paris; there is a huge outpouring of grief and reaction to the behaviour of the British royal family leads to change. **Romania** Former King Michael's Romanian citizenship is restored and he is once again free to visit the country; he now lives part of the year in Romania; he has no male heirs and the succession will revert on his death to the head of the Hohenzollern-Sigmarinen family, Prince Frederick William.

2000 **Luxembourg** Grand Duke Jean abdicates in favour of his son, Henri.

2003 **United Kingdom** Lady Louise Windsor is born to Prince Edward, the earl of Wessex; she is ninth in line of succession to the throne. **Liechtenstein** A referendum passes Prince Hans-Adam's revision of the constitution; Liechtenstein effectively becomes an absolute monarchy – he can dissolve parliament and call elections; he had threatened to leave the principality if the referendum had gone against his wishes. **Romania** Former King Carol II's remains are returned to Romania.

2004 **Liechtenstein** Prince Hans-Adam, a billionaire who owns a banking group and has an extensive art collection, hands the power of making day-to-day government decisions over to his son and heir, Prince Alois; Hans-Adam remains head of state.

2005 **United Kingdom** Prince Charles marries Camilla Parker-Bowles, who becomes the duchess of Cornwall. **Monaco** Prince Rainier dies, the second-longest reigning Monogasque monarch at 56 years; Prince Albert II becomes sovereign prince. **Norway** Prince Sverre Magnus, son of Crown Prince Haakon, is born; he is third in line to the throne. **Rome** Amid an unprecedented display of grief at the death of Pope John Paul II, Cardinal Joseph Alois Ratzinger is elected pope as Benedict XVI.

POPE JOHN PAUL II
1920–2005

Karol Józef Wojtyła is better known as Pope John Paul II. He was one of the most popular members of the papacy and it has been said of him, '. . . he reminded humankind of the worth of individuals in the modern world'. He was born in Wadowice in Poland on 18 May 1820, the son of a retired army officer and school teacher. In his early years he studied literature and philosophy and later became a playwright and a poet.

By the age of 36 he had two doctorate degrees and became a professor of ethics. He became cardinal at the age of 47 and led a force in Poland to try and counter communism.

In October 1978, Wojtyla became the first Slavic pope ever and the first non-Italian pope in 455 years, taking the name John Paul II. Within months of his election, he returned to his homeland and some historians say he helped bring about the end of the Cold War.

He survived an assassination attempt in May 1981 and had to spend more than two months recovering in a hospital in Rome. Amazingly he could communicate his messages in eight different languages. Pope John Paul II died at the age of 84 in his private apartment at the Vatican on 3 April 2005.

2007 **United Kingdom** James, viscount Severn, son of the earl of Wessex, is born; he is eighth in line of succession to the throne.

2008 **United Kingdom** A large slice of cake made to celebrate the wedding of Lady Diana Spencer and Prince Charles is sold at an auction house in Gloucestershire for £1000.

APPENDIX

ALBANIA

Following many years as a Roman province, Albania was ruled successively by Normans, Serbians and Bulgarians. It became an autonomous state for a brief spell before being overrun by the Ottoman Turks, who ruled for almost 500 years.

In 1912, following the Balkan War, Albania became a principality, before becoming a republic in 1925. This lasted only three years before a monarchy was introduced.

Italy annexed the country in 1939. After the Second World War, in 1946, it became a communist republic under the leadership of Enver Hoxha, who ruled for four decades, dying in 1985.

ARAGÓN

Aragón was a small county in north-east Spain. Following its absorption by Navarre in the 10th century, it was revived as an independent monarchy in 1035 by Sancho the Great, king of Navarre, who, having done his utmost to unite the kingdoms of Spain, divided his kingdom between his three sons. His illegitimate son, Ramiro, became king of Aragón. In January 1516, Ferdinand of Aragón became the first king of a united Spain.

AUSTRIA

Austria – the Osterreich, or eastern state of Bavaria – was a duchy from the middle of the 12th century. In 1267, Rudolf of Habsburg took possession of it, and, as territories were added to it over the years, it became the Habsburg Empire.

On the dissolution of the Holy Roman Empire by Napoleon I, in 1806, Archduke Franz of Austria took the title, emperor of Austria.

In 1867, the dual monarchy of the Austro-Hungarian Empire was created, being dissolved at the end of the First World War. The central section became the country of Austria, and the remainder became Hungary and Czechoslovakia or was absorbed by Italy, Romania, Poland and Yugoslavia.

BAVARIA

Bavaria was a kingdom located in southern Germany, at one time the second largest state in the German Empire, in terms of both population and area.

The House of Wittelsbach provided the rulers of the Duchy of Bavaria from 1375. In 1623, it became an electorate and, finally, in 1805 it became a kingdom. The last king, Ludwig III, fell from power after the First World War, ending 538 years of rule by the House of Wittelsbach.

BELGIUM

Belgium was for centuries known as the Southern Netherlands. Provinces such as Flanders, Brabant, Limburg and Hainault often came under German rule. The 1815 Congress of Vienna, which reorganized Europe at the end of the Napoleonic wars, created the United Kingdom of the Netherlands, uniting Belgium and Holland. William I of the House of Orange-Nassau became king.

In 1830, following a revolution, the Kingdom of Belgium was formed, under the Coburg family; Leopold I became king in 1831, and his descendants still rule today.

BOHEMIA

The greater part of what was once the Kingdom of Bohemia is now part of the Czech Republic. It was established as a duchy in the 9th century and then combined with Moravia to become a suzerain state of the Holy Roman Empire. In 1198, it became a kingdom, with Ottokar I becoming the first king of the Premyslid dynasty.

After being ruled by various families, in 1562 Bohemia was inherited by the Habsburgs, who retained possession until the end of the First World War, when the state of Czechoslovakia was created from the ruins of the Austro-Hungarian Empire.

BOSNIA

Bosnia was ruled from the 12th until the 14th century by Slavic *bans*, or noblemen. The first Bosnian state was established by the Ban Kulin, in the 12th century, and reached its most powerful point under the rule of King Tvrtko, towards the end of the 14th century.

After 1463, when Bosnia was conquered by the Ottoman Turks, it remained within the Ottoman Empire for four centuries. The Ottomans ceded administration of the country to the Austro-Hungarian Empire in 1878, and it was formally annexed by the empire in 1908.

Following the First World War, Bosnia was incorporated into the new Slavic Kingdom of Yugoslavia.

THE BULGARIAN EMPIRE

A khanate, Great Bulgaria, collapsed in the 7th century, and the Volgar Bulgars who had lived there moved to the area of the Lower Danube, which was annexed by the Byzantine Empire, remaining this way until the Asen brothers created a powerful kingdom there. The first ruler to use the name tsar (emperor) was Simeon I, after his crushing defeat of the army of the Byzantine Empire, in 913. His successors styled themselves this way until the country fell to the Ottoman Turks in 1396.

When Bulgaria was finally freed from Ottoman rule, almost 500 years later, in 1878, Alexander I, of the Coburg family, first monarch of the newly liberated nation, adopted the title 'kniaz'. Then, when complete independence was achieved in 1908, his successor, Ferdinand, changed the title once more to tsar. This was the title used by him and his successor, Boris III, until the abolition of the monarchy by the communist regime, which established a republic in 1946.

BURGUNDY

The original Burgundians were Germans who settled the eastern area of France in the 5h century AD, only to be conquered by the Franks a century later.

The last Burgundian king was Conrad II, who was also Holy Roman Emperor. The kingdom was divided up and eventually absorbed by the French monarchy.

DENMARK

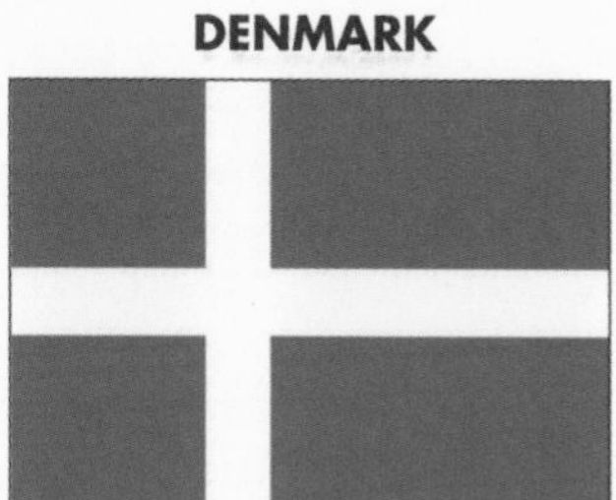

The Danish monarchy is one of the oldest monarchies in the world, with only the Japanese monarchy having been in existence longer. The first ruling dynasty was that of Gorm the Old, founded in 960, a dynasty that ruled until 1448.

The House of Oldenburg then reigned from 1448 to 1863, when the crown passed to the House of Schleswig-Holstein-Sonderburg-Glücksburg, another branch of the same house, which enjoyed a line of descent from King Christian III. The kingdom had been nominally elective, but was, in practice, hereditary and absolutist.

The House of Oldenburg occupies the throne to this day.

Denmark has been involved in various unions with its Scandinavian neighbours. From 1380 to 1397 it was joined with Norway; from 1397 to 1536, it was part of the Kalmar Union when it joined, with some interruptions, with Norway (with Iceland, Greenland, the Faroe Islands, Shetland and Orkney) and Sweden (including part of Finland) under a single monarch; from 1536 to 1814 it was part of the Kingdom of Denmark and Norway.

ENGLAND

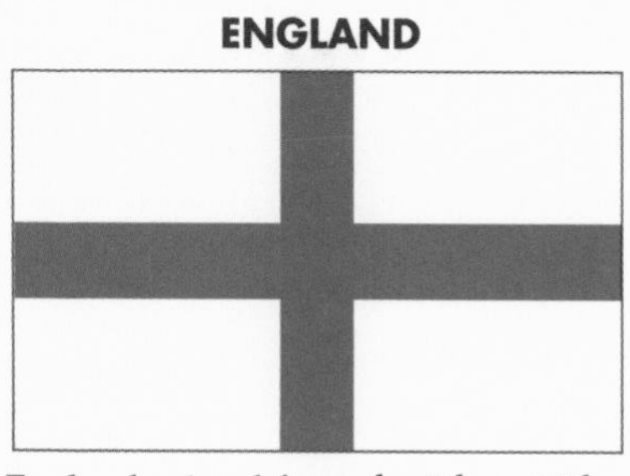

The Kingdom of England existed from the 9th or 10th century until 1707, when it became part of the Kingdom of Great Britain. Its history, however, stretches back far beyond the 9th century. Part of the Roman Empire, it was then overrun by Teutonic invaders from northern Germany, the indigenous Celts being driven westwards. These Anglo-Saxons took control of the richer lands of southern and south-east England and created a number of Anglo-Saxon kingdoms. Now and then, a powerful ruler would arise who would, for a time, gain supremacy over the others, kings such as Offa of Mercia, who ruled towards the end of the 8th century.

When Viking invaders from Scandinavia began to threaten the country's independence and prosperity, there was a growing necessity for the English to unite to repel them. At the end of the 9th century, Alfred, king of Wessex, and his descendants who ruled for the next 100 years, led the resistance.

In the 11th century, West Saxon and Danish kings ruled, and succession was irregular. The Normans seized the throne in the mid 11th century, with the slaying of the English King Harold at the Battle of Hastings.

Since 1066, six families have ruled England, both on their own and as part of the United Kingdom of Great Britain. Following the reign of the Normans, the English throne passed to the Plantagenets, from Anjou in France. The wars of the roses brought an end to the Plantagenet dynasty when Welshman Henry Tudor deposed Richard III. The Scottish Stuarts came to the throne when Elizabeth I died childless, and the crowns of England and Scotland were united under James I of England and VI of Scotland.

In 1714, the first king of German origin took the throne, George I of the House of Hanover. When Queen Victoria married Prince Albert of Saxe-Coburg and Gotha, another German family arrived. During the First World War, the royal family changed its name to the more English-sounding Windsor, and the present queen, Elizabeth II, and her family are of the House of Windsor.

ETRURIA

Etruria is also known as Tuscia, from which originates the modern name of Tuscany.

In 1800, Napoleon I dispossessed the grand duke, Ferdinand, whose family had ruled since 1531, and restyled the Grand Duchy of Tuscany as the Kingdom of Etruria. The crown prince of Parma was crowned the first of two kings who reigned before Ferdinand was restored in 1814. In 1860, it was annexed by the Kingdom of Italy.

FRANCE

Although it is not entirely certain when the Kingdom of France came into being, the name France comes from a Germanic tribe known as the Franks. The first rulers were chieftains, the oldest known of whom is Pharamond Clovis I, who was the first to become a king. Around the time of his rule, about 486, the last Roman official was defeated and driven from Gaul, and Clovis ruled a Merovingian Frankish Kingdom that existed until the Treaty of Verdun in 843, whereby the Frankish Kingdom splintered and three great states were created – the Eastern Kingdom would become Germany; the Middle Kingdom became Lotharingia, later part of the Holy Roman Empire, and the Western Kingdom became France, with Charles the Bald as its first truly independent ruler. It was the Carolingian kings who eventually united the Frankish kingdom for the first time since Clovis, becoming the first true French monarchy.

In 987 Hugh Capet became king, and members of the Capet family would rule France until 1328.

The monarch was called king of the Franks until around the reign of Philippe IV, who came to power in 1285, but the title was also used later for the brief period during the French Revolution, when the Constitution of 1791 was in effect, and after the 1830 Revolution, when the king was styled 'King of the French' instead of king of France, in something of a public relations effort to link the monarch in the popular mind to the people of France rather than to the country.

For centuries, the power of the French kings was not consolidated in their own realm, exemplified by the fact that, in 1340, Edward II of England called himself king of France as well as England. Again, in 1420, Henry V called himself *Regens Franciae*.

GERMANY

After the fall of Rome, the Franks, Agilulfings and the Carolingians divided Germany between them. This remained in place until 800, when Charlemagne created the Holy Roman Empire.

Germany became a powerful force in Europe, but was hampered by being divided into a number of duchies and minor states, such as Swabia, Saxony and Franconia. By the 16th century, the Habsburgs were in power, but it was not until 1871 that national unity was created with the formation of the German Empire by the Hohenzollern family, who controlled most of northern Germany. Wilhelm I, who had been king of Prussia for 10 years, was persuaded, against his better judgement, to accept the title of kaiser (emperor).

After the end of the First World War, Wilhelm became a private citizen, living the last 23 years of his life in Holland.

GREAT MORAVIA

The Principality of Great Moravia came into existence in 833, when Mojmír I unified the two neighbouring states, Nitra and Moravia. Although occasionally, during its brief existence, its leaders would submit to the king of the East Franks, it endeavoured, on the whole, to maintain its independence.

Internal strife and incessant war with the Carolingian Empire weakened the country, and eventually it was overrun by the Magyars around 896. Great Moravia disappeared later when it was shared between Poland, Hungary, Bohemia and the Holy Roman Empire.

GREECE

Greece finally threw off the shackles of centuries of Ottoman rule in the 1820s. The new kingdom, founded in 1829, lasted until 1967, when a military coup ousted the last king, Constantine II, from power to live in exile.

HANOVER

Hanover became a kingdom by the Treaty of Vienna in 1814, following the Napoleonic wars. Prior to that date, the rulers had been styled elector.

The country's first three kings were also kings of Britain – George III, George IV and William IV.

Hanover was separated from Britain on the death of William IV, making it an autonomous country, with Ernest-Augustus – the duke of Cumberland – as king.

Cumberland's son, George V, was the last king of Hanover; the kingdom was annexed by Prussia in 1866 and George went into exile in Paris.

HOLY ROMAN EMPIRE

The Holy Roman Empire consisted, in the beginning, of the Kingdom of Germany and the Kingdom of Italy, which incorporated the north of the country. The emperor was elected by seven German prince-electors and, following his election, had to travel to Italy to be crowned king and then to Rome for his coronation as emperor, by the current pope.

The elected Holy Roman Emperor used the title 'king of the Romans', until his coronation, which was usually performed by the pope in Rome. Coming into common usage in the 11th century, during the reign of Henry IV who ruled as emperor, but had still not been crowned by the pope, it later came to be used by the heir to the imperial throne, who was elected during the lifetime of his predecessor.

The question of succession was always a thorny issue, due to the fact that it was an elective monarchy, but, once crowned, the emperor was free to pursue the election of his heir as king. The heir would become king of the Romans.

The Habsburgs effectively took possession of the title of Holy Roman Emperor following the election of Charles V in 1500. The Habsburg heir-apparent became king of Rome or king of the Romans, and after 1556 the rulers of the Holy Roman Empire no longer sought coronation by the pope. They styled themselves emperor-elect on assuming the throne. 'King of the Romans' ceased, therefore, to be used by reigning monarchs.

Napoleon I revived the title king of the Romans for his son and heir, Napoleon II, although after 1815 he was more commonly known as the duke of Reichstadt.

HUNGARY

After the collapse of the Roman Empire, various tribes occupied the land that would become Hungary, until the empire of Attila the Hun was centred there. By the middle of the 10th century, however, the warlike Magyars were in control, eventually seizing Croatia, too, in 1095, and stretching the country's borders all the way to the Adriatic.

The Arpad family ruled until 1301, when Wenceslaus of Bohemia became king. Two hundred years later, the Ottoman Turks took over, remaining in power until the end of the 17th century, when the Habsburgs gained control. It was then one half of the Austro-Hungarian Empire until its dissolution at the end of the First World War.

IRELAND

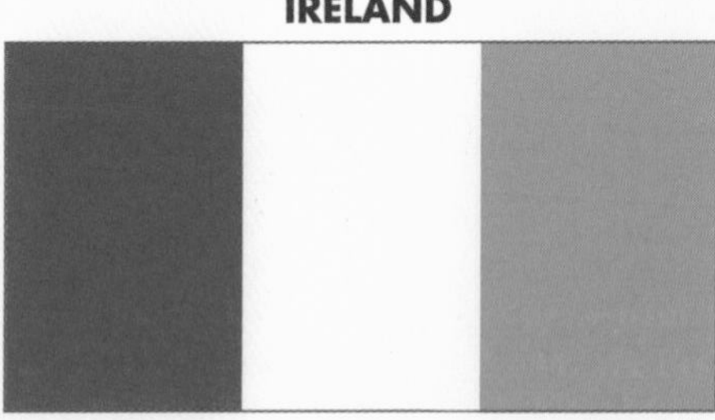

From 500 until 900, there were numerous kingdoms and hundreds of kings in Ireland. In the 9th century the Vikings controlled the country, founding small kingdoms centred on Dublin and other parts of the country. They were expelled in 1014. The Normans wiped out the remaining Irish kingdoms, and from 1170 the island was a lordship until it was attached to the English crown in 1541.

ITALY

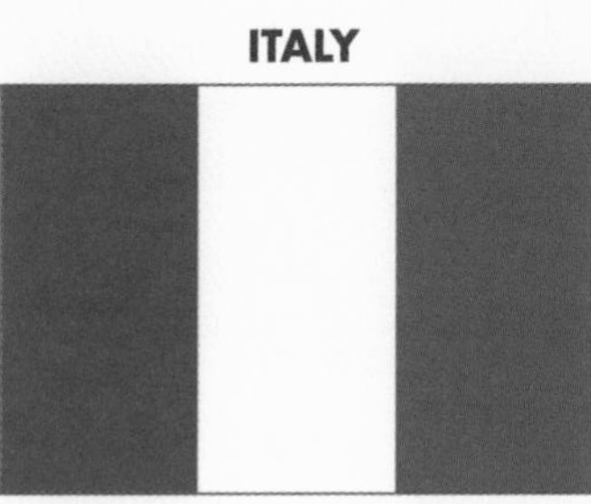

The Scirian Kingdom that followed the fall of the Roman Empire lasted until the end of the 5th century, being replaced by the Ostrogoths. Italy was then briefly part of the Byzantine Empire, and from 951 the Holy Roman Emperor also styled himself king of Italy.

The country was divided into small states over the next two and a half centuries, before being unified, in 1860, under the House of Savoy.

The king of Sardinia, Vittorio Emanuele II, became king in 1861, and the last king, Umberto II, abdicated in 1946, after reigning for a matter of weeks. A referendum had shown that the Italian people had had enough of the monarchy.

LEÓN AND ASTURIAS/ LEÓN AND CASTILE

León, a city in north-west Spain, became a kingdom under Garcia, when his father, Alfonso III, divided his kingdom between his sons, around 910. In 1035 it merged with Castile when Ferdinand I killed Vermudo III at the Battle of Tamaron.

NAPLES

Naples was, at one time, part of the Kingdom of Sicily. Following the revolt known as the Sicilian Vespers, when the Anjous were ousted from Sicily, they retained control of Naples. In December 1816, Naples and Sicily were absorbed into the new Kingdom of Italy.

NAVARRE

The Kingdom of Pamplona, later Navarre, occupied the strategically important southern slope of the western Pyrenees and a section of coastline of the Bay of Biscay. Following Roman occupation, neither the Visigoths nor the Arabs managed to establish a permanent occupation. The Franks tried several times to establish control over the area, but in 842 the Basque chieftain Íñigo Arista was chosen as king of Pamplona. The state expanded under his successors into the Kingdom of Navarre.

Eventually, a large part of Navarre became part of the Kingdom of Spain, but a small section, north of the Pyrenees, survived as an independent kingdom until 1620, when it was fully incorporated into France.

THE NETHERLANDS

Before the Napoleonic wars, the state of the Netherlands was a confederated republic, most of the semi-independent provinces being led by stadtholders from the powerful House of Orange-Nassau. Most of these eventually came into the possession of Burgundy and then the Austro-Spanish Empire, until revolution ousted Philip II and the United Provinces came into existence.

When Napoleon Bonaparte installed his brother Louis as king of Holland, in 1806, the Netherlands became nothing more than a puppet state. However, that particular monarchy lasted only until 1810.

Three years later, when the French had gone, the Dutch monarchy, as it exists today, was founded. The Prince of Orange was declared sovereign prince of The United Netherlands (made up of a number of northern provinces), and the new monarchy was confirmed by the 1815 Congress of Vienna, which reorganized Europe at the end of the Napoleonic wars.

The House of Orange-Nassau was given rule over the Netherlands, as it exists today, plus Belgium; it would be called the United Kingdom of the Netherlands. The king of the Netherlands was also given the title of grand duke of Luxembourg. William I was descended directly from John the Elder, younger brother of William of Orange, who had spearheaded the Dutch fight for independence from the Spanish in the 16th and 17th centuries. The 'Orange' part of the title came from William's 1544 inheritance of the principality of Orange, in southern France.

Dutch monarchs are in the habit of abdicating. Queen Wilhelmina (1962) and Queen Juliana (1980) both abdicated in favour of their daughters. However, the current monarch, Queen Beatrix, has stipulated that she has no intention of abdicating in the near future in favour of her son, Crown Prince Willem-Alexander, as she says he and his wife need to spend as much time as possible with their family.

NORWAY

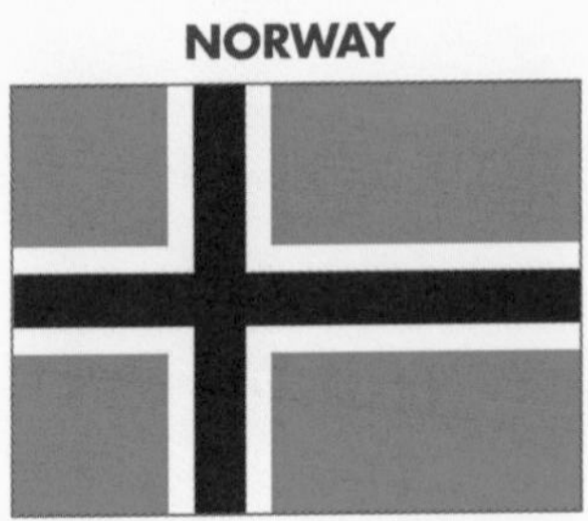

Norway was a more or less united country by the time that Harald Fairhair came to the throne in the 9th century. His descendants ruled until 1319. In 1387 Norway and Denmark were united with Sweden, in the Scandinavian Kalmar Union. Norway would share a sovereign with Denmark for 400 years.

In 1814 the Swedish king was installed as king of Norway. By 1905, the House of Oldenburg was back on the throne that it occupies to this day.

POLAND

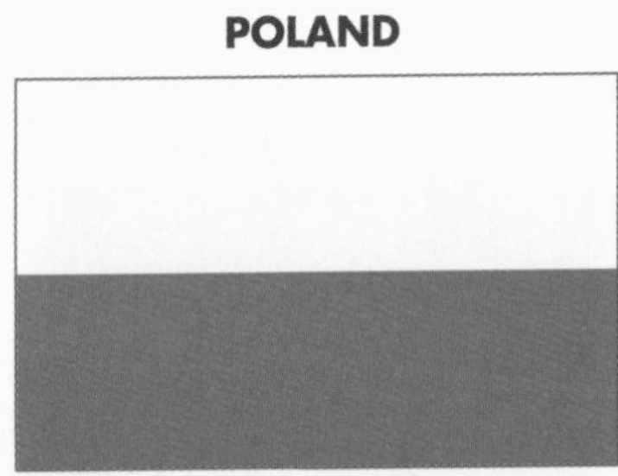

In the 10th century Poland was a major European power and a kingdom was created, with Boleslav I as its first king.

In 1370 the crown passed to the Angevins and then to a Lithuanian dynasty. Poland was a vast kingdom, stretching from the Baltic in the west to the Ukraine in the east. This continued until the fall of the Jagiellon family in 1572, when Sigismund II August died childless, despite three marriages, and Henri of Valois, brother of Charles IX of France, was elected King Henry III of Poland and grand duke of Lithuania.

The Swedish Vasa family were on the throne in the early 17th century, a time when the crown was elective and powerful. However, by the 18th century it was declining in power.

In 1795 the country was split between Austria, Russia and Prussia, and Napoleon established a grand duchy, which was overrun by the Russians in 1813. Until 1918, when the country became independent as a republic, the Russian tsars styled themselves kings of Poland.

PORTUGAL

It was not until the 11th century that Portugal emerged as a kingdom. Under French control, through the ruling Burgundian House of Capet, it drove southwards, pushing the Moors out of the country.

By the 16th century it was a global power, founding fantastically lucrative colonies in India and Brazil. However, in 1580 the Spanish Habsburgs gained the throne, remaining there until the Braganzas in 1640. The House of Braganza occupied the throne until the abolition of the monarchy in 1910. A republic was declared the following year.

PRUSSIA

Prussia was once the single most powerful part of the German Empire. It had become a duchy during the Reformation, when the last Grand Master of the Teutonic Knights had become a Lutheran and seized power as duke of Prussia. The territory of Brandenburg was added in 1618, and in 1701 it became a kingdom, with Frederick I of the House of Hohenzollern as the first king. Prussia disappeared into the German Empire in 1871.

ROMANIA

Romania is something of an ethnic curiosity. The people living there can, in all likelihood, claim Roman ancestry, as is evidenced by the country's name. However, by the late 1200s the inhabitants of the Wallachian state that occupied this land were of mixed origins. The rulers or governors of Wallachia and Moldavia, which was joined to it in the 1300s, were called *Voivodes*. Like most other Balkan states, Wallachia and Moldavia became vassal states of the all-conquering Ottoman Turks in the 16th century.

In 1862, following the merging of Wallachia and Moldavia three years earlier, the newly created larger state became the Principality of Romania. Alexander John Cuza became prince of Romania, or, to give the role its local name, 'domnitor'. The Romanian parliament deposed Cuza in 1866, inviting a German prince of the Hohenzollern family, Carol, to become prince of Romania. At the 1878 Conference of Berlin, Romania achieved complete independence from the Ottomans, becoming a sovereign kingdom in 1881, with Carol promoted to king as Carol I.

Romania enjoyed a constitutional monarchy, apart from the years 1938 to 1944 under the dictatorships of Carol II and Marshal Ion Antonescu. In August 1944 King Michael, during his second reign, restored the 1923 Constitution, but actually reigned as an unconstitutional monarch, suspending parliament until 1946.

The Soviet Union occupied Romania in 1947, announcing the abolition of the monarchy.

In 2008 King Michael of Romania announced his return to Romania, to live in the castle of Peles, near Bucharest, 60 years after the communists forced him to abdicate.

RUSSIA

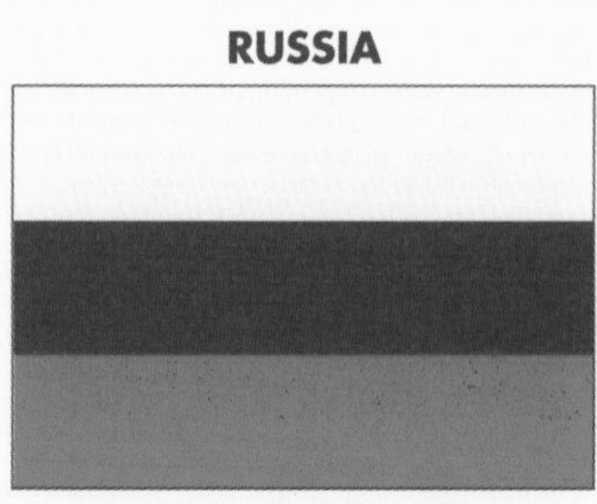

Slavic tribes are the ancestors of modern Russians, moving into lands vacated by migrating Germanic tribes.

From the 9th to the 12th centuries, the ruler of the state of Kievan Rus', centred around the city of Kiev, was called grand prince. The dynasty began with a semi-legendary Varangian (Viking) called Rurik; his dynasty would rule Kievan Rus' and Russia for the next 700 years. The Scandinavians merged, before long, into the indigenous population and helped to make Kievan Rus' the richest state in Europe by the 11th and 12th centuries.

However, after centuries of invasions by Mongols and others, and internecine fighting between princely families, the area's power had waned, and Kiev was finally destroyed in 1237.

The area of Galicia-Volhynia was eventually absorbed by the Polish-Lithuanian Commonwealth, while the Mongol-dominated Vladimir-Suzdal and the independent Novgorod Republic, two regions on the periphery of Kiev, became the basis for the modern Russian nation.

The Grand Duchy of Moscow became the most powerful state after the decline of Kievan Rus'. It annexed rival states, such as Novgorod and Tver. Ivan III the Great threw off the control of the Mongol invaders, consolidating the territory around Moscow, and became the first to style himself 'Grand Duke of all the Russias'.

In 1547 Ivan the Terrible became the first tsar of Russia, annexing the Tatar khanates of Kazan and Astrakhan, along the Volga river, making Russia a multi-ethnic state. By the mid 17th century there were Russian settlements in eastern Siberia, on the Chukchi Peninsula, along the Amur river and on the Pacific coast.

Peter I, of the Romanov dynasty, founded the Russian Empire in the 17th century, but the Russian Revolution of 1917 brought the monarchy to an end, with the execution of Nicholas II and his family, and the introduction of Soviet Russia.

SARDINIA

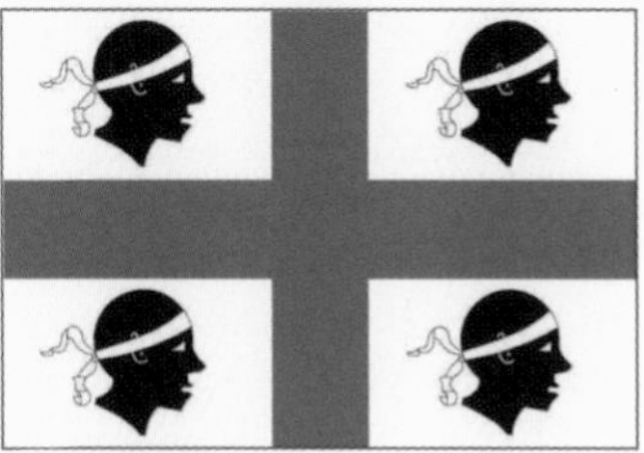

In 1720 a kingdom was created by the Treaty of London consisting of Sardinia, Nice, Savoy and Piedmont and, after the Napoleonic wars, Liguria. When, in 1859, Lombardy, the Two Sicilies, the Papal States and the Central Duchies were appended, the Kingdom of Italy came into existence.

Vittorio-Emanuele, king of Sardinia, became the first king of Italy in 1861.

SAXONY

Conquered by Charlemagne, this region of Germany obtained the imperial crown in the 10th century, becoming an electorate in 1423. In 1485 it was split between two branches of the Wettin family. Then in 1547 it was reunited, and became a kingdom in 1806, which lasted until the end of the First World War in 1918.

SCOTLAND

Like Ireland, the history of Scotland is shrouded in myth and legend. The Picts lived in the northern part of the country and Celts occupied the south. Irish, Scandinavians and Anglo-Saxons completed the mix.

The country's inhabitants provided fierce resistance to the Romans, who failed to conquer Caledonia, the area north of the Antonine Wall, stretching from the River Clyde to the River Forth. In fact, Roman occupation of any significant part of the country was limited to about only 40 years.

Pictland developed in response to the Roman threat, and this would become the Kingdom of Alba during the reign of King Constantine II. By 1018 Malcolm II had pushed the border of Scotland to roughly its present-day position. The gradual addition of the Kingdom of Strathclyde expanded the country until, by the end of the 13th century, it had assumed its present shape.

The name 'Scotland' derives from the Latin 'Scoti', the name given to the Gaels, an ethno-linguistic group originating in Ireland and subsequently spreading to Scotland and the Isle of Man. The Latin 'Scotia' referred, initially, to Ireland. By the 11th century 'Scotia' was being used to describe the land north of the River Forth, but 'Albania' and 'Albany' were also being used, both from the Gaelic 'Alba'. It was not until the late Middle Ages that 'Scots' and 'Scotland' became common currency for the land and its people.

Scotland became a kingdom in 843, when Kenneth, king of Dalriada, of the House of Alpin, became king of the Picts, and the first of the dynasty that would create Alba and rule until 1034. The Houses of Dunkeld and Moray ruled the country before several interregnums and the reign of John Balliol, which punctuated an unsettled period in the Scottish monarchy. The House of Bruce preceded the House of Stewart, which ruled Scotland for 336 years, between 1371 and 1707.

The crown of Scotland was merged with the English crown following the death of Queen Elizabeth I in 1603, when James VI of Scotland also became James I of England.

SERBIA

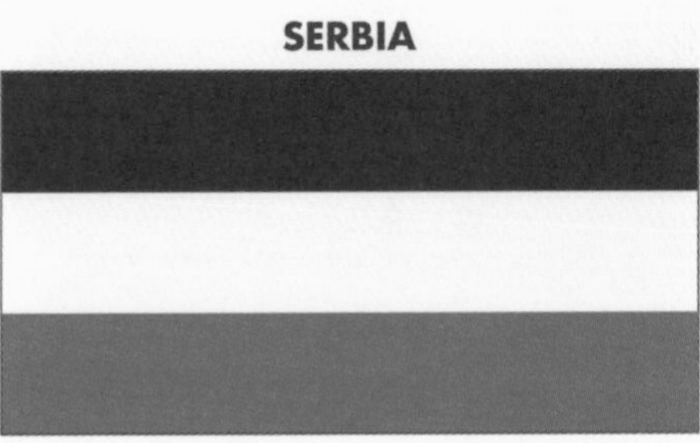

Serbia was established as a kingdom before 1200, by the powerful ruling Nemanjich family who had ousted the Byzantines and who remained in power until 1389 when the Ottoman Turks conquered the country.

In 1804 Czerny George, founder of the Serbian House of Karađorđević, drove the Turks out, and when they returned eight years later they were again expelled, this time by Milosh Obrenovitch, who became prince of Serbia in 1817.

Following the First World War, Serbia merged with other countries to form the Kingdom of Yugoslavia, with the Serbian king, Peter I, being elected king.

SICILY

Having been ruled in ancient times by Carthage and Greece, early in the 9th century, the Muslims seized control from the Byzantines. Next, the powerful Norman Hauteville family moved in, and by 1130 King Roger was in control of not only Sicily but all of southern Italy.

The year 1194 saw the Hohenstauffens gain control, but they lost it to the French Angevins. A rebellion in 1282 introduced Aragonese rule, and they also acquired the Kingdom of Naples. Both kingdoms passed into the hands of the Habsburgs and then to the Spanish Bourbons.

Sicily was annexed by the Kingdom of Italy in 1860, and the last king, Francis II, died in exile in Austria.

SPAIN

The marriage of Ferdinand of Aragon and Isabella of Castile, and the conquest of Granada at the end of the 15th century, unified the entire country of Spain, apart from Navarre, for the first time.

The House of Trastamarsa reigned until the arrival on the throne of the Habsburgs in 1504. They remained there until 1700, when the House of Bourbon came to power.

With only the interruptions of Napoleon and dictator General Francisco Franco, they have occupied the throne ever since.

SWEDEN

The Roman historian Tacitus makes the first mention of a Swedish king – the king of the Suiones – in his work *Germania*, written around AD100. There is little recorded about the rulers of the country, however, until around the 10th century, when lists of Swedish kings traditionally begin, around the time of the reign of King Olof Skötkonung, of the house known variously as the House of Munsö, the Old dynasty or the House of Uppsala. Olof Skötkonung united the Swedes with the Goths and introduced Christianity. Before this date, history is embellished with saga and mythology and cannot be relied upon.

The ruling Skoldung family was replaced by the Folkungs in the 13th century, and Sweden joined Denmark and Norway in the Kalmar Union from 1397 until 1523.

Breaking with the Union in 1523, Sweden elected Gustav I, of the Vasa family, to the throne, and during his reign Sweden became a powerful country. The Wittelsbachs succeeded them, but by the time the House of Oldenburg took the throne in 1751, Sweden was a weakened and bankrupt country.

Remarkably, in 1818, the former French military commander, Marshal Count Jean-Baptiste Bernadotte, who had been 'adopted' at the age of 47 by the previous king, Charles XIII, became king as Charles XIV. The Bernadotte family have occupied the Swedish throne ever since.

WALES

By the time of the complete withdrawal of the Romans from Britain, around 436, a number of Welsh principalities had been formed. These were briefly united by Rhodri in the 9th century, but he was killed by the Angles in 878. Although the Normans never really conquered the country, it was eventually joined to England in 1542.

WESTPHALIA

Westphalia was another kingdom created by Napoleon Bonaparte, of which he made a member of his family monarch. He did so in 1807, when it comprised nearly all of Hesse-Cassel, all of Brunswick and large parts of Prussia, Hanover and Saxony.

Westphalia ceased to exist after the Battle of Leipzig in 1813.

WÜRTTEMBERG

Having been ruled by the same family for more than 700 years, Württemberg became a kingdom in December 1805.

YUGOSLAVIA

Yugoslavia was created after the First World War, out of Serbia, Croatia and Slovenia. Its first king was the colourful Peter I, who was the son of Alexander, prince of Serbia. He had lived in exile since 1858, had joined the French army in 1870, and fought the Turks under the name of Mrkonjic.

Having been king of the Serbs since 1903, he was elected king of the Serbs, Croats and Slovenes in 1918.

The third and last king of Yugoslavia, Peter II, was exiled when Marshal Tito came to power in 1945, and the country became a dictatorship.

GLOSSARY OF ROYAL TERMS

Absolute monarchy A system of monarchy where the monarch has total power over the land and people he or she rules, including the apparatus of government, aristocracy and, often, the clergy.

Agnatic descent (also known as patrilineal) is where descent is traced exclusively through males from a founding male ancestor. Agnatic seniority, or patrilineal seniority, ensures that succession to the throne passes to the monarch's next-eldest brother (even if the monarch has his own sons), and then only to the monarch's children (the next generation) after males of the eldest generation have all been exhausted. Females of the dynasty and their descendants are excluded from the succession.

Antipope A person in opposition to the true pope, who makes a claim to be pope.

Apostolic king A hereditary title of the king of Hungary, reputedly given to Saint Stephen by Pope Sylvester II.

Appanage Derived from the Late Latin term for 'giving bread', appanage was the term used for the giving of an estate and titles to the non-heirs of a sovereign prince. It was widely used throughout Europe.

Boyar A term used, from the 10th until the 17th century, to describe a member of the highest rank of the feudal Moscovian, Kievan Russian, Bulgarian, Wallachian and Moldavian aristocracies, who were second only to the rulers.

Bretwalda An Anglo-Saxon term used, from the 5th century onwards, to describe Anglo-Saxon kings who had achieved overlordship over the other kingdoms.

Consanguinity Being descended from the same person, a factor that is considered when deciding whether two people should marry – important in royal families when monarchs often married cousins.

Constitutional monarchy A type of constitutional government in which a monarch is head of state and his or her government legislates. Most constitutional monarchies (such as the United Kingdom) utilize a parliamentary system of government.

Crown prince The heir to the throne in a monarchy.

Dauphin The title given to the king's eldest son, the heir apparent to the French throne.

De facto Latin term meaning 'in practice', but not stipulated by law.

De jure Meaning 'stipulated by law'.

De jure uxoris Meaning 'by right of his wife' – used when a person inherits a title through his wife.

Doge Descended from the Latin *dux* (as are duke and the Italian *duce*), meaning 'leader', and used for the head of state in a number of Italian city states, but principally Venice.

Domnitor The title given to the ruler of the principalities of Wallachia and Moravia, from 1859 to 1866, and in the Kingdom of Romania, from 1886 until 1881.

Heir apparent A term used for an heir who cannot be deposed from his or her inheritance.

Imperator Romanorum Emperor of the Romans.

Primogeniture The right of the first-born son to inherit.

Interregnum The period of time between one monarch and the next.

Khan A title for a prince, chieftain or governor in Turkish or Mongolian languages.

King consort Husband of a reigning queen.

Knyaz A word indicating a prince or nobility in Slavic languages.

Partible or divisible inheritance The division of property, rights or kingdoms between children; common in tribal societies.

Queen consort Wife of a reigning king.

Queen regnant A ruling female monarch, as opposed to a queen consort.

Salic Law The rule forbidding females from the inheritance of a throne.

Theocracy A form of government in which a god or deity is recognized as the supreme civil ruler.

Titular Used to describe a person in an official position who has no actual power (e.g. King Michael I, titular king of the Romanians).

Tsar 'Emperor' in Russian, Bulgarian and Serbian.

Witan (also Witenagemot or Witena gemot) A national assembly in England from the 7th to the 11th century, the function of which was to advise the king. It comprised the most important noblemen in England, both ecclesiastic and secular.

Without issue Without children.

PICTURE CREDITS

The publisher would like to thank the following for permission to reproduce photographs:

Cover:

Top band L–R © Master John, Getty Images, Carlo Maratta / Centre band L–R © FPG, Getty Images, Getty Images / Bottom band L–R © Getty Images, AFP/Getty Images, Tim Graham/Getty Images.

Internal:

2, 6, 41, 73, 118, 126, 129, 132, 135 © Getty Images / **2, 21, 74, 134, 133** © Time & Life Pictures/Getty Images / **2, 136, 137** © Tim Graham/Getty Images / **100** © Jean-Marc Nattier / **121** © Roger Viollet/Getty Images / **139** © National Geographic/Getty Images / **2, 6, 8, 19, 28, 36, 46, 66, 123** © The Stapleton Collection/The Bridgeman Art Library / **2, 6, 24, 30, 34, 60, 77, 88, 92, 97, 94** © Look and Learn/The Bridgeman Art Library / **2, 108** © Agnew's, London, UK/The Bridgeman Art Library / **6, 85** © National Gallery, London, UK/The Bridgeman Art Library / **6, 110, 113** © Chateau de Versailles, France, Lauros/Giraudon/The Bridgeman Art Library / **11** © Westminster Abbey, London, UK,/The Bridgeman Art Library / **13** © Lambeth Palace Library, London, UK/ The Bridgeman Art Library / **38** © Musee de Tesse, Le Mans, France, Lauros/Giraudon/ The Bridgeman Art Library / **50, 119** © Ken Welsh/The Bridgeman Art Library / **58, 130** © The Bridgeman Art Library / **59** © Bibliotheque Nationale, Paris, France/The Bridgeman Art Library / **62** © Collection of the Earl of Leicester, Holkham Hall, Norfolk/ The Bridgeman Art Library / **65, 95** © Philip Mould Ltd, London/The Bridgeman Art Library / **67** © Kunsthistorisches Museum, Vienna, Austria/The Bridgeman Art Library / **68** © Schloss Ambras, Austria/The Bridgeman Art Library / **70, 78** © Musee des Augustins, Toulouse, France/The Bridgeman Art Library / **81** © Scottish National Portrait Gallery, Edinburgh, Scotland/The Bridgeman Art Library / **87** © Victoria & Albert Museum, London, UK/The Bridgeman Art Library / **90** © Prado, Madrid, Spain, Giraudon/The Bridgeman Art Library / **96** © Montclair Art Museum, New Jersey, USA/The Bridgeman Art Library / **102** © The Crown Estate/The Bridgeman Art Library / **105** © The Drambuie Collection, Edinburgh, Scotland/ The Bridgeman Art Library / **106** © Musee Ingres, Montauban, France, Lauros/ Giraudon/The Bridgeman Art Library / **109** © Galleria Sabauda, Turin, Italy/Alinari/The Bridgeman Art Library / **114** © Pushkin Museum, Moscow, Russia/The Bridgeman Art Library / **116** Scottish National Portrait Gallery, Edinburgh, Scotland/The Bridgeman Art Library / **117** © Chateau de Versailles, France/The Bridgeman Art Library / **17** © Chris Hellier/CORBIS / **55** © Bettmann/CORBIS / **131** © Hulton-Deutsch Collection/ CORBIS.

Box section details:

Charlemagne to medieval kingdoms © French School/The Bridgeman Art Library / Renaissance monarchs © Croatian School/The Bridgeman Art Library / Rise of Empire © English School/The Bridgeman Art Library / Rebellion and Revolution © English School/The Bridgeman Art Library / The struggle to survive © Jerry Driendl/ Photographer's Choice.